The Second City

# The Second City

## THE ESSENTIALLY ACCURATE HISTORY

**THE SECOND CITY**

WITH SHELDON PATINKIN

AND LIZ KOZAK

MIDWAY

AN AGATE IMPRINT

CHICAGO

Library of Congress Cataloging-in-Publication Data

Names: Patinkin, Sheldon, author. | Kozak, Liz, author. | O'Hara,
    Catherine, writer of foreword. | Ramis, Harold, writer of afterword. |
    Second City (Theater company), issuing body
Title: The Second City : the essentially accurate history / the Second City
    ; with Sheldon Patinkin and Liz Kozak ; foreword by Catherine O'Hara ;
    lastword by Harold Ramis.
Description: Second edition. | Chicago : Midway, an Agate imprint, [2019] |
    Includes bibliographical references and index. | Summary: "New and
    updated second edition of The Second City, which tells the story of the
    comedy institution in with photos and stories from the cast"-- Provided
    by publisher.
Identifiers: LCCN 2019026836 | ISBN 9781572842816 (hardcover) | ISBN
    1572842814 (hardcover)
Subjects: LCSH: Second City (Theater company)--History. | Second city
    television (Television program)--History. | Comedy
    sketches--Illinois--Chicago--History.
Classification: LCC PN2277.C42 S4524 2019 | DDC 792.09773/11--dc23
LC record available at https://lccn.loc.gov/2019026836

Design by Morgan Krehbiel

Midway is an imprint of Agate Publishing. Agate books are available in
bulk at discount prices. For more information, visit agatepublishing.com.

This book is dedicated to Viola Spolin, Paul Sills, and Bernie Sahlins for their undying commitment to the work, and to the countless alumni and staff members who have kept The Second City living and breathing since 1959.

**–Andrew Alexander**
CEO and executive producer,
The Second City

"Our laughter is at once a protest and an acceptance of our common destiny."

**–Bernie Sahlins**

# CONTENTS

"THE SECOND CITY, LIKE THE GIFT OF HUMOUR ITSELF, LETS US KNOW WE ARE NOT ALONE IN THIS WORLD."

—Catherine O'Hara

# FOREWORD

Catherine O'Hara
in the 1970s

I BELIEVE WE'RE all born with the gift of humour. If you're lucky, life will let you keep it. If you're really lucky, you'll get to nurture it, feed it, and maybe even grow it into a career.

Lucky for me, The Second City opened a theater in my hometown, Toronto, in 1973. It became my comedy and acting university. I began my studies from the audience, as a Second City waitress. Gilda Radner, Danny Aykroyd, Valri Bromfield, John Candy, and Eugene Levy were my hilarious professors, teaching by example. After graduating grade thirteen (Does that grade still exist anywhere?!) I was hired by dear John Candy for the Touring Company, then by Joe Flaherty as the understudy to Rosemary Radcliffe and dear Gilda.

Now I was training on the job, and there are so many wonderful lessons to be learned at The Second City. Sketch work teaches you everything you need to know about scene structure. Any good story, in any form, is made up of scenes, each with a beginning, a middle, and an end. It's not just by chance that the best improvisers I know are also great writers.

I learned to think on my feet, or, at least, to have the confidence to go out onstage with an idea or direction to offer, yet be willing to let it go and trust my castmates to guide me somewhere new. Surrounded by my smart and funny cohorts, I was encouraged to take chances, to get way out of my comfort zone, to be open and willing to play. We all knew we were never without the greathearted support of each other.

I had always loved people-watching, and I always will, but while working at The Second City, I could note a snippet of conversation I heard on the subway, let my imagination run with it, and take it onstage that night in the improvs. In any scene, I could add a unique hairdo or fashion I happened to see on the street. Sometimes building a character from the outside is a way into their soul . . . even if it's just all in your head!

The Second City taught me to respect the audience—Second City audiences are a most generous, fun-loving crowd—and to play to their highest intelligence. It taught me to be curious, to listen, to empathize, to both follow and lead, to be in the moment with the future in mind, and, yes, do it all for the sake of a good laugh.

The Second City, like the gift of humour itself, lets us know we are not alone in this world. We're all lovely and ridiculous and we are right to laugh at ourselves.

CATHERINE O'HARA
2019

# NEXTWORD

**T**HE FIRST TIME I saw a Second City show in 1972 in Chicago, I was hooked. I remember exactly where I was sitting and who was in that wonderful cast. This funny, smart, and rebellious show sparked something in me, and I was on my way. And when I borrowed seven thousand dollars from a friend to restart The Second City in Toronto, I had zero notion that this might turn into something of a life calling.

In March 1974, we opened at the Old Firehall in Toronto with a cast made up of Gilda Radner, Eugene Levy, John Candy, Joe Flaherty, Rosemary Radcliffe, and pretty soon, Dan Aykroyd, too. I had little experience—but loads of persistence. I loved just sitting back and taking in the shows and the improv sets. I was in awe of improvisation and its magic, and, in particular, Joe Flaherty and Dan Aykroyd, who were undoubtedly the masters of this new art form to hit Toronto. Later that decade, through the inception and production of *SCTV*, I had a front row seat to one of the funniest, most creative ensembles ever to hit the airwaves.

Years later, Bernie Sahlins thought enough of what we had accomplished in Canada to offer myself and my business partner, Len Stuart, the opportunity to purchase the Chicago theater. I have had the good fortune to watch some of the finest talents in the comedy world develop their craft and move on to successful careers. One of the more gratifying developments has been the growth of our Training Centers, which have not only nurtured the next generation of Second City players, but have also inspired regular folks ages two to hundred and four to discover the joys of improvisation our performers share: increased empathy, an ability to collaborate, and a willingness to share the spotlight. By making a tremendous impact on the social, wellness, and workplace arenas, it's safe to say that improvisation has now become a worldwide phenomenon.

ANDREW ALEXANDER
2019

"This funny, smart, and rebellious show sparked something in me, and I was on my way.

**–Andrew Alexander**

# INTRODUCTION

The Second City opened its doors on a snowy Chicago night in December of 1959 and has evolved from a small cabaret theater into the most influential comedy empire in the world, entertaining and educating over one million people a year, both on and off the stage.

Along with developing a brand-new type of theater—improvisation—The Second City has proudly fostered generation after generation of comedy trailblazers, including Alan Arkin, Dan Aykroyd, Jim Belushi, John Belushi, John Candy, Steve Carell, Stephen Colbert, Rachel Dratch, Chris Farley, Tina Fey, Valerie Harper, Barbara Harris, Bonnie Hunt, Keegan-Michael Key, Richard Kind, Linda Lavin, Eugene Levy, Andrea Martin, Jack McBrayer, Adam McKay, Tim Meadows, Colin Mochrie, Bill Murray, Mike Myers, Bob Odenkirk, Catherine O'Hara, Gilda Radner, Harold Ramis, Joan Rivers, Amy Sedaris, Martin Short, Jason Sudeikis, Betty Thomas, Nia Vardalos, George Wendt, Fred Willard, and more than seven hundred others, all of whom you can find listed at the end of this book.

*The Second City: Backstage at the World's Greatest Comedy Theater* was originally published two decades ago. It covered our beginnings as a group of chain-smoking University of Chicago outliers and delved into The Second City's entire twentieth-century history, up through our fortieth year in 1999. Sheldon Patinkin, the book's author and The Second City's longtime artistic conscience, summed up the four-day anniversary celebration thusly: "That's a lot of years, a lot of memories, all crashing in at once."

We lost Sheldon in 2014. A prolific director, educator, and writer, he was a steadfast pillar in the Chicago theater scene, a pioneer of the city's improvisation community, and a beloved mentor to thousands of creative spirits. In his honor, we are proud to present this overhauled, updated edition that captures The Second City's legacy with archival photos, never-before-published artifacts, and the (mostly) true stories that make up our collective story. Commit to the definitive history of a place famous for making things up? It might seem futile, but The Second City was built on two words that have made something out of nothing for more than sixty years:

# "YES, AND."

# CHAPTER 1

## BUT FIRST, BEFORE THE SECOND CITY

I T ALL STARTED with children's games. Rooted in the groundbreaking theater games invented by the "High Priestess of Improvisation," Viola Spolin, a new art form was birthed by a rambunctious group of University of Chicago students in the 1940s. One of those trailblazers was Spolin's son, Paul Sills. Another one was Sheldon Patinkin.

To start any kind of improvisation, someone must initiate. In the 1999 book *The Second City: Backstage at the World's Greatest Comedy Theater*, Patinkin, who was involved with the theater for some fifty-five years, took on the immense task of unravelling The Second City's winding origin story.

Here, in his own words, is how his story—and The Second City's—began.

## *The Typewriter* Bangs Out the Beginning

In the late 1940s and early 1950s, among the people attending classes or hanging around at the University of Chicago were quite a few who were soon to become participants in Second City and/or its predecessor, the Compass. They included Paul Sills, David Shepherd, Bernie Sahlins, Mike Nichols, Elaine May, Severn Darden, Andrew Duncan, Roger Bowen, Eugene Troobnick, Bill Alton, Zohra Lampert, Tony Holland, and me. There were also quite a few others who've made theater and film their careers, including Ed Asner, Fritz Weaver, and Joyce and Byrne Piven. The irony is that the University of Chicago had no theater department—or theater classes.

But there was University Theatre (UT), a sort of after-school dramatic society for smart kids. It had a paid artistic director and a budget from the university. Everything else came from the students putting in the time around schoolwork or, as often happened, instead of schoolwork, leading to panic, craziness, and threatened suicides before final exams. The plays produced at UT were difficult, tending toward the obscure and the esoteric: Karl Georg Büchner, William Wycherley, unfamiliar Shakespeare, the Čapek brothers, Josef and Karel. And we had no instruction to help us over the rough spots, which were many. Some shows were considerably better than others.

In January 1952, Sills directed and acted in University Theatre's production of Jean Cocteau's *The Typewriter*. The cast also included Nichols and Joyce Piven. I learned how to run lights for it. *The Typewriter* was a rebellion against the dominant fourth wall method of acting. The concept of the fourth wall is part of the theory of acting developed by the enormously influential late nineteenth- and early twentieth-century Russian actor and director Constantin Stanislavsky and brought to the United States in the 1930s by Stella Adler, Elia Kazan, Lee Strasberg, and other members of the Group Theatre. In fourth wall acting, you're pretending that the front of the stage is the fourth wall of the room you're pretending to be in. In other words, the actor tries to leave out any sense of performing for an audience. (Apparently Marlon Brando, a fourth wall actor, couldn't even be heard in the back half of the theater when he played "Stanley Kowalski" in *A Streetcar Named Desire* on Broadway.)

By the early 1950s, fourth wall acting was the norm for any actor who wanted to be taken seriously. Thanks to Richard Rodgers and Oscar Hammerstein, it was even starting to be expected in musicals. Comedy, however, doesn't bounce well off walls. You have to play to the audience and their laughter—or silence—and therefore can't pretend to yourself that they're not there. It's one of the many reasons for the famous quote, attributed to several people, though most frequently to Groucho Marx: "Dying is easy; comedy is hard."

*The Typewriter* became a box office hit, and talk began about starting our own theater. Of course, none of us had any money, but when has that ever stopped the talk? (One big difference between then and now: there was no existing precedent in 1952 for starting your own theater company in Chicago.)

## Games On

With the talk getting stronger, a bunch of us got together for five hours every Saturday afternoon during much of the 1952–53 school year, and Paul Sills taught us the improvisational games and exercises he learned from his mother, Viola Spolin. There are many of them.

Exercises are usually used as warm-ups or to end a class and require no advance planning. Here's one: the group is divided into two teams who then have a tug-of-war, only the rope is mimed. Each game has a single rule of play and, with few exceptions, is

**REPORT CARD**
The 1999 edition of this book read: "The irony is that the University of Chicago had no theater department—or theater classes—and it still doesn't." This is no longer true. The school, which has been home to the student-run University Theatre since 1898, launched the Committee on Theater and Performance Studies (TAPS) in 2002.

# SHELDON PATINKIN

Sheldon Patinkin was a leading creative voice at The Second City for over five decades. Born in Chicago in 1935, Patinkin earned a master's degree in English at the University of Chicago when he was just nineteen years old. It was there that he developed friendships with Mike Nichols, Elaine May, and Second City co-founder Paul Sills. Patinkin explained how he was eventually bestowed the title of Second City artistic director:

> In November 1960, Bernie Sahlins called and asked if I wanted to be the manager of Second City and sort of assist Paul Sills. Since, by then, I was getting a stomachache every time I walked on the University of Chicago campus, I jumped at the offer. Six months later, I'd quit grad school, much to my parents' consternation. (It wasn't until my name started appearing in newspaper columns and relatives started calling them to try to get Saturday night tickets that they were able to accept my decision.) One day, Paul Sills, back from New York to direct, was yelling at the actors more than usual, then finally turned around and said, "See what you can do with them, Sheldon," and walked out. Usually when he did that, he would come back after a while. After about half an hour, he hadn't come back. I called Bernie at home and asked if he knew where Paul was. Bernie said he was on a plane back to New York and that I was now the director. And that's how I became the artistic director.

By the late 1960s, Patinkin had "directed about fifteen shows, plus fourteen Touring Company shows, a couple of our shows in New York, a couple of our shows at the Royal Alexandra in Toronto, including occasionally cooking the hamburgers, selling the tickets, seating the customers, and even filling in for the pianist a few times" in addition to teaching improv workshops. Next, he headed north to lend his expertise to The Second City's Toronto theater and worked as one of the associate producers and writers for the first season of *SCTV* before returning to Chicago and helping to formalize the first Second City Training Center.

In addition to his work with The Second City, Patinkin led the first workshops for the now-legendary Steppenwolf Theatre Company, co-founding The School at Steppenwolf, where he taught for seventeen years, and worked as an artistic consultant at the theater, mentoring actors like John Malkovich, Laurie Metcalf, and Gary Sinise. For three decades, he was chair of the Theatre Department at Columbia College Chicago and assumed the title of chair emeritus in 2009. Patinkin also co-created the Comedy Studies program in 2007, a groundbreaking educational partnership between Columbia and Second City.

The beloved mentor to thousands of performers, directors, and creative spirits—and a true pioneer of Chicago's improvisational community—passed away in September 2014 at the age of seventy-nine. "He had a terrific relationship with the younger generation. He just loved to be around young people and loved mentoring and teaching. He was embraced by that community," Andrew Alexander, CEO and executive producer of The Second City, told the *Chronicle*, Columbia College's student newspaper. "He just loved the theater, and was very instrumental in the early years of the beginning of the small theater community. He loved them and they loved him. Chicago is well-known for taking care of its own, and Sheldon represented that very well."

Sheldon Patinkin

Mike Nichols (left) and Elaine May

# ELAINE MAY AND MIKE NICHOLS

Elaine May and Mike Nichols formed their legend-ary comedy duo, "Nichols and May," after leaving the Compass. Their live improv acts were a smash hit on Broadway, resulting in three albums, the first of which won them a Grammy. After disbanding in 1961 and walking away from their combined success, they each went on to have tremendous careers. Nichols directed Broadway classics and iconic films, including *Who's Afraid of Virginia Woolf?*, *Catch-22*, and *The Graduate*, which earned him an Academy Award. In fact, Nichols's Emmy, Grammy, Oscar, and Tony wins made him a member of the elite EGOT club. He was married to journalist Diane Sawyer for twenty-six years, until he passed away in 2014.

May found herself in Hollywood, acting in films and becoming a two-time Oscar-nominated screen-writer, a playwright, and a talented director in her own right. In 2018, May made a "funny, maddening

and heartbreaking" (so said the *Hollywood Re-porter*) lauded return to Broadway after a fifty-year absence in the revival of Kenneth Lonergan's *The Waverly Gallery*. Her performance won her the Tony Award for Best Performance by an Actress in a Leading Role in a Play, May's first major acting award, at the age of eighty-seven.

Among the duo's many fans is Dan Aykroyd, who credits the pair with leading him toward The Second City. "My first introduction to Second City-style humor was a 'Nichols and May' album," he said. "It was the one for their Broadway show, *An Evening with Mike Nichols and Elaine May*. I remember hear-ing that on the radio, seeing them on *Ed Sullivan*, and being inspired by their work." Her performance won her the Tony Award for Best Performance by an Actress in a Leading Role in a Play, May's first major acting award, at the age of eighty-seven.

performed on an empty stage, with no costumes, and everything mimed except chairs. A game begins with the class counting off into two, three, or four people per team for that particular game. Then each team privately plans the three basic questions needed for any improvised scene: who? (who you are), what? (a mutual physical activity), and where? (the setting of the scene).

After planning that much, and usually only that much, you are given the rule for the game you're about to play. It might be to do the scene in gibberish or as a silent movie. It might be to make as many entrances and exits as you can, but only while everyone else onstage is looking at you and without your saying anything about the fact that you're trying to make an exit or entrance. Some games and exercises help work on character (the who), some on the where, some on the what, some on focusing on the other, and there are many other kinds as well, all helpful to the actor in creating an individual character within an ensemble.

Sills, of course, had started learning the games from Spolin when he was a child (as had Paul Sand and Alan Arkin). By 1953, he knew he was teaching us the games on those Saturday afternoons in order to build an acting ensemble for his dreamed-of new theater, and that's what happened to us. That's what always happens when a group plays Spolin's improv games together for a while; they learn to trust each other, to more or less cope with each other's foibles, and to work off what's happening between them and the others instead

Viola Spolin

# VIOLA SPOLIN

Born in 1906, actress, social worker, and educator Viola Spolin became drama supervisor for the Works Progress Administration Recreation Project in Chicago, where she invented a series of theater games designed to teach dramatics to children and recent immigrants. Her son, Paul Sills, then brought these games to his theatrically inclined friends. Spolin remained an active teacher, artist, and writer until her death in 1994. Her 1963 book, *Improvisation for the Theater*, remains a classic. The book defends the position that "it is highly possible that what is called talented behavior is simply a greater individual capacity for experiencing."

# "EVERYONE CAN ACT. EVERYONE CAN IMPROVISE. ANYONE WHO WISHES CAN PLAY IN THE THEATER AND LEARN TO BECOME 'STAGE WORTHY.'"

—Viola Spolin, *Improvisation for the Theater*

of just off themselves. After all, in an improv, as opposed to a play, you don't know what you're going to say or do next, and whatever it is has to come off what you see and hear from the others, combined with what you want from them.

The last show of the 1952–53 University Theatre season was Sills's extraordinary production of Bertolt Brecht's *The Caucasian Chalk Circle* in its Chicago premiere and second production anywhere. The cast of twenty, between us, played about sixty characters without ever leaving the stage—a perfect chance to use the ensemble techniques we had been learning in the workshops. With the arrival of David Shepherd, who had as strong a vision as Sills's and a little money, talk also began on the possibility of opening a political cabaret for working-class audiences, which was Shepherd's dream.

## Playwrights Theatre Club

Since no one was really ready for a political cabaret yet, Paul Sills, David Shepherd, and Eugene Troobnick opened Playwrights Theatre Club on June 23, 1953, with a restaged and somewhat recast production of *The Caucasian Chalk Circle*. Playwrights was located at the corner of North and LaSalle (a block from the current Second City) on the outskirts of the area known as Old Town, far from the University of Chicago and slightly off the beaten track. Our space was a tile-floored converted Chinese restaurant upstairs from a drugstore and an all-night diner. We incorporated as a club, because that was the only way you could be not-for-profit in those days—our lawyer had to invent a lot of that stuff as we went along. We sold memberships instead of tickets. The seats were wood-frame director's chairs with detachable red, blue, or yellow canvas seats and backs; each color was a different "membership" price.

There was a record heat wave on opening night and no air-conditioning, but the critics loved us anyway, and we were an instant hit in our 125-seat house with individual memberships priced at one to two dollars. (The diner downstairs sold an excellent barbecued beef sandwich with fries, lettuce, tomato, and coffee for seventy-five cents, if that helps you understand the economy. Somebody always seemed to be playing Eartha Kitt's "I Want to Be Evil" on the jukebox down there.) We were the first local theater in years, the beginning of a movement that wouldn't see its major growth until the late 1970s.

In two years, we did close to thirty productions. The shows ran an average of three weeks each, some less, some more, depending on business. We did six performances a week, no matinees. We would close on a Sunday and open the next show on Tuesday. We were young and didn't know you couldn't do all that. We were learning our craft by doing it six nights a week.

We rehearsed daytimes and after the shows and made sets, costumes, and everything

**GAME CHANGER**
According to Joyce Piven, Viola Spolin was better at creating exercises than she was at remembering the mechanics of them. "When we asked Viola about particular points of improv games," the founding Playwrights member recalled, "[Spolin] said, 'I really don't know how that game goes—or any of them, really. I was in a state of revelation when I wrote them.'"

> "When they create a pantheon of theatrical gods, Paul Sills should be Zeus. He freed the actor."
>
> **—Ed Asner**

# PAUL SILLS

Revered as the godfather of modern improvisational sketch comedy, Paul Sills was the original director of Playwrights Theatre Club, the Compass, and The Second City; he was also one of Second City's three co-founders. "Without Paul, there would have been no improv movement. He had the very highest ideals, and he never compromised," Bernie Sahlins told the *Chicago Tribune*. An avid evangelist of the improvisational games he learned from his mother, Viola Spolin, Sills's genius (and frequent volatility) was transmitted as often as not with grunts, groans, hollering, and throwing chairs around the room. "He's a fucking genius, and there isn't anybody from all of this that doesn't know that, whether they love him or hate him," Sheldon Patinkin said in Jeffrey Sweet's 1978 oral history of The Second City, *Something Wonderful Right Away*. In Mark Siska's 2014 documentary, *Compass Cabaret 55*, Ed Asner proposed that "when they create a pantheon of theatrical gods, Paul Sills should be Zeus. He freed the actor."

Sills got more out of people than they knew they had in them. He insisted that improvisers stay in the moment, never going into their heads to find what to say and do next. He also understood how to place all of a show's separate scenes, songs, and blackouts into a running order that made the whole thing feel unified—while still managing to make all the performers look good—setting the standard for every Second City director to follow. "He was the first, and he was the best," Patinkin upheld. After Sills's death in 2008, Andrew Alexander called him "the unsung hero of Second City."

Sills once said, "There's no laugh like the explosion of laughter after improvisation." Thanks to his unique genius, those explosions of laughter continue to this day at The Second City and around the world.

Paul Sills

"No air-condition-
ing" is not a prob-
lem that audiences
at The Second City
have to contend
with in the modern
age. In fact, it is
the opposite—the
thermostat is set
pretty low these
days. That is be-
cause the weather
up onstage under
the lava-hot lights
is vastly different
for the performers
than it is for the
audience down
below. . . . And no
one wants a bunch
of overheated ac-
tors raining sweat
down onto the
front row.

else whenever we could. We lived communally off the take, earning five, ten, or fifteen dollars a week, each according to need. (Since Barbara Harris and I still lived more or less at home—we were both seventeen when Playwrights started—we were among those who got five bucks a week, as did those few with day jobs. I sometimes brought food from home for everyone, since my wonderful parents worried about whether anyone was getting enough to eat.) Many of the men in the company lived in little alcoves around the back and one side of the theater, separated from the main auditorium by curtains, not doors, leaving privacy at a premium.

As we were approaching our first anniversary, we decided to move to a bigger space and join Actors' Equity, the actors' and stage managers' union, which provided a mini-mum guaranteed salary of fifty-five dollars a week, allowing the guys who had been living in the theater to move into their own small apartments and still have enough money to eat. By then, Bernie Sahlins, at the time a businessman with Pentron tape recorders and a travel agency—and therefore someone with some money—had replaced Troobnick as one of the producers. Troobnick did not want to be a boss anymore, or at least that's what we were told.

The second Playwrights space, a two-hundred-seat theater, was a converted photogra-pher's studio at the corner of Division and Dearborn, upstairs from an expensive restau-rant and across the street from the art film house. Membership prices went up a little. Business was usually excellent, but there were more seats to fill and more expenses. Actors started leaving for New York because there wasn't enough work in Chicago, and most of it didn't pay much better than Playwrights. Also, after eighteen months of productions, we were getting tired—especially Sills, who had directed most of the shows.

In early spring of 1955, the fire department descended. To this day, some people believe it's because we were suspected of being fellow travelers and possibly even communists in that Joseph McCarthy era. Among other things, we had started at the University of Chi-cago, which had been labeled "pinko" by anti-communist government investigators of the time. Quite a few of us came under suspicion because we were poor but Jewish. Also, we had produced works by Brecht, who had recently lied to the House Un-American Activities Committee, fleeing the country the next day to take up residence in communist East Berlin, and we had just done an original play called *Rich but Happy*. Whatever started the inves-tigation, we were certainly in violation of the outmoded fire codes and had been all along, and they closed us down. We did a few shows in rented spaces, but the spirit was gone, as were many of the original ensemble members.

# ED ASNER

Ed Asner

Many talented people were drawn to Playwrights Theatre Club in those days by the opportunity it offered young actors to learn their craft and to work on a regular basis. Ed Asner, a former assembly-line worker for General Motors, was one of them. He was in charge of cleaning up the theater before the show every night. As he had only recently gotten out of the U.S. Army Signal Corps, he ran the place "like he was the master sergeant and we the buck privates," Patinkin recalled. "If Ed was angry with someone, that person got latrine duty that night." As much an activist as he is a performer these days, Asner holds the distinction of being the only actor to win both comedy and drama Emmys for playing the same role, "Lou Grant."

## The Compass

During the nearly two years of Playwrights, we had worked on Viola Spolin's improv games with Paul Sills whenever we could. Spolin herself, who was living in Los Angeles, came in toward the end, when excitement was building about opening David Shepherd's political cabaret theater. She arrived just in time to do improv workshops and help form the ensemble that became the first company of the new place, which Shepherd decided to call the Compass because he wanted it to point in whichever direction society was already going. It was to be informal and close to where people lived so they could come without dressing up, where there would be food and drink, and where they would see shows dealing with the life they led, rather than the illusions, dreams, and lies being put out by Hollywood, New York, and Washington.

Shepherd wanted to open it in a working-class neighborhood in Gary, Indiana, a steel mill town an hour's drive from Chicago, or in the neighborhood of Chicago's stockyards; fortunately (though not from Shepherd's point of view), neither of those worked out.

Fred Wranovics, a popular bartender at the Woodlawn Tap (known as Jimmy's) on Fifty-Fifth Street in the University of Chicago neighborhood, had just bought the Hi-Hat Lounge, also on Fifty-Fifth Street, and had also bought the empty store next door. After knocking a hole in the wall between the two buildings, the Compass ensemble, with a lot of

Bernie Sahlins

"Bernie saved my life. Second City wasn't a theater ensemble to me; it was a halfway house."

–Alan Arkin

# BERNIE SAHLINS

After selling his share in a tape recorder factory, Bernard (but "Bernie" to everyone, always) Sahlins became one of The Second City's three co-founders and original owners, serving as producer for the theater's first twenty-six years. He also produced several television projects in the United States, England, and Canada, and he co-developed *SCTV* and produced the show's first season. He met his incredible wife of over forty years, Jane Nicholl Sahlins, in 1963 while working on a TV series in Manchester called *Second City Reports*.

Sahlins began directing at The Second City Chicago in 1969, proving himself to be more intellectually oriented than the directors who had preceded him. He insisted on keeping the reference level of the show material as high as possible and—like every director before and after him—he had his own agenda for the kinds of shows he wanted to create.

Andrew Alexander and Len Stuart bought The Second City from Sahlins in 1985, but he remained artistic director for three more years. "Bernie Sahlins was charming, smart, and influential. He used those gifts to not only create one of the theater world's most treasured institutions, he gave that institution the cultural fortitude to sustain itself through seismic sea changes in the way the world works," Second City stalwart Kelly Leonard said about the man who hired him in 1988.

The comedy impresario famous for sporting mustard stains on his tie passed away on June 16, 2013, at the age of ninety. "Bernie Sahlins made no small plans, and his legacy will be felt for generations to come," Alexander told the *Chicago Tribune*. A few months later, a packed-to-the-gills memorial was held in the Chicago Shakespeare Theater, where a group that included Bill Murray sang Sahlins one last "Goodnight Song."

Alan Arkin, a 1960 alum, said of Sahlins:

*Bernie saved my life. Second City wasn't a theater ensemble to me; it was a halfway house. I think it was true of all of us for the first few years of the place. We didn't know that there was any future in it; we just knew that our lives were being saved by getting up and railing against everything we hated. When you ran out of things to hate, you went on and did something else with some other theater group. Bernie not only gave me a job, he took me in. I became his family; he became my family—the first family that I ever had and loved.*

hard work—especially by cast member Andrew Duncan—converted the empty store into a playing space. The storefront windows were left unblocked so passersby could see the show, an excellent way of getting them inside. Wranovics rechristened the place the Compass Tavern, and the show opened on July 5, 1955. (It was supposed to open on the Fourth of July, but the air conditioner broke down.)

Sills directed all the shows the first summer, and Shepherd was the producer and one of the performers. Among the many performers that summer along with Shepherd and Duncan were Roger Bowen, Barbara Harris, and Elaine May.

David Shepherd

# DAVID SHEPHERD

Simply put, there would be no Second City without David Shepherd. In 1952, he hitchhiked his way to Chicago after studying at Harvard and getting his master's degree in theater history at Columbia University. Shepherd helped opened Playwrights Theatre Club in 1953, where he created tirelessly as a producer and occasional director before the project collapsed "because I'm not a businessman," Shepherd admitted at The Second City's fiftieth anniversary, nine years before his death at age ninety-four.

Shepherd's vision of a political cabaret for working-class audiences became a reality with the debut of the Compass. "I was a student of literature. I thought the three-act play had turned theater to shit, and I wanted to get rid of it," he told Newcity in 2015. "It's an unnatural trap for talent. Improvisation puts the burden on the player, takes it off the writer, and becomes a whole exploratory method."

"David was a passionate scholar and champion of the work. His mind was always in innovation mode, and he was never lacking for fresh new ways to explore the world of improvisation," said Andrew Alexander about the Second City forefather.

The Compass began with a format that included a short opening piece or two to get the audience laughing, followed by the "Living Newspaper," twenty minutes of improvs on and narrated reenactments of articles in that day's paper (not unlike *SNL*'s "Weekend Update" segment or *The Daily Show*). Then came an original politically or socially conscious short play created from a bare bones plot outline the cast wrote out ahead of time, which they would improvise for the audience. These scenario plays dealt with such subjects as teen-age parental and peer pressure, high-powered salesmen, tax evasion, and the university neighborhood itself.

At the conclusion of the act, the actors would take suggestions from the audience in such categories as political events, authors, pet peeves, and so on and, after a short break, do a set of improvisations based on the suggestions. All this, done with some chairs and hats as the only props, was performed five nights a week: two shows on Friday, three on Saturday, with a new "Living Newspaper" every day and a new scenario play every week or two.

Shepherd and business manager Charley Jacobs moved the show on October 1, 1955, to a larger space on Lake Park Avenue near Fifty-Third Street, on the fringe of the University of Chicago area. They dubbed it the Compass at the Dock. There were some changes in the personnel: Sills had gone to England on a Fulbright, taking his then-wife, Harris, with him; Bowen was about to be drafted; Shepherd was now the director; May was running the improv workshops and performing along with Duncan and a company enhanced by the arrival of, among others, Mike Nichols and Severn Darden. Shepherd also decided they needed a pianist at the new Compass space.

"I did audition for David Shepherd, who heard a few bars and asked if I wanted to be the intermission pianist for the Compass at the Dock, opening in a few weeks—five dollars a night, drinks at cost. I said yes," recounted William Allaudin Mathieu. "It never occurred to anyone, least of all me, that the club pianist should become part of the show."

Mathieu recalled the widespread influence the Compass had:

> There were many who came to see us who recognized the Compass as not only
> a new level of freedom in making theater, but also, more tellingly, a new level
> of creative social thought. We were the darlings of the university cognoscente,
> especially the social scientists. One day, a scene of Mike and Elaine's even came
> up for discussion in my Social Sciences II class. . . . Something new was clearly
> in the air, something people found entertaining, intellectually stimulating, and
> useful in their lives.

Compass shows started running a good deal longer than a week or two each, but business was not great. In May 1956, Shepherd moved the show to the Argo Off-Beat Room on Broadway near Devon, very far away from the university. By then, along with Shelley Berman, Duncan, May, and Nichols, the cast included Mark and Bobbi Gordon, and music was supplied by the Eddie Baker Trio. In July, Harris rejoined the company, Sills directed again for a while, a few other people came, a few went, and the show closed in January 1957. The now-legendary and highly influential Compass had played in Chicago for only eighteen months, about the same length of time as Playwrights, although most audience members who remember those days are surprised when they are reminded that's all it was.

## JERRY STILLER AND ANNE MEARA

Jerry Stiller and Anne Meara formed their own act after leaving the Compass and turning down Paul Sills's offer to join the new group at Second City. "Stiller and Meara" were popular in clubs, on records, and on TV, appearing on *The Ed Sullivan Show* thirty-six times. In addition to their plum professional partnership and equally fruitful individual careers, the two shared a loving marriage for sixty-one years, until Meara's passing in 2015.

Their son, Ben, is an avowed lifelong *SCTV* fan. An *Entertainment Weekly* review of *The Ben Stiller Show*, his early-nineties sketch series, called it "*SCTV* with better hair."

Clockwise from top left: Alan Arkin, Jerry Stiller, Nancy Ponder, and Anne Meara

# JOYCE AND BYRNE PIVEN

Director and actress Joyce Piven, along with her late husband, Byrne, were among the founding members of Playwrights Theatre Club. "We did *Henry IV*, Chekhov—I played 'Nina' in *The Seagull*. . . . Viola Spolin came on Saturdays and taught us theater games to make us more present and creative. Those games changed everything. And it all came from Chicago—all the seeds for future forms," Joyce said in a 2015 interview with *Newcity*.

*The Typewriter* remains a significant point in the group's rule-bending approach to theater. "Even at an early date, Paul was pushing the envelope, breaking the so-called fourth wall between the actors and the audience," she said. "It was very exciting, because we would enter through the audience. I remember many nights standing next to someone as I was emoting, with people sitting there either chewing gum right in my ear or knitting very diligently."

The Pivens opened the famed Piven Theatre Workshop in Evanston, Illinois, in the early 1970s. The workshop includes amongst its alumni their son, Jeremy Piven, Lili Taylor, John and Joan Cusack, and Aidan Quinn. Daughter Shira Piven, also a director, married Second City alumnus Adam McKay.

## The Compass Points Away

On April 2, 1957, David Shepherd and his new partner, Ted Flicker, reopened the Compass at the Crystal Palace in St. Louis, by invitation of the owner, Fred Landesman. The show closed in September, presumably to reopen in New York, but the New York booking fell through, so Mike Nichols and Elaine May started their own nightclub act.

Shepherd produced other incarnations of the Compass in various places, using such performers as Alan Alda, Alan Arkin, Jack Burns, Diana Sands, and Jerry Stiller and Anne Meara, who formed their own act after leaving the Compass.

In the late 1950s, nightclubbing was very popular and comedy records were selling in the millions. Moreover, comedy was changing: more personal, more laid-back, filled with ideas, characters, and stories rather than jokes. Some of it was even political. Severn Darden and Del Close started doing stand-up acts. Paul Sills and his friend Howard Alk, who had made occasional appearances at the Compass, got jobs at the Gate of Horn, a popular Chicago folk music and comedy club where Lenny Bruce appeared frequently. Sills was house manager, and Alk ran the lights. They began talking a lot between themselves and with others about starting another Compass-like place in Chicago. Although Shepherd was firmly into other ways of doing things and not interested in joining up, he gave them his blessing—but not the name.

# CHAPTER 2

## 1959

### A COMEDY REVOLUTION BEGINS

**W**HEN BERNIE SAHLINS, Paul Sills, and Howard Alk took over a storefront at 1842 North Wells, the former site of Wong Cleaners & Dyers, they didn't know how soon the public would come a-knocking. "For several weeks after we took occupancy," Sahlins wrote in his 2001 memoir, *Days and Nights at The Second City*, "people would knock and mournfully enter brandishing their laundry tickets." (Today, the location is home to a condo building that aptly boasts a 24-7 laundry room.) The trio had originally envisioned the new club as a coffeehouse where friends and even strangers could sit around and talk, but they soon decided they might as well put on a little show, too. All they needed was a name.

"Naming the theater was a collective endeavor that took weeks," Sahlins remembered. "At about this time, a series of articles about Chicago entitled 'Second City' was appearing in the *New Yorker*. As the appellation implied, their author, a wonderful journalist named A. J. Liebling, did not think much of our metropolis on the lake. In fact, he was relentlessly negative about its citizenry and culture. I think it was Howard Alk who suggested we defiantly carry the title of the articles as our banner."

## Setting the Scene

Inspired by the aesthetic and feel of German cabarets, the team brought in a self-taught St. Louis designer named Jimmy Masucci to make magic on their tight budget. Masucci pulled apart old telephone booths, painted them black, and paneled the club's walls with them. "In the center of each," Bernie Sahlins described, "under the glass, he installed prints from a set he had cut from a book on Roman antiquities. The effect was stunning."

Paul Sand (left), Andrew Duncan, Mina Kolb, Howard Alk (in helmet and glasses), and Eugene Troobnick

# HOWARD ALK

Howard Alk was "born with self-confidence," said his ex-wife, Jones Cullinan, in the film *Howard Alk: A Life on the Edge*. Alk was a larger-than-life iconoclast, described by Chicago Black Panthers member Bob Lee as looking "like Paul Bunyan." At just fourteen years old, he enrolled at the University of Chicago and became a member of the Compass. Along with Bernie Sahlins and Paul Sills, Alk was a co-founder of The Second City and is credited with coining the theater's name. Alk "couldn't act, play the guitar, or sing, but he managed to do all those things convincingly," Sahlins wrote. "Howard stayed with us only a few months and then went off to do whatever his thing was, but his incisive knowledge of young, avant-garde thinking was invaluable at the start."

William Allaudin Mathieu, The Second City's first musical director, has a rather colorful story about Alk in those early days. "I thought of him at first as a kind of night worker in the 'Intellectual Mafia,' but after the actual Mafia bombed Second City for refusing to pay [for] protection, Howard showed up to work packing a piece and peeking out of the newly replaced windows from behind the velvet curtains, like a film noir scene."

After leaving The Second City in the early sixties and selling his stake in the company to Sahlins, Alk entrenched himself in the New York counterculture scene while devoting himself to independent filmmaking as a writer, editor, and director. He made the 1971 documentary *The Murder of Fred Hampton* about the charismatic Black Panthers leader who was murdered by Chicago police. He wrote and directed the popular 1975 biopic of Janis Joplin, *Janis: A Film*, and was a longtime friend and collaborator of Bob Dylan's.

Alk, whom Sahlins called "a great bear of a man with a highly developed sense of irony, a voracious appetite for high-level gossip, and a well-developed nose for trends and fakery," died of a heroin overdose in 1982.

The most resourceful of shoppers, Sahlins and company purchased 150 bentwood chairs at an auction for a dollar each, cleaned up on bar equipment thanks to the ruin of a recently bankrupted restaurant, and bought carpet remnants for a dollar a yard—which were still being nailed down as the audience entered the room on opening night. The red velvet banquettes and Formica-topped tables sat 125, but Violet Torre, the first hostess, claimed she could squeeze in 150 if everyone promised to breathe in unison. In the theater's very small lobby, the "box office" was a little metal cashbox sitting atop a card table—which doubled as the office during the day.

As for the actors' backstage respite, "We used the first of the two basically uninhabitable floors above the theater at 1842 North Wells as a dressing room, entered through a separate street door or from backstage," wrote Sheldon Patinkin. The dressing room was "a totally unpainted, unadorned, cold-in-winter, hot-in-summer room in the semi-decayed building over the club." Expanding the theater's footprint into the great outdoors, they opened a summer beer garden in the vacant lot next door to the north, which eventually served ice cream and screened silent movies.

## The First Cast

With Bernie Sahlins producing and Paul Sills directing, The Second City hired its first ensemble. The original eight consisted of co-founder Howard Alk, along with Roger Bowen, Severn Darden, Andrew Duncan, Barbara Harris, Mina Kolb, Eugene Troobnick, and musical director William Allaudin Mathieu.

### ROGER BOWEN

Actor, author, and chess competitor Roger Bowen wrote the outline for a stage story that was developed by a group of University of Chicago actors into a full play, all through improvisation. By demonstrating the power of their improvisational techniques, the play served as the impetus for David Shepherd to create the Compass. "He of devastating wit," as Bernie Sahlins called Bowen, left The Second City after the first show but continued sending in scripts. He returned in 1961 for a stint in the sixth revue, *Six of One*.

A prolific writer, Bowen authored eleven novels. He appeared frequently on television, but his most notable film role was as "Colonel Henry Blake" in Robert Altman's 1970 movie, *M*A*S*H*. Bowen's final on-camera appearance was in *What About Bob?* with Bill Murray, which was released five years before his death in 1996.

## SEVERN DARDEN

Intellectual clown Severn Darden was infamous across the University of Chicago campus long before he joined the Compass and The Second City. As a student, the eccentric—who was born Francis Xavier Severn Teakle Darden Jr.—drove around in an old Rolls-Royce and often wore formal clothes with tennis shoes. Darden habitually chewed on handkerchiefs, napkins, or anything else at hand, including, occasionally, people. "All Second City performers are good, but Severn Darden most personifies the quintessential Second City talent," said Fred Willard, 1965 Second City alumnus. "One night, he was in the audience and joined us in the set. He took off on one of the most imaginative improvs I've ever seen. Afterwards, he said, 'Boy, that was a bomb.' It was then I felt I still had a long way to go."

One of Darden's favorite characters to play was "Dr. Walther von der Vogelweide," a German professor who was an expert in whatever subject the audience suggested. In real life, he seemed quite a bit like an absentminded professor, although he was anything but. Blessed (or cursed) with a "vacuum cleaner mind," as Bernie Sahlins described it, Darden could "instantly call forth every obscure fact, philosophical tenet, and literary work ever produced by man."

Not everyone was a fan. "Severn pinched my boobies the first time I met him. It was just madness. I could never relate to Severn. He wore a cape and carried a walking stick," said Joan Rivers, 1961 Second City alumna.

### BEHIND THE BENTWOOD

Named for the method in which wet wood is literally bent into shape, the bentwood chair was invented in 1859 by German cabinetmaker Michael Thonet. His timeless, simple design—six pieces of wood, ten screws, two nuts—is now one of the most familiar silhouettes in the world, and we wouldn't be The Second City without it. Six of those chairs served as the scenery on opening night . . . and have continued to do so every night since.

ABOVE: Andrew
Duncan onstage in
1961. Sir Edmund
Hillary (third from
left) and his sherpa,
Tenzing Norgay
(second from left),
are in the front row.

RIGHT: Barbara
Harris (left) and
Mina Kolb

Later in his life, Darden appeared in various films and television series. His most notable film role was the coldhearted "Kolp" in *Conquest of the Planet of the Apes* and *Battle for the Planet of the Apes*. Darden lived in semiretirement in Los Angeles before moving to Santa Fe in 1992, and he passed away at age sixty-five. The Second City Training Center Severn Darden Graduate Program is named in his honor.

## ANDREW DUNCAN

The quintessential straight man at both the Compass and The Second City, Andrew Duncan was tasked with welcoming the audience and introducing the first scene of the night. "Somehow it fell on me to come out and say, 'Welcome to Second City. Tonight, we'd like to bring you our show *Too Many Hats*,' or whatever it was," he said in *Something Wonderful Right Away*.

Because Duncan was also very politically and socially conscious—he had been a social worker—and had an organized mind, he was the glue that held together every company he was a part of. After his years at The Second City, he has continued to work in theater, television, and film, including roles in *Love Story* and *Slap Shot*.

## BARBARA HARRIS

Barbara Harris joined Playwrights as an apprentice when she was still a high school student. As a founding member of both the Compass and The Second City, her contributions to the art of improvisation and the legacy of The Second City are incalculable. "My favorite Second City memory is when Todd Cazaux, the only male on our waitstaff, ran to help some of his customers who were stuck in the snow," she once said. "When he finally pushed their car out, he came back wet and cold and covered with snow, only to find they did not pay or tip him."

More than anything, her wit and warmth are what paved the way for so many performers at The Second City. However, Harris's physical appearance often caused her colleagues to underestimate her talent. Intended compliments like "the innocent-looking ingenue with the unexpectedly rapierlike mind" and "beautiful and clearly vulnerable. . . . Nearly every man in the audience fell in love with her" detract from how truly rare her gifts were.

Once named by Robert De Niro as one of his four favorite actors, Harris went on to much acclaim on Broadway and in Hollywood, earning a Tony nomination for the show *On a Clear Day You Can See Forever* and winning in 1967 for *The Apple Tree*. Harris received an Oscar nomination in 1971 for *Who Is Harry Kellerman and Why Is He Saying Those Terrible Things About Me?* Other celebrated film performances were in Robert Altman's *Nashville*, *A Thousand Clowns*, Francis Ford Coppola's *Peggy Sue Got Married*, *Grosse*

"Everyone gets acting mixed up with the desire to be famous, but some of us really just stumbled into the fame part, while we were really just interested in the process of acting."

**–Barbara Harris**

*Pointe Blank*, and opposite a teenaged Jodie Foster in *Freaky Friday*. (The 2003 *Freaky Friday* remake starred Lindsay Lohan, who also infiltrated the Plastics in the Tina Fey–penned movie *Mean Girls*.)

"Barbara Harris established the role at Second City of ferociously smart women who refused to be mere adjuncts to the boys. She brought an emotional complexity that has rarely been matched," said Andrew Alexander upon her death in 2018.

"I just felt she was the greatest thing in the world," her friend and peer Ed Asner told the *Chicago Sun-Times*. "She had a great sense of humor, if you connected with her, and was a joy to work with."

### MINA KOLB

"Second City is about telling the truth. The reason Mina succeeded, and succeeded so beautifully, was that she always called them as she saw them," said Bernie Sahlins. "She told the truth." When Mina Kolb was hired, she was already a local celebrity. She and Ray Rayner had spent five years on a local Chicago TV show called *Rayner Shine*, where they lip-synced live to records while teenagers danced. She had never improvised before The Second City. "I didn't know what was going on," Kolb recalled. "I grew up in a little town, way out there somewhere. I didn't know what they were talking about. I never understood a word of it."

"I remember rehearsals with Paul Sills and Mina Kolb," Alan Arkin said. "Paul would be rehearsing us, screaming and yelling and ranting and raving and wanting to plumb the depths of the intellectual climate of Chicago and the country. Mina was the only person in the group who was just sitting there, reading the newspaper, and I think it was the comics! She paid no attention, but it worked."

Kolb's onstage character was so clearly defined that, for a long time, Chicago ad agencies frequently asked for "Mina Kolb types." You might recognize her as Jeff Garlin's mother on *Curb Your Enthusiasm*, as Kolb eventually relocated to California, where she moved on to movies, TV, and both teaching and performing improvisation. Her most recent acting credit again teamed her with Garlin. She appeared in his 2006 film, *I Want Someone to Eat Cheese With*. The independent rom-com featured a smorgasbord of Second City and Compass players, who, if we were to list them all here, might take up an entire chapter of this book.

## EUGENE TROOBNICK

One of the original producers and company members of Playwrights, Eugene Troobnick was a go-to character actor at The Second City, taking on diverse roles from businessman to Satan (though some might say those two examples aren't diverse in the least). Bernie Sahlins said Troobnick "was close to embodying the stereotype of the classical actor but self-aware enough to parody the type brilliantly."

He went on to teach and perform at the Yale School of Drama and had a recurring role on the soap opera *Guiding Light*. Troobnick helped make an indelible mark on the world before passing away in 2003. "I do think that we did help start changing the consciousness of the country," he said in *Something Wonderful Right Away*.

## WILLIAM ALLAUDIN MATHIEU

William Allaudin Mathieu, or "Bill," as he was called in the old days, was the first pianist and musical director for both the Compass and The Second City. A master at setting moods with improvised music and underscoring, he also wrote the original songs and musical parodies that dotted the shows. Mathieu, who had toured with the Stan Kenton Orchestra, sometimes even played the trumpet in the show—occasionally, he would play his trumpet with one hand and the piano with the other. His talents set a high audio bar for every Second City musical director after him. Here is how he explained his legacy:

> *I've written dozens of songs for Second City, but there were also the ten thousand cues playing the actors on and off, establishing mood, atmosphere, and context, and supplying references—a vast, amorphous opus of fragments. I think these fragments went a long way toward setting the tone of Second City in the early days, of giving it an eclectic aesthetic and in helping to make a coherent style out of the diversity of theatrical forms that were arising. I think the modus was passed intact to my successors, who elaborated on it and expanded it in wonderful, creative ways.*

"I watched the unfolding of events from a vantage point no one else had: the piano bench." **–William Allaudin Mathieu**

**OPENING DECEMBER 16**

THE SECOND CITY, located at 1842 North Wells, will be Chicago's first combination coffee house and night club.

THE SECOND CITY, began five years ago as a cabaret theatre, using the talents of Elaine May, Mike Nichols, Shelley Berman and many others. In those days it was called Compass. Since then fame, military service, and Fulbright fellowships have scattered that company. Now Paul Sills, director of both Compass and Playwrights Theatre Club has assembled a new company, including several of the former Compass players.

THE FIRST PRODUCTION, an improvisation by the company entitled Excelsior! (and Other Outcries) is a satire with music, illustrating a startling new trend in American business, as yet undetected by the sociologists.

THE COFFEE HOUSE, in an adjoining room, provides a depressurized atmosphere where one can nurse a mocha or a martini, play chess, converse, or listen to quiet music. Coffee house hours will be from 5 P.M. to 2 A.M.. Sandwiches, pastries, continental coffees and mixed drinks will be served in both rooms. There is no minimum at any time in either room.

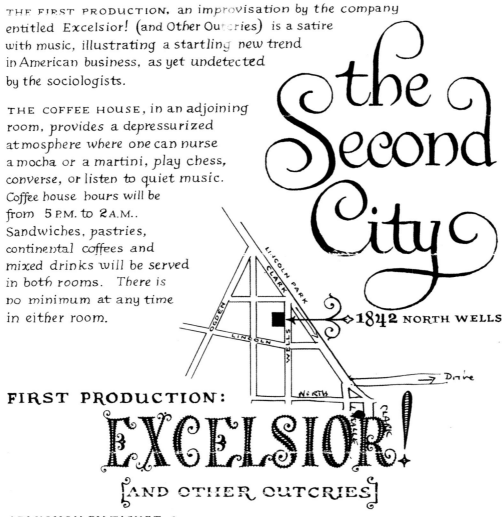

the Second City

1842 NORTH WELLS

**FIRST PRODUCTION:**

**EXCELSIOR!**

[AND OTHER OUTCRIES]

ADMISSION BY TICKET⤳

    $1.50 ⤳ Wednesday, Thursday, and Sunday, at 9:00 P.M.

    $2.00 ⤳ Friday and Saturday, at 9:00, 11:00 P.M, and 1:00 A.M.

FOR RESERVATIONS,

    Phone⤳ DElaware 7-3992

Service during performances ⤳

    No Minimum.

ON MONDAYS AND TUESDAYS ⤳

    Film society screenings and/or special events.

## Opening Night

It was a cold, snowy night in Chicago when The Second City opened its doors on Wednesday, December 16, 1959. Admission was $1.50 with a no-drink minimum (a policy that's still very much in effect). Bernie Sahlins and Paul Sills spent the night flipping burgers in the kitchen. As there was no stage manager, the lights were run by whichever warm body was not onstage at the time. The coat check person was Melinda Dillon, who had her work cut out for her.

"They didn't have a coat check room yet," she said in the 2009 book *The Second City Unscripted*, written by former *Chicago Sun-Times* arts and entertainment writer Mike Thomas. "I was just collecting coats and putting them in the ladies' room."

The very first show, dubbed *Excelsior and Other Outcries*, began with Barbara Harris, bathed in a spotlight, performing a song called "Everybody's in the Know":

> Everybody's in the know but me,
> Knows who Eisenhower has to tea;
> Knows what's wrong with education,
> Specialization, automation;
> Are clear as to what they would have done
> Had they been tempted by Twenty-One.
> Me, I'm not so sure of myself.
> No, I don't have it all clear.
> But if you don't like your drink,
> The next one will taste better . . .

"On that first night, when the entire company was taking its bow, there was no one left to bring the lights up and down, a situation none of us had thought of before and that I realized in the nick of time," said Sahlins. "I ran backstage and twirled the dimmers through indeterminable curtain calls . . . we were a hit!"

**FACING PAGE:** A flyer advertising opening night in 1959

The makeup of a Second City show—or "revue," as we call them—has remained virtually the same since the very beginning: two acts that are (mostly) scripted, followed by our famed third act of improvisation. The show is actually written by the cast over an eight- to ten-week rehearsal period. We call this sacred time "process," and it's a comedy gauntlet. The cast and crew rehearse all day long and perform at night, constantly testing and adjusting material based on the audience's reactions and suggestions. Most new material is generated in those third-act improv sets, and if an improvised piece is particularly strong, it will be further refined the next day in a rehearsal with the director. During process, the new material is introduced into the scripted show. Themes begin to develop, and the actors and directors craft the scenes into a brand-new production. A few months later, we do it all again.

## NAMING RIGHTS AND WRONGS

Revue titles have rarely had anything whatsoever to do with the content of the shows. Severn Darden liked coming up with titles from Shakespeare; *The Seacoast of Bohemia*, for instance, refers to a Shakespearean location, even though Bohemia doesn't have a coast. Other favorite titles from our archives: *Hello Dali*, *Orwell That Ends Well*, *Taming of the Flu*, *Take Me Out to the Balkans*, *To Mock a Kilogram*, *Freud Slipped Here*, and *The Madness of Curious George*. And the longest show title in our history? The Second City e.t.c.'s 1992 revue *The Heliotrope Players' Production of Thornton Wilder's American Classic, Our Town, as Directed by d'Eric Blakemore, or Cash Stations of the Cross*.

## Improv Sets Are Free

After the shows, the cast began returning to the stage to take suggestions for new scenes from the audience, just as a way to have a little extra fun. They soon realized it was a prime opportunity to try out material and test it in real time, essentially allowing them to develop the next show in public, instead of behind a closed rehearsal door. To this day, no Second City show has ever officially closed—the subsequent one just organically takes the place of its predecessor.

The original schedule saw the cast doing thirteen shows and five postshow improv sets a week, but, as Mina Kolb put it, "We were young, you know." (The schedule now for the Mainstage is eight shows and five improv sets a week.) It cost one dollar to come in for the improv set, but very quickly that experience became free—and will remain free as long as our doors are open. That promise has been made in neon.

The first audiences were largely well-educated, well-read young professionals, many of them graduates of the University of Chicago—doctors, lawyers, psychiatrists, professors. Many of them smoked, and all of them (hopefully, for profit's sake) drank and ate before and during the show. The theater served half-pound burgers served on thick black bread and pastries from the Bon Ton, a nearby Viennese bakery.

The hours after the show finished and before the sun came up had their own associated rituals as well. It was nearly impossible to just go home and go to bed after the final curtain call; the adrenaline was too high. Most nights, many of the artists would sit around in the theater after the audience was gone, the tables had been bussed, and the waitstaff had been

checked out and had finished moaning over the size of their tips. Sometimes the front-of-the-house employees would do parodies of the onstage employees, and vice versa. Sometimes Bill Mathieu would play the piano, and there would be group singing. They would have a drink or two; everyone got a free drink after work in those days. And there would be talk—such talk—about the next show, about that night's audience, about politics, religion, sex, philosophy, books, foreign films, clothes, gossip, and whatever else was on their racing minds. Opinions differed on almost everything, but rarely did they turn into serious arguments. When whoever was locking up that night wanted to go home, the ones who were left would often move across the street to the Lincoln Hotel for a snack or a meal and more talk. Some balmy nights, they didn't even get to the Lincoln. They just stood outside the darkened theater to continue talking.

Mathieu summed up those early days well:

> *The first few months of The Second City were special in the lives of those who lived it. A new societal mirror was being cast that enabled us all to see ourselves openly and critically in real time. The new theater was based not only on the immediacy of daily social and political life, and the humor to be found in those, but also on trust. The actors had to develop the capacity to tell themselves and each other the truth and trust the audience to understand and accept it. The audience was in on the act, and as our audiences grew and our fame spread from local to national, the terrific feeling of good work well done grew also. This doesn't mean there weren't harsh words, or even fistfights, because there were, and often. But they didn't last long. What was at stake was too valuable. For me, one of the most important indicators of value was the temperament of the staff— waiters, cooks, ticket seller, and hatcheck girl. We were all glad to get to work, glad to be in each other's presence, glad to be party to the audience's delight, and, especially, glad to party when the audience went home.*

*Excelsior and Other Outcries* ran for eight weeks. Three more revues opened during the first year: *Too Many Hats* (an organizational costume problem the actors seemed to endlessly experience backstage), *The Third Programme*, and *The Seacoast of Bohemia* were all well reviewed and well attended. By 1960, The Second City was the hot new thing, though that fact gave little solace to some. The first time a table stood empty during a show—it was at an eleven o'clock performance on a snowy Thursday night about a year after opening— Paul Sills was heard to moan that the end was near.

**THE SECOND CITY SCRIPT**
The first Second City logo was designed by Selma Quateman, a girlfriend of Sheldon Patinkin's. Today, the theater's original banner hangs in the atrium of Piper's Alley, the historic Old Town building that houses The Second City in Chicago.

# CHAPTER 3

# THE 1960s

## COMING OUT SWINGING

**W**ITHIN A YEAR of its opening, celebrities visiting Chicago knew The Second City was the place to be. The hearts of staff and patrons alike would flutter when famous faces like Cary Grant, Anthony Quinn, or Hugh Hefner were spotted in the audience. "I practically lived at Second City. . . . That kind of improvisational theater was truly unique and innovative and very exciting," Hefner said in *The Second City Unscripted*. "You never knew from night to night what was going to happen."

The first year of business brought in plenty of unknown faces, too. Paul Sills had spotted a talented young actor performing at the Compass in St. Louis and presented him with an open invitation to come to Chicago. In 1960, an out-of-work Alan Arkin took Sills up on the offer and joined the rest of the underdogs and outliers at The Second City. "A lot of mavericks and displaced people end up here," explained Arkin. "I mean 'displaced' in the best sense of the word; displaced because we don't fit into a tightly structured, well-organized society. . . . I'm happy about it."

As America in the 1960s collectively experienced tremendous change and upheaval, so, too, did the artists who sought to reflect their world on the stage. For Second City, which *Time* magazine hailed a "temple of satire," the decade opened up the gates for the artists to experiment with new places, new people, and new ways to express themselves, four-letter words and all.

**PICTURED ON PREVIOUS PAGE:**
Severn Darden (left), Eugene Troobnick, Howard Alk, Roger Bowen, William Allaudin Mathieu, Alan Arkin, Paul Sills, Mina Kolb, and Paul Sand afloat on the Chicago River in a 1960 promotional image

Alan Arkin (left), Andrew Duncan, Zohra Lampert, Anthony Holland, and Eugene Troobnick in 1961

# ALAN ARKIN

Prior to joining The Second City, Alan Arkin spent time at acting school and in a singing group called the Tarriers, with whom he co-wrote "The Banana Boat Song" (which was made famous by Harry Belafonte and would one day provide the soundtrack for a memorable scene of Catherine O'Hara's in the film *Beetlejuice*). Although he had wanted to be an actor since the age of five, getting his professional start proved to be quite a challenge:

*I couldn't get arrested trying to get a career started in New York. I felt total despair. Paul Sills had seen me at the Compass in St. Louis, and Paul and Bernie Sahlins asked me to come and join Second City. I did, and it gave me, for the first time in my life, an opportunity to work all day long. I would come in at nine in the morning, wait for a workshop or rehearsal, do whatever workshop or rehearsal was going on, spend a whole day waiting for someone to talk to and improvise with, do the show, and then*

*talk about the show afterwards. For the first time in my life, I had an opportunity to do what I always wanted to do. I thought it, breathed it, and ate it from the moment I got up in the morning until late every night.*

Arkin found himself cast in an ensemble that was "an amazing and eclectic mix of people," he said. "My sense of the actors in the early years was that we were a diverse and multi-talented bunch of misfits. We all had broad interests and abilities, but no real specialties. We had nowhere else to go. We were saving our lives by being at Second City."

In addition to Arkin's wildly successful career as an actor on Broadway and in film (he won an Academy Award in 2007 for *Little Miss Sunshine* with Steve Carell), he has also devoted himself to producing and directing. "Second City was the first time I'd gotten any substantiation that this was a career I belonged in," he said.

## The Mother of Second City

Early in 1961, a young woman appeared in the lobby. She asked if she could aid the theater by coordinating group sales, proposing to sell out shows as benefit performances for local organizations. At the same time, Bernie Sahlins was busy expanding in the south half of the beer garden next door by adding a second theater, so he made her an offer: sell out a week of previews in the new space, and she had the job. She did it, and that is how Joyce Sloane began her five-decade-long impact on The Second City.

"Everybody who comes to Second City has issues," 1978 alum Tim Kazurinsky told the *Chicago Tribune*. "She was the mother to the largest dysfunctional family in the world."

Sloane recalled her first season at The Second City as the new theater's construction progressed:

*Bernie and I crawled in and out of that theater as it was being built. He asked me to sell out the first week. I was so young and so stupid, I guess, I didn't know theaters don't open with the first week sold out, so I did it. But I had two groups that wanted the opening night. One was the University of Chicago Cancer Research Foundation, and the other was the Junior Board of the Travelers' Aid Society. Sheldon said, "That's easy. We'll make one the first preview." I didn't even know what a preview was. That first night, the carpet people were still tacking down the carpeting. The University of Chicago people arrived, and it was spring, so ladies were in their lovely dresses. They forgot to connect the flue in the kitchen, so all the smoke backed up into the lobby. Even before the show started, we had the fire department over, and everybody was out on the street.*

Joyce Sloane conducts business.

> "He asked me to sell out the first week. I was so young and so stupid, I guess, I didn't know theaters don't open with the first week sold out, so I did it."

# JOYCE SLOANE

Joyce Sloane

During her fifty years with The Second City, Joyce Sloane did just about everything—except get up onstage and perform. From selling tickets to founding The Second City Touring Company to bringing The Second City to Toronto and opening The Second City e.t.c., Sloane wasn't just a producer to her colleagues, she was their den mother.

"She was it," said Jim Belushi. "She gave herself up to the people in that theater. She gave us confidence, strength, and support. Gave me money; I didn't have money. She gave me her car. She took me to the dentist. She was the heart of that theater."

"She cared about every waitress and dishwasher, not just the famous alumni. If you got some good news or a gig or something, you called your mom and then you called Joyce," Second City alumnus George Wendt told the *Chicago Tribune* after Sloane's death in 2011 at eighty years old.

Tina Fey added that Sloane "would be just as happy if you came out of Second City with 'a nice husband' instead of a movie career." (How thrilled she must be up in heaven that Fey came out with both.)

"Joyce Sloane's impact on the Chicago theatre community cannot be measured," Andrew Alexander said. "She nurtured thousands of young performers— she encouraged them, fed them, even housed them when needed. She was the mother of The Second City, and she cannot be replaced. The loss is monumental, but Joyce Sloane's legacy carries on forever in the work of the artists of whom she was so proud."

# MELINDA DILLON

Melinda Dillon

Melinda Dillon was the first coat checker at The Second City before taking over onstage for Barbara Harris in 1961—and long before receiving an Oscar nomination for Steven Spielberg's *Close Encounters of the Third Kind*. (You probably also know her as the staunchly anti-leg-lamp-and-Red-Ryder-BB-gun "Mother Parker" in *A Christmas Story*.) Here is how Dillon told the story of getting her big break at The Second City:

> It was soon after the opening of the club. When I got to work, I found our three producers in a panicked and heated discussion as to whether the show could go on or not without Barbara–Barbara Harris was ill! They were still at it when the patrons began to arrive. I already had twelve hats. So, knowing what I had to do, I interrupted them.
>
> "What do you want?" Bernie Sahlins yelled.
>
> "Sorry, sorry," I said. "I know the show. I can do it."
>
> They looked at each other. Then Bernie said, "No! She's not smart enough to wait tables, you gonna let her ruin the show?" They looked at each other some more. Then Howard Alk said he had a "feeling" about me. Then Paul Sills smiled and, always the one to welcome a jump into the great unknown, said, "Let's do it. You're on." So we did, and it was grand. . . . (Bernie was right about the tables.)

Dillon was not the last nonperformer staff member to make it to the stage that way. *My Big Fat Greek Wedding*'s Nia Vardalos took a similar path (which is covered in chapter 7), and both women's stories prove Oprah Winfrey's adage that "luck is preparation meeting opportunity."

## Playwrights and Wrongs

The larger new theater was sentimentally called Playwrights at Second City. The street-level entrance glass doors were surrounded by stone arches that had originally graced the facade of the Garrick Theater, an 1891 jewel designed by renowned nineteenth-century architects Louis Sullivan and Dankmar Adler. When the building was demolished in 1961, the arches found a new home at The Second City, thanks to the efforts of photographer and heroic historical preservationist Richard Nickel. (Tragically, Nickel was ultimately killed by his unwavering passion for preservation in 1972 when he was crushed during an attempt to salvage pieces of the Chicago Stock Exchange building.)

The new Playwrights opened with Pulitzer-winning cartoonist and satirist Jules Feiffer's first theater piece, a revue called *The Explainers*, a staged version of his two-dimensional cartoon creations. The cast had several future Second Citizens in it, including Del Close and Paul Sand, who took a break from The Second City's show next door to participate. Paul Sills directed *The Explainers*, and William Allaudin Mathieu wrote the show's music, but his vacation replacement—a jazz pianist named Fred Kaz who was short a few fingers thanks to an old factory accident—took over performing duties.

Business at the secondary theater proved to be disappointing, so in November 1961, the two theaters swapped addresses, with The Second City moving into the larger space at 1846 and Playwrights into the smaller one at 1842. Opening Playwrights was one of a few misses that took place that year. The company's first record, *Comedy from The Second City*, was somewhat of a flop. A Broadway show composed of scenes from the theater's first five revues, *Live from The Second City*, was sniffed at by the press, who shunned it as "semi-pro." (One major problem with the production was that the New York producer, Max Liebman, would not allow the cast to improvise.) "True satire is not just poking cheerful fun at something," wrote John Chapman of the *Chicago Tribune*. "It must be wicked, cruel, destructive criticism, and these nice people from Chicago aren't up to it." The show closed after two months at the Royale Theatre.

**CLOCKWISE FROM TOP LEFT:** Playbill from an early New York performance; Dick Schaal (left) and Judy Harris in 1963; Dick Schaal (left), Severn Darden, and Del Close in a scene from the 1962 revue *My Friend Art is Dead*, directed by Paul Sills (pictured on facing page)

Del Close

# DEL CLOSE

Infamously dedicated to establishing improv as a unique art form in its own right, Del Close was an influential teacher and director, an impassioned, complicated guru, and a true comedy maestro who pushed all artistic boundaries and trained many of the most celebrated performers of the late twentieth century. Born in Manhattan, Kansas, the trained fire-eater (Azrad the Incombustible!) was a second cousin of Dwight D. Eisenhower. He joined The Second City cast in 1961, having already performed with the Compass in St. Louis and as his own solo stand-up act. In and out as a member of the company for years, he also directed The Second City's twelfth revue, *20,000 Frozen Grenadiers or There's Been a Terrible Accident at the Factory.*

Close struggled with multiple addictions for years until giving up drugs after John Belushi's death in 1982. One evening, when he was still performing in the show, Close attempted suicide shortly before curtain time. Discovered in time by his coworkers, Close was rushed to the ER to get his stomach pumped. Hospital authorities were insistent that he be committed to a psychiatric facility, at least for observation. Bernie Sahlins called a friend, who called a friend, and Close was committed to a private sanatorium. After a few days, Sahlins and Sheldon Patinkin were informed that, in

> "Del Close, though older, was of our generation. He had always been possibly a century ahead of his time. There was no hope of catching up with Del, but he took us to new places spiritually and in consciousness that none of us had been before." **–Harold Ramis**

order for Close to be allowed to start performing again, one of them would be required to travel to the sanitorium, check him out, take him to The Second City, and bring him back to the sanitorium after the show. For several weeks, six nights a week, they—usually Patinkin—did exactly that.

After moving west and hooking up with a San Francisco improv group called the Committee, Close invented a long-form improv structure he named the "Harold." He returned to Chicago in the early seventies, directed several more Second City shows, and became one of the country's most revered improv teachers. Close also wrote comic books, acted in the film *The Untouchables*, was an advisor for *Saturday Night Live*, and co-founded Chicago's ImprovOlympic (now called iO) with Charna Halpern. "He was a comedy genius who had taught all of my heroes," said Amy Poehler, whose Upright Citizens Brigade ensemble first met and formed in Close's classes.

A controversial figure both on and off the stage, Close died in 1999 at the age of sixty-four. The night before he died, he held a "living wake" in the hospital, complete with jazz musicians, balloons, Bill Murray, and a pagan ceremony. According to Halpern, his last words were "I'm tired of being the funniest person in the room." Close also famously willed his skull to Chicago's Goodman Theatre for use as "Yorick" in any future productions of *Hamlet*; Halpern admitted in 2006 that his entire body had in fact been cremated and that she had supplied the theater with a proxy, despite her best efforts.

Second City alumna Betty Thomas is set to direct an upcoming film about Close's life based on the book *Guru: My Days with Del Close* by Jeff Griggs.

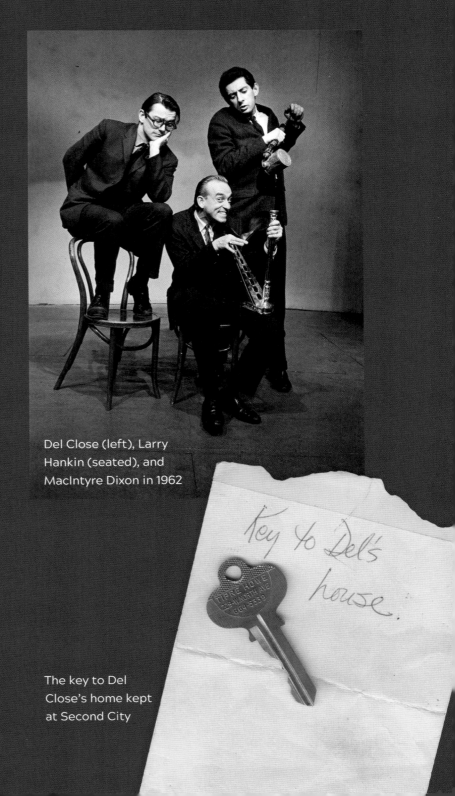

Del Close (left), Larry Hankin (seated), and MacIntyre Dixon in 1962

The key to Del Close's home kept at Second City

## Joan Rivers Flings an Ashtray

The "nice people from Chicago" had no clue what they were in for the day Joan Rivers came and waited five excruciating hours to try out for The Second City in 1961. "They auditioned sixty ladies," she said in *Something Wonderful Right Away*, "and I was sixty-first." Unfamiliar with either improvisation or the theater itself, Rivers flew into a rage after learning there was no script with which to audition. "I was insane now, screaming, 'I don't care about you, don't care about your goddamn show. You can go to hell.' . . . I grabbed a glass ashtray and flung it," she recounted in her 1986 memoir, *Enter Talking*. Rivers got the job. She made her debut in the theater's seventh revue, *Alarums and Excursions*.

"You were able to say what you thought was funny," Rivers said about her time at The Second City in a PBS interview five years before her death. "You never had to ask would the audience get it. You didn't care."

Rivers went east with The Second City in 1962 for a second Broadway experiment—this time at the Square East. This show, unlike the first, flourished on and off for nearly five years. Rotating performers included New York recruits Alan Alda, who would become best known as "Hawkeye Pierce" on all 251 episodes of the iconic television series *M\*A\*S\*H*, and Valerie Harper, whose beloved television alter ego was "Rhoda Morgenstern" on *The Mary Tyler Moore Show* and its spin-off, *Rhoda*, and who took workshops with the cast.

# JOAN RIVERS

Joan Rivers admittedly was never really happy at Second City. Her style was different enough from the other performers that she was not able to blend easily into the ensemble—she was a born stand-up. But Rivers did create a sketch called "Our Children" that is still very much part of our Touring Company's repertoire. In it, a man and a woman are saying goodbye to some unseen departing guests. As they close the door, the wife goes into a rant against the guests, how boring they are, how disgusting their eating habits are, and on and on, ending with, "I don't ever want them here again," to which her husband reasonably responds, "But honey, they're our children!"

Avery Schreiber (left), Joan Rivers, and Bill Alton in *Alarums and Excursions*, 1961

# "I WAS REALLY BORN AS A COMEDIAN AT SECOND CITY. I OWE IT MY CAREER."

—Joan Rivers

Paul Sand (left), Mina Kolb, and Eugene Troobnick in 1960

# PAUL SAND

Paul Sand began studying with Viola Spolin as a child before working with mime Marcel Marceau in Paris and touring with Judy Garland. Sand joined The Second City as a replacement for original cast member Roger Bowen and went to Los Angeles with the cast of *Live from the Second City* for its successful pre-Broadway trial at the Ivar Theatre before going on to appear in dozens of television and film projects, winning a Tony Award in 1971 for *Paul Sills' Story Theatre*, and co-founding Santa Monica Public Theatre in 2016. At Second City, Sand's characters were often sweet, vulnerable, and socially inept. He brought one of them back to life for The Second City's fiftieth-anniversary

celebration, which the *Chicago Reader* described as "a once-in-a-lifetime collaboration among artists of different generations."

In a 1961 scene named "Phono Pal," created by Sand and Eugene Troobnick, Sand played a lonely guy listening to a record by a motivational speaker. As the record spun, Sand began to interact with it, forming a one-sided relationship. During the fiftieth-anniversary performance, Sand "sat on a cane-back chair and pantomimed playing a record on a turntable, just as he had done 48 years ago," wrote the *Chicago Reader*. "But since Troobnick died in 2003, his lines were spoken by another Second City alum . . . Stephen Colbert."

## The Second City Goes International

In 1962, *The London Show*, a "best of" revue featuring Mina Kolb, Bill Alton, Del Close, Avery Schreiber, and Dick Schaal, came together. The Second City used the show to swap stages with Peter Cook and Dudley Moore's London club, the Establishment. The Second City performers arrived just in time to catch a lot of flak about the Cuban missile crisis from the very rowdy English audiences, both in the club and on the streets. The Second City played London again the next year, when Bernie Sahlins also produced a television series in Manchester for Granada TV called *Second City Reports*.

The Second City also took its first of many annual excursions north of the border to Toronto's Royal Alexandra Theatre in spring of 1963. On opening night, a snowstorm canceled most flights into the city, so Bernie Sahlins chartered a plane for the cast. However, the US plane was not allowed to land on Canadian soil. The owner of the "Royal Alex," Ed Mirvish, pulled all sorts of strings to get it down. Joyce Sloane and Sheldon Patinkin waited anxiously at the theater, both ready to do a poetry reading if necessary. When the cast finally arrived, it was impossible not to notice Severn Darden wearing a full-length fur coat for his trip to the Great White North.

Toronto audiences were more than receptive to The Second City. Casts that included Bob Dishy, Valerie Harper, Linda Lavin, Dick Schaal, Omar Shapli, David Steinberg, Penny White, and the comedy duo of Jack Burns and Avery Schreiber prompted *Toronto Star* critic Nathan Cohen to write in his column, "What a wonderful gift it would be to have a permanent Second City here." Cohen's words got Sahlins to start thinking seriously about expanding north.

Though a generation later everything would change, in the sixties, Toronto was clearly second city to Montreal. In those days, Montreal had it all—size, wealth, glamour—but Toronto, once seen by performers as a gray Presbyterian town where bars were scarce and everything closed up tight on a Sunday, was developing some flair of its own. A bright counterculture was thriving in and around the University of Toronto and the adjacent Yorkville district, where the coffeehouse scene featured young talent like Gordon Lightfoot, Ian & Sylvia, Joni Mitchell, and Neil Young. The city was developing a strong music scene of its own, but a night out at a club for comedy was still a new idea. Even so, each time Sahlins and Sloane brought their show north from Chicago for a Toronto run, it was a smash.

VIENNA'S ENGLISH THEATRE
Regular European performances remained an exciting part of the company's calendar for decades. In 1992, The Second City began booking yearly shows at Vienna's English Theatre, the oldest and most established English-language theater in continental Europe. "Bringing the intelligent social and political satire of The Second City to English speakers in Austria was a dream come true," said Beth Kligerman, a producer on some of The Second City's more exotic excursions. "Vienna is a city oozing with art, culture, and history like no other. It was a perfect fit for us."

Fred Kaz (left), Bernie Sahlins, and Del Close on Wells Street

# FRED KAZ

A consummate musician, artist, and poet, Fred Kaz holds the honor of being The Second City's longest-running performer. He was the company's musical director for nearly thirty years, using his extraordinary talents to compose the music and lyrics for countless revues and serving as a teacher and artistic compass for everyone whose path he sailed across. Described by Bernie Sahlins as the "master of the musical pun," Kaz's wisdom and astuteness saved many a scene from behind the piano.

According to Richard Kind, "Fred Kaz told you more with his fingers on the keys than most directors could tell you with an afternoon of rehearsal."

In the late eighties, the "Captain of Cool" retired to live on a boat given to him by Andrew Alexander and Len Stuart, and it was there that he died in 2014.

"He was my master, my father, my friend, and my spiritual leader," said Jim Belushi about Kaz to the *Chicago Tribune*. "He'll be gigging in heaven on Day One."

## Dropping the F-Bomb

In the early to mid-sixties, profanity onstage was not as commonplace as it would eventually become. In 1963, The Second City debuted the use of the word *shit* on its stage in a scene called "Lenny Bruce," named for the controversial stand-up. Bruce—who was famously found guilty of using "obscene, indecent, immoral, and impure" material onstage—had recently been arrested in New York. When the lights came up, all but one member of the cast was onstage. The missing cast member hurriedly entered, brandishing a newspaper, and asked, "Hey, did you hear? Lenny Bruce was arrested for obscenity." The rest of the cast replied in unison, "No shit!" Lights out.

Second City's first use of the f-word happened the night after the assassination of President John F. Kennedy, and, appropriately, it was improvised. The theater was closed the Friday of the assassination. On Saturday night, the audience clearly wanted a respite from weeping in front of their televisions, and laugh they did, perhaps even harder than the show warranted. When the time came to take audience suggestions for the improv set, someone called out, "the assassination." The entire audience gasped; Del Close turned angrily to the man and asked, "Just what the fuck did you want to see, sir?" Everyone burst into applause.

## Bob Curry Makes History

There were other important firsts made in this period. Bob Curry was a former student of Viola Spolin disciple Jo Forsberg's improvisation workshops—which predated The Second City Training Center. The first African American cast member in The Second City's resident company, Curry joined the ensemble in 1966 for *A View from Under the Bridge or Enter from Above*, directed by Sheldon Patinkin. An award-winning actor and inspiring director, Curry coached and mentored many actors in Chicago's theater community and helped widen the path for many more performers of color at The Second City before his passing in 1994 at the age of fifty-one.

The Bob Curry Fellowship program launched in 2014 to honor its namesake's trailblazing contributions and encourage diverse voices to pursue careers in comedy at The Second City and beyond. "Bob was brilliant and fearless and was famous for getting naked at any time for no particular reason," said Aaron Freeman, who kick-started The Second City's Outreach Program in 1992.

In fact, when Freeman came in to speak to the inaugural group of Bob Curry fellows, he "completely disrobed in Bob Curry fashion. He talked the entire time in the nude about improv and the art form to honor Curry," recounted The Second City's director of diversity talent inclusion and development, Dionna Griffin-Irons. "Aaron's lovely wife just crocheted in the corner, not batting an eye."

**ALL YOU CAN EAT**
The next actor to regularly exercise his First Amendment rights onstage was John Belushi. In the early seventies, he "introduced a whole new language to the stage with the classic line, 'Eat a bowl of fuck,'" Harold Ramis said in 1999. "I still don't know what it means." According to Bob Woodward's *Wired: The Short Life and Fast Times of John Belushi*, the comedian only used the line when Bernie Sahlins—who was not a fan of actors going for shock value—wasn't around.

Bob Curry

David Steinberg
(left) and Ann
Elder in 1964

Top row: Dick Schaal (left), Richard Libertini, and Del Close; bottom row: Avery Schreiber (left), Judy Harris, and MacIntyre Dixon in 1963

## Off the Road

This era introduced many of our most memorable alumni. One of comedy's most beloved oddballs, Fred Willard, auditioned for The Second City with Robert Klein. Klein, who had started out in life intending to be a doctor (until a few things "like calculus, physics, biology, zoology, reading, spelling, comprehension, inclination, aptitude, attitude, and talent" got in the way), and Willard were total strangers, but the pairing worked beautifully, despite the improvisational curveballs thrown at them by their competition. "They wanted the job, so they gave you hard ones," said Klein. "Fred and I were given the suggestion that he was a club owner and I was a performer. I had a crude improvisational talent. I was creative. We got the job."

In 1965, Willard and Klein found themselves in a company with resident star David Steinberg for the eighteenth revue, *Off the Road*. Though cast friction ensued due to a rivalry between Klein and Steinberg, Willard was immune to the comedy sword fight. "You never saw anything like Fred," Steinberg said in *The Second City Unscripted*. "Weird characters. And Fred himself is offbeat, even to this day."

# FRED WILLARD

Fred Willard called his time at The Second City "really one of the best years of my life artistically" because "at Second City, you can do something during the day, have an idea, and have it up on-stage that night," he told WGN Radio in 2016. With credits in more than seventy films—including improvised masterpieces like Christopher Guest's *Waiting for Guffman* and *Best in Show*—and more than one thousand episodes of television, it is not at all surprising to find out that the hardest-working man in comedy has always been unflappable. In fact, nothing ever seemed to upset Willard. He was so laid-back that sometimes it seemed he wasn't present at all, but he was acutely aware of his surroundings—and what got a laugh—at all times. One of his favorite characters at Second City was a clumsy vampire whose fangs were two cigarettes hanging out of the sides of his mouth.

**FACING PAGE:** Fred Willard (right) examines Robert Klein

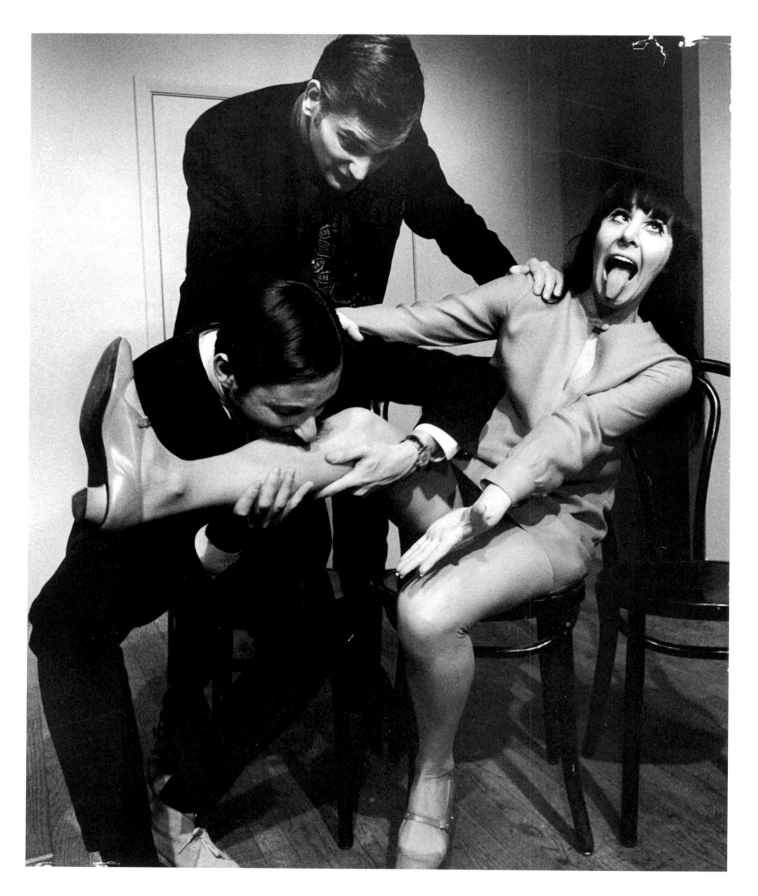

**LEFT:** Standing: Roberta Maguire; top row: Judy Morgan; middle row: Brian Doyle-Murray, and Jim Fisher; bottom row: David Blum, Harold Ramis, and Joe Flaherty

**RIGHT:** Clockwise from top left: Dennis Cunningham, Omar Shapli, Jack Burns, Melissa "Sally" Hart, Dick Schaal, Ann Elder, and Avery Schreiber in 1963

Joe Flaherty (left) and Brian Doyle-Murray

**FACING PAGE:** Burt Heyman (left) bites Carol Robinson as Martin Harvey Freidberg looks on in 1967.

## On the Road

The company kicked off an eight-city tour in 1965 in Detroit as part of the Theatre Guild subscription season. The generally elderly subscribers were expecting their usual fare—road companies touring shows like *My Fair Lady* or the latest Broadway comedy. The Second City's brand of satire so infuriated some of them that the Guild most likely lost several hundred subscribers during those ten weeks.

Trying another tactic, The Second City franchised a show to a Bourbon Street nightclub in New Orleans. The show used local talent, but Second City retained artistic control from Chicago. This 1967 artistic fiasco was the wrong show in the wrong place and lasted a very short time. The customers, usually drunk before they even arrived, expected to see strippers and cheap comics. They were sorely and audibly disappointed.

After realizing the need for experienced bench strength to rely on for out-of-town gigs (and an easier way to scout new talent), The Second City Touring Company was born. Members learned material from old shows, and Joyce Sloane began booking the company at colleges.

## Sweet Home Chicago

Old Town—Second City's home turf—had become a major entertainment hub in Chicago by 1967, with restaurants, bars, head shops, and boutiques popping up all over the neighborhood. Wells Street was also the home of the very first Crate & Barrel (and the world's *second* most famous bentwood chairs), which had taken over an old elevator warehouse five years earlier. That summer, The Second City, stone arches and all, moved two and a half blocks south into a former bakery on North Wells, part of the Piper's Alley building. Just as she had done before, Joyce Sloane sold out a week of previews. Peter Boyle was in the first show in the 350-seat theater, and on opening night, the paint on the walls was still wet. The Second City has called 1616 North Wells Street home ever since.

# PETER BOYLE

When Peter Boyle was hired, he found himself in a company with a group of actors who mostly knew nothing about politics or tough satire—and didn't care to learn. Boyle was just the opposite and found the experience almost constantly frustrating, especially as the country became increasingly divided. The conflict ultimately led to his departure. A gifted character actor, Boyle went on to play some well-known roles after Second City, including "Frank Barone" on *Everybody Loves Raymond* and "the Monster" in Mel Brooks's *Young Frankenstein*, in which he co-starred with Gene Wilder, who later married Gilda Radner. Boyle met his own future wife, a reporter for *Rolling Stone*, while filming the 1974 comedy classic. The best man at their wedding was their good friend John Lennon.

Peter Boyle (right) embraces Sandy Holt in 1967.

Judy Morgan (left), Jim Fisher, David Blum, mystery guy in park, Roberta Maguire, Brian Doyle-Murray, Nate Herman, and Harold Ramis in 1969

# HAROLD RAMIS

Harold Ramis was the "Party Jokes" editor of *Playboy* magazine before coming to The Second City, where he didn't make it into the Touring Company after his first audition. Thankfully, he got another shot—eventually crossing the streams of his two worlds during an epic party at Hugh Hefner's place, a night involving the entire cast of *Hair* singing naked in the pool.

Even in his early days at the theater, where he joined the Mainstage cast in 1969, Ramis already showed his instincts for what would lie ahead in his career. "I love the process of improv, but as soon as I had the opportunity, I started writing what everyone else was going to say," the *Ghostbusters* writer and *Groundhog Day* director said.

We lost Ramis in 2014, when he was sixty-nine. It was much too soon, but his impact on comedy is ever present in the incredible work he left behind and the generations yet to be influenced by his genius. At a Los Angeles memorial attended by six hundred of his friends, family, and colleagues, Martin Short told the crowd, "I adored Harold. I don't think anyone didn't adore Harold. You couldn't have a soul or an understanding of the human condition and not adore Harold."

In 2015, The Second City opened the Harold Ramis Film School, the world's only film school dedicated entirely to comedy. "Much of Harold's greatest learning came as a result of his time at The Second City in Chicago," said Trevor Albert, Ramis's producing partner for over twenty years and chair of the program. "It only makes sense that the film school named in his honor is right where Harold learned to be Harold."

Harold Ramis

## A *Plague* Comes to Town

In 1968, "Chicago was erupting," described Harold Ramis. "We had the race riots in the spring, the Democratic [National] Convention in the summer, and then a year later the Chicago Seven trial. Abbie Hoffman used to come to The Second City then. He improvised with us as an alibi during the trial. When the Weathermen were in the streets, he was with us. He actually played Judge [Julius] Hoffman [who presided over the Chicago Seven conspiracy trial] onstage."

On the heels of the DNC, *A Plague on Both Your Houses* opened, co-directed by Sheldon Patinkin and Michael Miller, who was Patinkin's successor as artistic director. Earlier that year, businesses along Wells Street—including The Second City—had been ordered to close for a couple of days and nights during the riots following the assassination of Dr. Martin Luther King Jr. while the National Guard patrolled the streets in open vehicles, carrying heavy weapons. During the convention, there were no such orders; the police could "handle it." Second City is located very near Lincoln Park, and shortly after eleven o'clock each night during the whole week, staff could hear protestors being chased out of the park, could smell the tear gas, and could see the police pushing people up against the wall of the drugstore across the street.

In an article commemorating the fiftieth anniversary of the infamous Chicago Seven conspiracy trial, *Chicago Tribune* theater critic Chris Jones expounded:

> *Hoffman surely knew that it would not be good for his courtroom fate if he was seen to be, or assumed to be, roaming the Chicago streets with the Weathermen, the militant group that came to be known as the Weather Underground, who were smashing cars pretty much outside the door of the theater. And so he came to Second City almost every night, usually losing the investigators he assumed to be on his tail by melting into the night as fast as he arrived.*

In 1969, Bernie Sahlins took the entire Chicago cast to New York, opening up an opportunity for a whole new generation of Second City performers to bring a different style and attitude to the stage. They called themselves the "*Next Generation*."

# CHAPTER 4

# THE 1970s

## NEW BLOOD, NEW HORIZONS

THE 1970s PROVED to be a pivotal decade for The Second City, despite some very lean times. Refusing to increase prices (tickets in 1971 cost $3.95 on weekends and $2.95 on weeknights), Bernie Sahlins took out a loan from his father to help pay the bills—bills that only increased when he and Joyce Sloane opened a second theater in Canada. The Second City Toronto provided a new pool of incredible talent, but that didn't immediately translate to financial success. However, the debut of *Saturday Night Live* in 1975—and the fact that Second City alumni made up nearly half the cast—began to turn the tide. By the end of the decade, with the advent of *SCTV* and films like *Animal House* and *Meatballs* making John Belushi a household name and Bill Murray a certifiable movie star, comedy business was booming.

## The Next Generation

More laid-back and less angst-ridden than their predecessors, performers of a new type emerged in the early seventies, and they were raring to take over the Chicago stage. They included David Blum, Brian Doyle-Murray, Jim Fisher, Joe Flaherty, Roberta Maguire, Judy Morgan, and Harold Ramis. They had long hair and wore blue jeans and tie-dye onstage, a sharp contrast from the buttoned-up casts of yesteryear. They called themselves—and their show—*The Next Generation.*

*The Next Generation* steered the material toward a different look and feel. Scenes became more direct in their criticism of politicians, corporations, and organized religion. They were

Judy Morgan (left) and Brian Doyle-Murray

# BRIAN DOYLE-MURRAY

The second of nine Murray siblings, Brian Doyle-Murray, Bill's older brother, was one of the *Next Generation* cast members before going on to write and act in a multitude of projects. (His hyphenated last name is the result of adding his grandmother's maiden name, as there was already a working actor named Brian Murray.) After leaving The Second City, he co-wrote *Caddyshack*, Harold Ramis's directorial debut, based on his own childhood experiences caddying in the Chicago suburbs. The gravel-throated Doyle-Murray also appeared in the film as "Lou Loomis" to utter the classic line "Pick up that blood."

The Murray brothers have kept their connection to golf—and each other—strong over the years, opening two Murray Bros. Caddyshack® Restaurant locations (Carl's crab cakes, anybody?) and hosting the annual Murray Bros. Caddyshack® Charity Golf Tournament. Established in 2001, the tournament was "created with the mission to partner with various charities to provide health care, educational and public safety assistance to many programs in the Northeast Florida area."

# JOE FLAHERTY

Joe O'Flaherty (who soon dropped the *O'* to avoid confusion with another actor) originally joined The Second City as a stage manager before making his way to the Mainstage. There, he wrote and performed in multiple revues along-side John Belushi, Brian Doyle-Murray, and Harold Ramis. Seven years after joining the company, Flaherty moved to Toronto to perform and direct, also joining the *SCTV* team. His impressions on the show included Kirk Douglas, Richard Nixon, and Art Garfunkel, and his solid character work left many *SCTV* fans unaware that he played both station owner "Guy Caballero" and newscaster "Floyd Robertson," a character who did double duty as "Monster Chiller Horror Theatre" host "Count Floyd." ("Count Floyd," who lived in an upright coffin and intro-duced bad horror movies, received special thanks from *SCTV* fan Alice Cooper on his 1981 album, *Special Forces*.) Younger fans might know Flaherty as the "jackass"-jeering heckler in *Happy Gilmore* or patriarch of the Weir family on Judd Apatow and Paul Feig's cult classic TV show, *Freaks and Geeks*.

Joe Flaherty (top) and Jim Fisher in 1972

also focused on being *funny*, rather than trying to out-intellectualize the audience. "The original companies of the late fifties and early sixties had been Freudian, alienated, postwar, beatnik, bohemian in their philosophy and outlook," said Ramis. "We were political in a different way. We were radical, born out of the 1968 Chicago convention. We looked like the guys who were in the streets getting clubbed by the police, but we weren't really in the streets."

## John Belushi Steals the Scene

Meanwhile, the *next* "next generation" was busy trying to get a restaurant-cleaning business off the ground. When that idea didn't pan out the way they had hoped, college students John Belushi, Tino Insana, and Steve Beshakes came up with a new way to occupy themselves. They formed an improv group that routinely "borrowed" Second City material and staged it at nearby schools, coffeehouses, and churches. Joyce Sloane remembered her introduction to Belushi:

> *I went out to the College of DuPage to sell a series of short experimental films to the head of student activities. As long as I was there, I thought I'd try to sell them Second City. He said, "We don't need Second City. We've got a student who goes to see your shows and comes back and does the whole thing for us . . . he's right over there playing foosball." He took me over, and this student looks up, raises one eyebrow, and, of course, it was John Belushi.*

John Belushi (right), Joe Flaherty, Jim Fisher, Roberta Maguire, and Judy Morgan in *No, No, Wilmette*, 1971

Instead of suing the scene-stealers, Sloane called the cohort in to audition for her and Bernie Sahlins in 1971. "One of them was not tall, not handsome, not prepossessing, but unforgettable," recalled Sahlins of his first impression of Belushi in *Days and Nights at The Second City*. "Once he walked on stage, neither of us could take our eyes off him." Belushi was hired on the spot.

Belushi's younger brother Jim described the moment he realized he also wanted to make it to Second City one day:

> *My brother John was in the company when I was sixteen years old. I went to see the show, and it was the best show Second City has had in the last forty years. The cast had John, Harold Ramis, Brian Doyle-Murray, Jim Fisher, Joe Flaherty, Eugenie Ross-Leming, and Judy Morgan. Fred Kaz at piano. Those names are tattooed on my arm. . . . It was the single funniest show I had seen in all my life. At that moment, I wanted to be here. I wanted to be part of this.*

Harold Ramis (left), Eugenie Ross-Leming, and John Belushi mime a western in 1972.

Eugenie Ross-Leming (left), John Belushi, Jim Fisher, and Judy Morgan

# JOHN BELUSHI

John Belushi was just twenty-two years old when he made his Second City debut in the theater's forty-first revue, *No, No, Wilmette*, but audiences immediately singled him out for future stardom. Called a "lodestar for his generation" by Bernie Sahlins, among his many characters onstage were Chicago mayor Richard J. Daley, Marlon Brando, Truman Capote, Joe Cocker, and an inept taxman who asked a client, "About how many children do you have?" His explosive dynamic riveted audiences and his peers alike.

His widow, Judith Belushi Pisano, explained:

*John was a rare blend of characteristics. He had a classical beauty, and he was funny looking. He could be impishly sweet or outrageously funny. He could frighten you or melt your heart with a smile. His eyes told all. He had the power to make people think, to shake things up . . . he had the energy to make things exciting. He had the spirit to make things fun. His reward was to hear people laugh.*

# DAN AYKROYD

Dan Aykroyd studied criminology and deviant psychology before enlisting with The Second City along with his comedy partner, Valri Bromfield. "It was joyous," the former mailman said of his time with The Second City. "Those were beautiful days. We learned generosity with your fellow actor, how to give onstage, how not to worry about failing, how to write, how to shape material."

While performing with the troupe, Aykroyd famously ran a speakeasy out of his apartment at 505 Queen Street East. "Club 505," which opened at one a.m., served as an after-hours hangout for the cast, their friends, and other night owl members of Toronto's arts scene. John Belushi visited the joint one particularly fateful night, and he and Aykroyd struck up a conversation about the blues—more

specifically, Belushi's unfamiliarity with the genre. Shortly thereafter, the "Blues Brothers" were born.

Aykroyd left the theater in 1975 to make television history with the first cast of *Saturday Night Live*. He later co-wrote *Ghostbusters* with Harold Ramis (the two also co-starred alongside Bill Murray) and received an Oscar nomination for his performance in *Driving Miss Daisy*. Along the way, Aykroyd also co-founded the House of Blues chain of live music venues and the Crystal Head Vodka spirits brand. In 2017, he returned to his Toronto roots for *Take Off, Eh*, a benefit that raised over three hundred twenty-five thousand dollars to aid Second City and *SCTV* alumnus Dave Thomas's nephew, Jake Thomas, and Spinal Cord Injury Ontario.

## The Second City Toronto Opens Its Canadian Doors

As John Belushi wrapped up his time at The Second City in Chicago, Bernie Sahlins, Joyce Sloane, and Del Close held auditions in Toronto. Ten years after that first Canadian engagement at the Royal Alex, the Americans were readying The Second City's second location for opening. Among the many talented hopefuls in the spring of 1973 were a one-time Kleenex salesman named John Candy and the ever-eager Danny Aykroyd, who concurrently had an application in to join the Royal Canadian Mounted Police.

During this same time, future cast members Jayne Eastwood, Gerry Salsberg, and Gilda Radner were already performing in the local cast of *Godspell*. The production also featured future Second City and *SCTV* alumni Martin Short, Andrea Martin, Dave Thomas, and Eugene Levy. Expected to run just a few dozen performances, *Godspell* was a massive success and closed over a year—and 488 performances—later. And the musical director? Future *Late Night with David Letterman* bandleader and sidekick, Paul Shaffer.

That summer, Sahlins and Sloane opened their new 250-seat cabaret on Adelaide Street in association with "corned beef king" Sam Shopsowitz, owner of a successful Toronto delicatessen called Shopsy's. The first ensemble—a mixture of locals and imports from Chicago—was composed of Aykroyd, Valri Bromfield, Brian Doyle-Murray, Eastwood, Joe Flaherty, Radner, and Salsberg, with Fred Kaz as the pianist and musical director. The theater had no air-conditioning, no liquor license, and almost no audience. Sloane described some of their more desperate cost-cutting solutions:

> We needed to have food to justify a liquor license in Toronto, but we really didn't have the ability at that time to provide food service. We used to sneak across the alley to the creperie next door any time a customer ordered a food item. We would then run back across the alley with the pastries, or whatever, and serve them to the customers. Things got so bad, I remember, that Gilda came in with a roll of our toilet paper—the cheapest you could buy—and said, "I know that money is tight, but can't we please get a better brand of toilet paper?"

Financially, things only got worse. Aykroyd remembered coming to work one night with Radner and finding a padlock on the door. "We were hugging each other and crying," he said. "We felt like the gypsy theater group that had been shut down by the mean old sheriff." Adelaide Street did indeed close after just six months—six months bereft of a liquor license.

**FACING PAGE:** Dan Aykroyd (left) and Eugene Levy in Toronto's fifth revue, *Alterations While You Wait*

# JOHN CANDY

John Candy was tricked into auditioning for The Second City. "I was invited by Dan [Aykroyd] and Valri Bromfield to join them for lunch," he explained, "and they'd put my name on the list to audition, unbeknownst to me. While I was standing around waiting for Dan and Val to finish their work there, my name was called. They pushed me into a room."

At just nineteen years old, the kid dubbed "Johnny Toronto" was immediately asked to relocate to Chicago, where he and Bill Murray started the very same week. A larger-than-life figure in every sense of the word, Candy was even kinder than he seemed onscreen.

"It was the small things that counted to John," said Andrew Alexander, "the things that said you cared for John Candy the human being, not John Candy the star. And being in a business where it's often only the big things that count, John was a man who got hurt a lot. Maybe he had a hard time believing everyone wasn't as true and caring as he was."

John Candy (left) and Bill Murray

# GILDA RADNER

Though she was born in Detroit, Gilda Radner was a member of the original Toronto cast of The Second City starting in 1973. "There would be nights when this magical, chemical, extraordinary thing would happen between you and the others," she said about her time at the theater in *Something Wonderful Right Away*. "You'd be so excited about what had happened, you couldn't sleep all night."

Radner went on to become the very first cast member hired for *Saturday Night Live*, where she created her iconic characters "Roseanne Roseannadanna" and "Baba Wawa." Radner's one-woman Broadway show, *Live from New York*, was directed by Mike Nichols, and her work in film included *The Rutles*, *First Family*, *Haunted Honeymoon*, *The Woman in Red*, and Sidney Poitier's *Hanky Panky*, where she met her the love of her life, Gene Wilder.

Her book, *It's Always Something*, was published shortly before she succumbed to ovarian cancer in 1989 at the age of forty-two. Andrew Alexander described her legacy:

> Gilda had a tremendous impact on all of us because she was so good, so human, so much herself, and so loved by the audiences and her colleagues. She had this innate ability to be sweet and vulnerable, but at the same time, there was a side to her that wasn't afraid to go for the jugular. She is still very much with us today. . . . Gilda would be amazed at the effect she's had on people—not simply because of her comedy, but because of the legacy of her fight with cancer and the philosophy that emanated from that battle.

"Life is about not knowing, having to change, taking the moment and making the best of it, without knowing what's going to happen next. Delicious ambiguity." **–Gilda Radner**

Gilda Radner

## Legends in the Making

By 1973, a whole new cast was poised to take over in Chicago. John Candy, Tino Insana, Bill Murray, David Rasche, Ann Ryerson, Jim Staahl, and Betty Thomas made their Second City debut in *Phase 46 or Watergate Tomorrow, Comedy Tonight*. The theater's forty-sixth revue was directed by Del Close to much acclaim in the press, with *Chicago Sun-Times* critic Glenna Syse writing, "Close has gathered together what I think is the best group of actors the theatre has had in a few years." A scene in the show between Insana and Staahl about the self-sabotaging reality of group therapy hit especially close to home for an audience member catching his first Second City show, a Toronto transplant named Andrew Alexander.

## STRONG FEMALE LEADS

Betty Thomas returned to The Second City in 1988 to direct Mike Myers and Bonnie Hunt in *Kuwait Until Dark or Bright Lights, Night Baseball*. The Chicago Mainstage's seventieth revue was also its first directed by a woman. The list of female resident stage directors at The Second City has thankfully been getting longer and includes the names Sandra Balcovske, Bernadette Birkett, Jen Ellison, Sue Gillan, Nancy Hayden, Carly Heffernan, Shari Hollett, Melody Johnson, Linda Kash, Anne Libera, Jane Morris, Catherine O'Hara, Leslie Seiler, Tracy Thorpe, Anneliese Toft, and Barbara Wallace.

# BETTY THOMAS

Betty Thomas got her start at The Second City not on the Mainstage, but as a server. At the time, Harold Ramis, Joe Flaherty, and John Belushi were the ones onstage, and there was no better comedy education for Thomas than seeing the same show, every night, with minor adjustments. "I had seen or heard their show probably a hundred times, and I started to understand their process of self-editing," she told Harold Ramis Film School students in 2017. "Things that would kill one night wouldn't necessarily kill the next night, and that was an important lesson to learn."

Thomas joined the Chicago cast in 1973. "We used to call her 'Broadway Betty,'" recalled Joyce Sloane. "She drove a truck—when women didn't drive trucks." Thomas was also notorious for her lack of modesty backstage, where she spent most of her time before and after the show naked.

After leaving Chicago, Thomas landed the role of "Lucy Bates" on *Hill Street Blues*, for which she received an Emmy in 1985. She is also an acclaimed director whose films have grossed over five hundred sixty million dollars worldwide and include Howard Stern's autobiographical *Private Parts*, *Dr. Dolittle*, and cult classics *28 Days* and *John Tucker Must Die*. 2009's *Alvin and the Chipmunks: The Squeakquel* became the first female-directed film to gross more than two hundred million dollars. Thomas received a second Emmy for her directing work on the HBO series *Dream On*, making her one of the few artists in the award's history to win in both the acting and directing categories.

**FACING PAGE:** Top row: Bill Murray; middle row: Betty Thomas, Paul Zegler, and Ann Ryerson; bottom row: Mert Rich

"THERE ARE A LOT OF ACTORS THAT ARE MORE TALENTED THAN ME AT SECOND CITY WHO QUIT IT BEFORE THEY EVEN GOT TO A PAYING STATUS. WEIRD LUCK. I HAD NO OTHER OPTION."

—Bill Murray

Tino Insana (left) and Bill Murray in 1973

# BILL MURRAY

Onstage, you couldn't take your eyes off Bill Murray; he emitted a true sense of danger. Offstage, the unpredictable bon vivant is as much of an enigma as some of the characters he has played onscreen. Raised in Wilmette, Illinois, Murray initiated his comedy career at The Second City after following in the footsteps of his older brother Brian Doyle-Murray. As a member of The Second City Touring Company, he (not surprisingly) routinely got into trouble. In the van ride home after a show at an Indiana college, "everybody's giggling, and I can't figure out what they're giggling about," Joyce Sloane recounted in *The Second City Unscripted*. "Bill had taken it upon himself to take an Oriental rug from the president's home and put it in the back of the van. We drove right back."

### BILL MURRAY

Bill Murray, the fifth of nine children, is currently casting to replace himself in his family. Bill has lots of personal problems, most typically with his employer at The Second City. He is interested in organic foods, ecology, and human relations, but just doesn't have the time. Basically insincere, he hopes his experience in theatre, movies, and television can perhaps get him work as a <u>Playgirl</u> centerfold.

Bill Murray's orignal playbill bio, circa 1973

Murray graduated to the Chicago Mainstage in 1973, where he developed several characters that he later used to good advantage, most notably "Nick," the *Star Wars* theme-singing lounge lizard he played on *SNL*. "Bill Murray is a great stand-in for all the people I knew and admired growing up," Harold Ramis once said about his frequent collaborator. "Very brave comedian, very down-to-earth, very honest in his work, and extremely creative." Murray has credited much of his success to his early professional experience, telling *Parade* in 1999 that "I went to Second City, where you learned to make the other actor look good, so you looked good."

## The Old Firehall

Not ready to give up on their Canadian dream after the demise of Adelaide Street, Bernie Sahlins and Joyce Sloane found a partner in a young Canadian entrepreneur named Andrew Alexander.

"The whole idea of the spirit of improvisation I had a visceral connection to," Alexander explained to author Sam Wasson in his book *Improv Nation: How We Made a Great American Art*. Alexander took over The Second City Toronto in 1974 via a contract scribbled on a cocktail napkin and reopened the show at the Old Firehall, a converted nineteenth-century fire station. Alexander explained how the deal went down:

> *I happened to meet Bernie and Joyce because they were looking for a place to rehearse before they opened on Adelaide Street. I was working at the St. Lawrence Centre in publicity and marketing, and I found them a place. Then I moved to Chicago while they opened in Toronto. I had a job at a theater there called the Ivanhoe, but I hung out at Second City. Bernie and Joyce told me about the problems they were having in Toronto. They had an incredible cast, but they had to close after six months. Joyce was looking for investors, just trying to keep the doors open. She and Bernie asked if I'd be interested in trying to run it. I knew a guy from the meatpacking business named Jim Patry who'd actually invested in the last four weeks on Adelaide Street. I asked if he'd be interested in investing some more. He put up seven thousand bucks, I think. I worked out a deal with Bernie to pay him a royalty and cleared up some of the debts. We acquired the rights and opened at the Firehall in February.*

Located at 110 Lombard Street, the building had a discotheque on the first floor and a restaurant on the second when The Second City moved in. Previews for the first show were performed between rock bands' sets in front of a beer-swilling, uncomprehending audience. By the time the show actually opened, The Second City was the sole entertainment. In a 1976 review in the *Toronto Star*, critic Gina Mallet wrote, "The Old Firehall is ideal. It is hot, sweaty, overcrowded. It is also redolent of adventure and daring." *Daring*, indeed— the brass pole the firefighters used to slide down was just on your right as you entered the lobby, and many customers would put it to use after a couple of drinks.

Under Alexander's leadership, The Second City Toronto began developing its own voice. "Before, we had gotten some complaints that the show wasn't Canadian enough," American Gilda Radner explained in *Something Wonderful Right Away*, "so when we reopened, we really kept our nose to the Canadian angle." Joe Flaherty and Sahlins co-directed the first Firehall show, *Hello Dali*. Flaherty was also in the cast, along with John Candy (who had

# ANDREW ALEXANDER

Born in England and raised in Canada, Andrew Alexander worked as a cabdriver, truck driver, speakeasy operator, waiter, tree salesman, marketing manager, ad salesman, magazine editor, and producer in the alternative Toronto theater scene, positioning himself well for a career in the comedy business. The college dropout and questionable mariner (he once spent seven days marooned in the most desolate region of Baja, California) eventually found himself grounded in Chicago, where he worked for the Ivanhoe Theater on Wellington Street. He became a frequent patron of The Second City, developing an eye for and an appreciation of the work.

After borrowing money from a friend, Alexander—whom Dan Aykroyd once called the "white knight of Second City"—took the helm of The Second City Toronto in 1974. He then forged a partnership with two fellow Canadians, Scott Baker and bingo magnate Len Stuart, and in 1976, they established Second City Entertainment. (Stuart and Baker also became partners in The Second City Toronto in 1978, although Baker died later the same year.) The company's first production was the iconic series *SCTV*. Alexander co-created and produced all six groundbreaking seasons of the show, which received two Emmys.

Since acquiring The Second City Chicago with Stuart in 1985, Alexander has produced or executive produced over two hundred shows for The Second City, in addition to countless television and film projects, including an *SCTV* documentary directed by Martin Scorsese. He also launched The Second City Training Center, The Second City Alumni Fund, and the Harold Ramis Film School.

In 2018, Alexander was presented with a Lifetime

Andrew Alexander outside the Old Firehall

Artistic Achievement Award as part of the Governor General's Performing Arts Awards, Canada's most prestigious recognition for the performing arts. During his remarks at Ottawa's Rideau Hall, he noted, "Receiving this award is a tremendous acknowledgment of the thousands of talented young actors and students who have found a home at Second City, just like I have."

Alexander continues to keep his cab license valid . . . just in case.

moved back from Chicago), Eugene Levy, Rosemary Radcliffe, Radner, and pianist and musical director Allan Guttman. Flaherty soon was replaced by Dan Aykroyd and Radner by one of the theater's waitresses, Catherine O'Hara.

Audiences began showing up in decent numbers, but preventing the actors' paychecks from bouncing (which would happen sometimes to those who were last to try to cash them) came down to more than ticket sales. In those days, it was impossible to get a liquor license—a requirement for keeping a comedy club afloat—without also serving food. Every few weeks, the Liquor Control Board would check a club's receipts, and if it was selling more alcohol than food, it would lose its license. Alexander circumvented the problem by creating a dinner and show package that he marketed to groups. Customers who bought the package had their meal in the upstairs dining room then moved downstairs for the show. It was very successful, but some of the more rambunctious parties could be tough on the cast.

One particularly combative night, the show was sold out to the employees of a condom factory. They had all had dinner and about six drinks each upstairs before the show even started. Halfway through the first act, they were already throwing the contents of their drinks at each other and at the stage; Candy even got hit by a flying ice cube. He yelled at the group, but they just yelled back, their voices getting louder and their language fouler as the act went on. The actors plowed through somehow, ducking and weaving all the way, and then refused to return for the second act. The audience never knew the difference.

## The Second City Swap

In order to keep The Second City's name in front of the Toronto press, new owner Andrew Alexander persuaded Bernie Sahlins to swap the Toronto and Chicago casts for two weeks in 1974. That meant Dan Aykroyd, John Candy, Eugene Levy, Gilda Radner, and Rosemary Radcliffe went to Chicago to do a show called *The Canadian Show or Upper USA*, while Debbie Harmon, Bill Murray, Mert Rich, Betty Thomas, and Paul Zegler went up to Toronto.

"That was an incredible summer," Aykroyd said. "That was the summer Nixon resigned, and I was doing Nixon at San Clemente Dodge-Chrysler saying, 'Now that I have some time on my hands, I am trying to move some Chryslers off my back lot.'"

**ABOVE:** The Great Second City Swap: both casts on the Chicago stage on August 8, 1974: John Candy (left), Bill Murray, Mert Rich, Dan Aykroyd, Catherine O'Hara, Eugene Levy, Ann Ryerson, Gilda Radner, Paul Zegler, Betty Thomas, and Rosemary Radcliffe

**LEFT:** Standing: Eugenie Ross-Leming (left) and Betty Thomas; middle row: Tino Insana (left), Jim Staahl, Joe Flaherty, and David Rasche; floor: Jim Fisher

## THE SECOND CITY AND *SNL* CONNECTION

The Second City's deep ties with *Saturday Night Live* go all the way back to the show's 1975 premiere and original cast members Gilda Radner, Dan Aykroyd, and John Belushi. Over the last forty-plus seasons of the groundbreaking show, myriad Second Citizens have gone on to join the illustrious list of "Not Ready for Prime Time Players," as Lorne Michaels and his team continue to scout talent at The Second City at least once a year. No, it's not considered poaching. Yes, we are thrilled when one of our own goes "live from New York." Longtime Second City executive Kelly Leonard broke down the reasons why Second City talent has found such success at *Saturday Night Live*:

*What is it that makes a Second City actor such a good prospect for SNL? First and foremost, it is the improvisational training. Second City actors have to think quick on their feet, and a live TV show demands quick thinking. Another benefit is the experience one gets at The Second City from working in an ensemble. Learning to be successful within the group dynamic is no minor feat.*

According to Aykroyd, "Second City was my college, and *Saturday Night Live* was my university. I had to go through Second City's baccalaureate program before I could get my master's degree." Tina Fey, who became the show's first female head writer, backed up the theory that Second City training prepares people for the high-pressure environment, explaining, "You take a lot on because you come from Second City and know how to fix things quickly. If you're improvising, you have to fix things on your feet, so the luxury of having three or four days to fix a sketch is delightful."

Those who were part of The Second City—either as a resident stage alum or a member of the Touring Company—and became *SNL* players include Dan Aykroyd, Peter Aykroyd, Vanessa Bayer, Jim Belushi, John Belushi, Aidy Bryant, Brian Doyle-Murray, Rachel Dratch, Robin Duke, Chris Farley, Tina Fey, Mary Gross, Tim Kazurinsky, David Koechner, Julia Louis-Dreyfus, Tim Meadows, Jerry Minor, Bill Murray, Mike Myers, Mike O'Brien, Catherine O'Hara (who left the show before appearing in a single episode), Amy Poehler, Gilda Radner, Chris Redd, Tim Robinson, Tony Rosato, Horatio Sanz, Martin Short, Cecily Strong, Jason Sudeikis, and Nancy (Walls) Carell. The list of writers is just as long.

**ABOVE:** Amy Poehler (left), Chris Farley, and Tim Meadows. **FACING PAGE:** Top row: Bill Murray, Gilda Radner, Mary Gross, and Mike O'Brien; second row: Tina Fey, Robin Duke, and Jerry Minor; third row: John Belushi, Aidy Bryant, Rachel Dratch, and Tim Kazurinsky; bottom row: Vanessa Bayer, Jason Sudeikis, and Dan Aykroyd

# SHELLEY LONG

After taking workshops with improv pioneer Josephine Forsberg, Indiana native Shelley Long joined The Second City's Chicago cast in 1976 for *North by North Wells*. After leaving the Midwest for Hollywood, she attracted major attention with roles in films like *Night Shift*, *The Money Pit*, and *Troop Beverly Hills*—not to mention *The Brady Bunch Movie*, directed by fellow alumna Betty Thomas, and her iconic turn as "Diane Chambers" on *Cheers*, which she co-starred in with George Wendt.

**ABOVE:** Shelley Long (left) and Steven Kampmann in 1976

## *Saturday Night Live* Rocks the Comedy World

In 1975, a Second City company made up of both Chicago and Toronto alumni opened in a Pasadena, California, shopping mall with a show called *Alterations While You Wait*.

"John Candy and I drove thirty-eight hours from Toronto to Pasadena, straight through," recalled Dan Aykroyd. "We had a big Mercury Cougar, and we switched off driving. I went to only two rehearsals in Pasadena, and then [Lorne] Michaels called and had me in for an audition for *Saturday Night Live*." Aykroyd got the job. Although the remaining cast featured a dream lineup that included John Candy, Betty Thomas, and Eugene Levy, it was a big disappointment. The Second City Pasadena closed after nine months, but it existed long enough to witness pop culture history.

That October, Levy and his Pasadena castmates watched the premiere of a new comedy show from backstage on a little black-and-white TV. Their friends and peers Aykroyd, Gilda Radner, and John Belushi had been hired by Michaels—a Canadian, a former performer, and a sometime student at the Toronto Second City workshops—for his new show, *NBC's Saturday Night*. It was an immediate phenomenon.

The buzz surrounding the show (which was eventually rechristened *Saturday Night Live*) and its "Not Ready for Prime Time Players" was soon so intense that the media and the public wanted to know where this cutting-edge program had come from. The Second City was catapulted into the mainstream when the show's stars began crediting their time at The Second City for their current success, and our name started popping up in publications like *Rolling Stone*, *Time*, and *Newsweek*. Soon, both native and tourist audiences wanted to see "the place where Belushi got his start." They weren't disappointed with the casts they saw in Chicago or Toronto, which were made up in the mid- to late seventies with people like Jim Belushi, Mary Gross, Tim Kazurinsky, Eugene Levy, Shelley Long, Andrea Martin, Catherine O'Hara, Martin Short, Dave Thomas, and George Wendt.

**CLOCKWISE FROM TOP LEFT:** Gilda Radner (left), Brian Doyle-Murray, Gerry Salsberg, Dan Aykroyd, Joe Flaherty, Jayne Eastwood, and Valri Bromfield in Toronto's *Tippecanoe and Déjà Vu*, 1973; Andrea Martin performs in Toronto's *For a Good Time Call 363-1674*, 1976; Dave Thomas (left) and Catherine O'Hara in Toronto's sixth revue, *Also Available in Paperback*; Rosemary Radcliffe (left), Eugene Levy, and John Candy in a scene from 1974's *Hello Dali*

The cast of Chicago's revue *The First 100 Years or So Far, So Good*: Mert Rich (left), Deborah Harmon, Michael J. Gellman, Betty Thomas, Don DePollo, and Doug Steckler

## SCTV Is on the Air

*SNL*'s instant success led Bernie Sahlins and Andrew Alexander to ask themselves an obvious question: "If Second City could supply the talent to make a TV show like that work, why couldn't we do our own show?" Alexander recalled his initial reaction to breaking into television:

> *Bernie Sahlins had been bugging us to do TV, and I didn't want to. But then Lorne Michaels came out with Saturday Night Live, and we decided we wanted to do our own show. In a meeting with Allan Slaight, Global TV's owner, he said, "I can give you a studio and crew if you can come up with the rest of the money." My partner, Len Stuart, put up thirty-five grand, a lot of money in those days. Those were our above-the-line costs for the first seven shows. If Len hadn't come along, there would definitely not have been a television show. And I don't know how much longer I could have kept going at the Firehall.*

    *SCTV* premiered September 21, 1976, on the Global Television Network. The iconic sketch show went on to earn multiple accolades and a significant spot in TV history, as well as a devoted fan base. (Stay tuned, as the next chapter of this book is fully dedicated to *SCTV*'s indelible mark on comedy.)

### THE DAWN OF THE UTTERBACK ERA

Illustrator Bill Utterback drew his first signature caricature of Chicago's Mainstage cast for the 1976 show *North by North Wells*. He captured the theater's resident stage casts for over thirty years, until his death in 2010. It was a thrill for ensemble members to be "Utterback-ed," and it was one of the most-loved perks and time-honored traditions that came with the job. Utterback's work is still prominently displayed throughout the Piper's Alley building, both in the public spaces and The Second City's offices.

# LEN STUART

A brilliant entrepreneur and loyal friend, Len Stuart became the co-chairman and co-owner of The Second City in 1978. A native of Edmonton, Alberta, Stuart entered Alberta College and—with typical ambition and drive—became president of the student body, with his own office and company car. He took a job at Acme Novelty as a shipping clerk and ended up owning the company, which had twenty-six hundred employees and two hundred million dollars in annual revenue. His innovations turned community bingo games into huge revenue centers for government and charity organizations.

Stuart's partnership with Andrew Alexander provided business acumen and secure financing, two rare items in the world of theater. In addition to supplying the critical initial funds for the first seven episodes of *SCTV*, Stuart helped guide the show through some difficult business transactions in 1978, which resulted in the show being produced in Edmonton for two years. These negotiations, plus the securing of a deal with a major US TV distributor, cemented *SCTV*'s future.

With his many business ventures well established, the straightforward, imperturbable Stuart helped support The Second City and its interests through many defining challenges for nearly forty years. After his death in 2016, Stuart's wife, Angelika; daughter, Jessica; and son, D'Arcy, took over co-ownership of The Second City, along with Steve Johnston. D'Arcy is also now COO.

Len Stuart

# GEORGE WENDT

Long before everybody knew his name as "Norm" in all 275 episodes of *Cheers*, Chicago-bred George Wendt dropped out of Notre Dame with a 0.0 GPA. After visiting The Second City as a patron, he began taking workshops with Josephine Forsberg because "it turned out, the only thing I wouldn't hate doing was being in the cast of Second City," he said. "Second City looked for all the world like a bunch of people goofing off onstage. I was pretty sure they got paid for it." After spending time in the Touring Company, Wendt's first turn on the Mainstage was in 1975's *Once More with Fooling*. It earned him a ticket back to the Touring Company for further "seasoning." He admitted:

*It was the first of many firings and hirings for me. What was I fired for? For not being funny, for flagrantly sucking onstage. But eventually I learned what was funny and what wasn't. That's the thing about Second City. They teach you—or you learn— what works and what doesn't, what's funny and what isn't. That's what I learned.*

Wendt got another shot in 1978 for *Freud Slipped Here*. A brilliantly slow and grumpy clown, Wendt's languid side showed even when he played high-energy characters. Among his many creations at The Second City were a hip priest, a test-tube baby (complete with an oversize baby bonnet), and a barbershop quartet cowboy.

In September 2017, Wendt—who has been married to fellow Second City alum Bernadette Birkett for over forty years—graciously returned to The Second City Mainstage for *I Can't Believe They Wendt There: The Roast of George Wendt*, a star-studded reunion that raised more than two hundred thousand dollars for Gilda's Club Chicago and The Second City Alumni Fund.

Larry Coven (left) and George Wendt

# TIM KAZURINSKY

Australian-born Tim Kazurinsky was an advertising executive until he joined The Second City in 1978. Many of his characters were old men or hyperactive kids; he also played a naughty ventriloquist's dummy sitting atop George Wendt's knee. The camaraderie Kazurinsky and Wendt shared in their scenes transcended the stage. During one particular performance, there were only two people in the audience. Upon discovering it was the couple's twenty-fifth anniversary and they had driven in from Wisconsin to celebrate, Kazurinsky and Wendt went on with the show—one of their best.

Kazurinsky moved from The Second City to *SNL* for four seasons, played "Officer Carl Sweetchuck" in the *Police Academy* movies, became a successful screenwriter, and made his Broadway debut in 2015. The man who once spent a year as "the Wizard" in the national tour of *Wicked* maintains that the art of improv is a lot like sorcery:

> *You must fail for the audience to trust that you're truly creating. When you do an improv set, you're dying about a third to half of the time. In a weird way, the audience loves to see that. They don't want to see the tightrope walker go right across the canyon. The good ones, they'll pretend that they're going to trip and fall. That's what makes you more like a wizard. If you just did it well all the time, people wouldn't be impressed.*

Mary Gross (left) holds Tim Kazurinsky close in *I Remember Dada or Won't You Come Home, Saul Bellow?*

Utterback illustration for Chicago's fifty-seventh revue, *Another Fine Pickle*

Will Aldis (left) and Jim Belushi in 1978's *Sexual Perversity Among the Buffalo*

# JIM BELUSHI

Agnes Belushi, Jim Belushi's mother, made a deal with Joyce Sloane. She could hire her son to work at The Second City only after he graduated from college, and Sloane agreed. With one semester left to go, Belushi began touring on "June 6, 1976. I still have the check stub. I remember I did a lot of material on the bicentennial."

Soon, another deal was made—this time with Jim's older brother, John, who told Sloane he didn't want Jim performing any of his old scenes. Again, Sloane agreed. It was hard enough for Jim to develop his own comedic voice when everyone was comparing him to his famous older brother. Jim explained:

*My brother didn't give me any pointers. But that was good, I had to do it all myself. That's the way I look at it. I didn't study with anyone at Second City. I learned improvisation kind of the way you learn to drive a motorcycle, by grinding the gears and shifting into the wrong gears and slowly learning to do it right, so that by the time I got to Second City, I had learned the patter.*

Belushi joined the Chicago cast in 1978 for the show *Sexual Perversity Among the Buffalo*, returning in late 1980 for two more revues, *Well, I'm Off to the Thirty Years War or Swing Your Partner to the Right* and *Miro, Miro on the Wall*, both directed by Del Close.

"When I stepped onto the Mainstage," he said, "my two biggest surprises were that girls liked me more and how bad I felt when I had a bad improvisational set."

In addition to his successful career as a performer, musician, writer, producer, activist, and cannabis farmer, Belushi also took over for his late brother in the Blues Brothers band as "Zee Blues," alongside Dan Aykroyd, otherwise known as "Elwood Blues."

**CLOCKWISE FROM TOP:** Special guest Robin Williams (left) and Martin Short; Don DePollo (left) and Eric Boardman in *Wellsapoppin'*; Larry Coven (left), Audrie Neenan, and Will Aldis in Chicago's fifty-sixth revue, *Sexual Perversity Among the Buffalo*

**CLOCKWISE FROM TOP LEFT:** Brenda Donohue (left) and Catherine O'Hara; Ann Ryerson (left) and Steven Kampmann; PJ Torokvei (left), Cathy Gallant, Martin Short, Robin Duke, and Steven Kampmann in Toronto's twelfth revue, *Saturday Night Beaver*

Bruce Jarchow (left), Tim Kazurinsky, and George Wendt in the scene "Cowboys" from Chicago's fifty-eighth revue, *Freud Slipped Here*

By the twentieth-anniversary party in Chicago in December 1979, Second City's influence had begun spreading like a bad rash. With our boundary-pushing comedic sensibilities and an electric parade of talent, we had truly become a comedy force to be reckoned with.

# CHAPTER 5

# SCTV, 1976-1984

## WELCOME TO MELONVILLE

"*IT'S SECOND CITY Television, now beginning its programming day . . .*"

The Second City unveiled its answer to *Saturday Night Live* in 1976. *SCTV*, short for "Second City Television," had a simple premise. Set in the made-up Podunk town of Melonville, the show represented a day of programming on a fictional television network, also called SCTV.

"We thought, well, we're doing it at a really cheesy Canadian television station," said cast member and original head writer, Harold Ramis. "Let's *be* a cheesy television station." *SCTV* was an overnight phenomenon, with *Newsday* television critic Marvin Kitman declaring, "The premiere episode was quite simply the most superb half-hour of comedy . . . in a long time."

More than forty years later, *SCTV* remains a revered bastion of comedy beloved by millions of fans—fans that, at the time, the cast had no idea even existed. Speaking on an *SCTV* reunion panel with her co-stars at the U.S. Comedy Arts Festival in Aspen, Catherine O'Hara admitted, "We never second-guessed our audience, because we didn't know we had one."

At the same 1999 festival, panel host Conan O'Brien explained how the pioneering show led him to a career in comedy:

> *For me, and a lot of the comedy writers, performers, and producers of my generation, SCTV is the show. I started watching the show, and it literally changed my life. This is a show that had a relentless pace, it didn't hold for laughs, there was no studio audience. If you started laughing at something, you missed three jokes. SCTV was the reason that I got into television, the reason I wanted to go into comedy.*

**PICTURED ON PREVIOUS PAGE:** *SCTV* cast members, clockwise from top left: Eugene Levy, John Candy, Dave Thomas, Rick Moranis, Andrea Martin, Joe Flaherty, and Catherine O'Hara

## The First Season

The "show within a show" format of *SCTV* allowed the inexperienced group—made up entirely of Second City talent—to experiment with the characters, genres, and TV tropes of the time, all on their own (albeit thrifty) terms. "The quality of the show, which was all very low-budget, played into the reality because we did not have a lot of money," said series producer and resident check writer, Andrew Alexander. Along with broadcasting the day's faux programming, which parodied soap operas, films like *Ben-Hur*, local commercials, talk shows, station promos, and game shows, the audience also learned bits and pieces about the lives of the (mostly inept) brass who worked at the station. It was the ideal show-case for the cast of improvisers and comedians. Harold Ramis said:

> As far as a transition from Second City, we had this wonderful opportunity with SCTV to take all the things we'd learned onstage and directly translate them into television without any network sponsors or producers in authority. We were the authorities. We got to do what we wanted and operate the same way we did onstage, just in a different medium.

*SCTV* premiered on Canada's Global Television Network on September 21, 1976. The first season was produced by Bernie Sahlins and Alexander, with Joe Flaherty, Sheldon Patinkin, and Ramis as the associate producers and Milad Bessada directing. The original performers and writers were all alumni of the Chicago or Toronto theaters: John Candy, Flaherty, Eugene Levy, Andrea Martin, Catherine O'Hara, Ramis, and Dave Thomas.

"The cast was a young, active group of people who were very strong-minded and confident they knew how to relate to the generation that would be watching them," said Alexander. "They were, in a sense, their own artistic entity, with their own direction and sense of power. They really took the ensemble mentality from the stage to television."

Immediately, audiences sparked to the show. The response was swift, and it was glowing. "Global TV may have just pulled off the comedy coup of this season . . . the concept is as clever as the loony company members," wrote the *Toronto Star*'s Margaret Daly. Truth be told, the secret behind *SCTV* may have just been sheer ignorance.

"I can say now that *SCTV* probably succeeded because many of us did not know what we were doing," Alexander admitted. "Had we known what was involved—for producers, crew, writers—how hard it was, it would have been frightening. To do it 'by the book' would have been really quite difficult. The way we did it was quite anarchistic by comparison. And it worked."

**AN UNRELIABLE CREATION STORY**
Opinions differ regarding who actually had the idea for *SCTV*. According to Dave Thomas's memory, those present in the meeting at the Old Firehall that fateful day, besides himself, were Andrew Alexander, Del Close, Joe Flaherty, Eugene Levy, Sheldon Patinkin, Harold Ramis, and Bernie Sahlins. What exactly happened in that room remains a veritable mystery.

# CATHERINE O'HARA

Catherine O'Hara as "Dusty Towne" (top) and Brooke Shields (bottom)

Catherine O'Hara followed in her brother's and sister's footsteps by waiting tables at the Old Firehall. In 1974, without any formal training, she stepped in to replace Gilda Radner in the cast when Radner left for New York. "I basically imitated her for months," O'Hara said in a 2019 profile in the *New Yorker*. She wrote and performed in eight consecutive revues at The Second City Toronto, keeping her night job onstage even as she filmed the first season of *SCTV*.

As *SCTV* began gaining steam with Canadian audiences, co-star Andrea Martin came into the studio with an amusing story. A neighbor had stopped her on the way to work to tell her how much she liked the show, how much she liked Martin on the show, and how much she liked the other three women, too. The "other three women" were all O'Hara, already proving herself to be one of show business's strongest character actors.

In addition to her iconic *SCTV* characters, including "Dusty Towne" and the oversexed diva "Lola Heatherton" ("I wanna bear your children!"), O'Hara's impressions ranged from Meryl Streep to Brooke Shields to Lucille Ball. She was choosy about what portrayals she took on. "When we were doing *SCTV* and someone would say, 'What about this person? You want to play them in a scene? You want to do her?' If I didn't like them, I wouldn't play them. It takes too much of my time and energy," she told *Vulture* in 2019.

O'Hara and Eugene Levy have continued to pair up on-screen over the decades, co-starring as multiple iterations of dysfunctional lovebirds: "Cookie and Gerry Fleck" in *Best in Show*, "Mitch and Mickey" in *A Mighty Wind*, and "Moira and Johnny Rose" in *Schitt's Creek*. "She brings so much to whatever she takes on," Levy gushed about O'Hara in a 2019 visit to the Harold Ramis Film School. "We approach our work as actors, not as funny people. We don't consider ourselves funny people in real life." Agree to disagree.

# EUGENE LEVY

After taking over as "Jesus" in *Godspell* when much of the musical's cast defected to the new Second City outpost in Toronto, Eugene Levy also decided to find out what this improv thing was all about. The Hamilton, Ontario, native joined the first Old Firehall cast in 1974 and found the environment to be "the most amazing, exciting thing in the world," he told a group of Harold Ramis Film School students in 2019. Intoxicated by the proximity of the audience while simultaneously petrified by the improv, "I was learning as I was going," he admitted.

On *SCTV*, Levy's characters were just as inventive (and weird) as they had been onstage at The Second City, where he was known for a solo scene he did as a trainer for an amoeba circus. On television, he killed as "Bruno," the grunting hunchbacked assistant to John Candy's "Dr. Tongue"; one-half of the polka-playing "Schmenge brothers" (opposite Candy); or "Bobby Bittman," the leisure-suit-wearing sleazebag comic who couldn't seem to ask the question "How are ya?" enough.

Levy's improv and writing experience has come in handy many times since his Second City and *SCTV* days. He co-wrote and co-starred in Christopher Guest's improvised films *Waiting for Guffman*, *Best in Show*, *A Mighty Wind*, and *For Your Consideration*. Recently, the *American Pie* dad has been able to share screen time with his real-life children, Sarah and Dan, on *Schitt's Creek*, which Levy also co-created with his son.

## "Second City was the best school of comedy for me." —Eugene Levy

Eugene Levy as "Bobby Bittman"

## Season Two

As *SCTV* geared up for the second season, the team was faced with a stark reality. Head writer Harold Ramis had to leave for the West Coast to focus his attention on writing *Animal House*, and the team did not want to lose his guidance and instincts. Ramis "was the gauge as to whether something was good," Eugene Levy said. "Harold was the arbiter of what worked and what didn't work." Sometimes what worked was something rather uncouth. "For somebody so smart, he could write the cheapest punch line," Levy revealed.

In order to keep the group together to write, Andrew Alexander rented a house in Los Angeles—a sort of sun-soaked comedy lab, if you will—for the cast to live and work in for the summer. Ramis recalled how they spent their time at the retreat:

> *We'd meet every day, and there was a swimming pool and a pool table. It was kind of my dream: the comedy house where everyone was funny. You'd sit at that table, and John Candy would pull a napkin out of his pocket from a bar the night before. He'd unfold it, and it had an idea, but it was like, "Oh, all I can read is 'Davy Crockett hat.'" You'd try to piece that together for John. He would just keep throwing things in until the scene grew and grew. You knew everything was right because they were going to perform it. You wouldn't write anything that couldn't be performed because you were already laughing at the table, and that was exactly how it was going to go down. It eliminated a lot of problems.*

The group left Los Angeles with eight new episodes written. With Ramis out, Brian Doyle-Murray joined the writing staff. Among the other writers who worked on the show over the years were original Second City Toronto cast member Valri Bromfield; Joe Flaherty's brothers, Paul and David; Andrea Martin's then-husband (and Martin Short's brother-in-law), Bob Dolman; Martin Short's brother Michael; Jeffrey Barron; Dick Blasucci; Chris Cluess; Tom Couch; Jim Fisher; Eddie Gorodetsky; Judith Kahan; Stu Kreisman; John McAndrew; Brian McConnachie; Mert Rich; Jim Staahl; and Doug Steckler.

## American Airwaves

Global TV produced a total of fifty-two episodes of *SCTV*, which was syndicated in the United States starting in 1977. For US broadcasts, the show had to be trimmed down to be two minutes shorter than the Canadian version—more time for commercials—which meant that every episode had to be edited twice. The differing postproduction demands, combined with the differing demands of the cast and producers, did not make for a

---

**MORT FINKEL AND MOE GREEN**

As "Mort Finkel," Harold Ramis once delivered an (un)educational "Sunrise Semester"— *SCTV*'s version of an early-morning instructional show— on do-it-yourself dentistry, using vodka as the only painkiller. The crew put real booze in the bottle during the shoot, and Ramis ended up actually getting drunk. Ramis was also known for playing the authoritative station manager (and "Dialing for Dollars" host) "Moe Green." When he left the show after season one, the character's absence was explained as a kidnapping.

joyous time behind the scenes. Bernie Sahlins left *SCTV* after the first season, leaving Andrew Alexander in charge as executive producer. When Sahlins left, he took The Second City's name with him. (The show was supposed to be called *The Second City Television Show* in US syndication, which, in hindsight, doesn't have the same ring to it.)

To the great disappointment of the crew in Toronto, Global Television Network couldn't afford to keep producing the show there, and production ceased after the second season. *SCTV* suffered a year-and-a-half hiatus while Alexander and Len Stuart sought out a new place for Melonville to call home.

## Greetings from Edmonton

In 1978, Len Stuart helped guide *SCTV* through some difficult dealings with a large Canadian broadcast company called Allarcom. The success of these negotiations resulted in the show's production being moved over two thousand miles west to Edmonton, Alberta, for two years. "I was shocked at the knowledge Len had of our industry," said then-Allarcom president Doug Holtby. "You have to remember, his background was in printing at the time, so to have the understanding that he did at that time was quite impressive. The deal secured *SCTV* for years to come."

The location shift wasn't the only big change for the show. It had a revamped name, *SCTV Network*. John Candy was gone, off shooting a pilot; Catherine O'Hara took a year off; Andrea Martin and Eugene Levy could only commit to a few shows each. To make up for the missing actors, new faces Robin Duke, Rick Moranis, and Tony Rosato were hired. John Blanchard took over as director. With few distractions in the cold and rather isolated Edmonton, the company melded together quickly—what Andrew Alexander fondly chalked up to a "bunker mentality." However, the remote environs eventually proved too taxing for the cast. "They loved the crew and production staff but were burnt out by the hotel living and hard commuting between Toronto and Edmonton," Alexander explained in Dave Thomas's book, *SCTV: Behind the Scenes*.

**JOHNNY LARUE**

One of John Candy's most beloved characters on *SCTV* was the drunken, bad-tempered, vain "Johnny LaRue," who liked to think of himself—erroneously—as irresistible to women. The host of a number of man-on-the-street ("Street Beef"), dining, exercise, cooking, and even children's shows ("Mr. Science"), the shameless on-air personality and one-time city council candidate constantly chased his dream of getting that granddaddy of truly grand camera moves: the crane shot.

In reality, the biggest thing Candy was misguided about was how to cook a turkey. During the first year of *SCTV*, Canadian Candy—who fully appreciated American Thanksgiving traditions—invited some of the show's expat Americans over for a holiday dinner. The guests were to arrive around six p.m. At six fifteen, Candy was still dressing the twenty-two-pound turkey. The group didn't eat dinner until two in the morning.

# DAVE THOMAS

Before Dave Thomas joined The Second City, he was an ad man—a really good one. "I was working for McCann Erickson," he explained in a 1988 Show-time special celebrating The Second City Toronto's fifteenth anniversary. "[I] worked there for about a year and a half, wrote some commercials for Coca-Cola, and my creative director came to me, put his arm around me, and said, 'In three years, you'll be a creative director,' and I thought, 'Well, that's it. I'm out of here,' and I quit."

A cast member in the legendary Toronto production of *Godspell*, Thomas joined The Second City Toronto in 1975, where he made his debut in the theater's sixth revue, *Also Available in Paperback*.

The show also featured Thomas's future *SCTV* co-stars Catherine O'Hara and Andrea Martin. In 1976, he shared the stage with John Candy in two revues, *For a Good Time Call 363-1674* and *The Wizard of Ossington*. When *SCTV* premiered that same year, Thomas cemented his place in pop culture history with his "Great White North" character, "Doug McKenzie," the brother of Rick Moranis's "Bob McKenzie." Thomas also mastered an impression of comedian Bob Hope, thanks to a little help from a fake nose and the right angle at which he jutted out his chin. For an exhaustive, candid recounting of the making of *SCTV*, seek out a copy of Thomas's book, *SCTV: Behind the Scenes*.

## "GREAT WHITE NORTH"

"Bob and Doug McKenzie," *SCTV*'s beer-swilling, loon-calling, flannel shirt-wearing brothers, were the direct result of the Canadian Broadcasting Corporation's requirement that each episode have two minutes of "identifiable Canadian content." (See earlier: the two minutes that had to be cut for US TV.) Starting in 1980, the brothers, dreamed up and played by Dave Thomas and Rick Moranis, hosted an inane talk show called "Great White North." The segment became a fan favorite on *SCTV*, with the

actors' stereotypical portrayals of Canadians ("Take off, eh?") actually becoming a source of immense national pride. Moranis and Thomas found themselves nominated for the Order of Canada, the country's highest honor, for "contributing to [Canada's] sense of cultural identity." Suddenly, everybody wanted to be a "hoser," a word the characters entered into our lexicon; "hoser" became one of pop culture's most affectionate insults.

In 1981, an LP titled *The Great White North* sold more than one million copies and won a

Juno Award (Canada's answer to the Grammys) for Comedy Album of the Year. Moranis and Thomas then brought their iconic characters to the big screen in 1983 with the film *Strange Brew*, which became the highest-grossing Canadian film of that year. Since then, "Bob and Doug" have spawned commercial deals, an animated series, and even action figures. In 2017, Moranis and Thomas brought the brothers back to life one more time at The Second City Toronto for a one-night-only benefit, appropriately called *Take Off, Eh*.

**THE REAL *SCTV* SUPERHEROES**
*SCTV*'s many transformations were made possible by the tireless handiwork of the incredibly talented hair, makeup, and wardrobe team, who made makeover magic on a shoestring budget. Judi Cooper-Sealy (hair and wig wizard), Juul Haalmeyer (costume designer extraordinaire and leader of the left-footed "Juul Haalmeyer Dancers"), Beverly Schechtman, and Christine Hart (both makeup maestros) deserve as much credit for the success of the show as anyone else.

# RICK MORANIS

Rick Moranis was the only *SCTV* regular who was never part of The Second City. With experience as a writer for CBC radio and television and appearances on a few TV shows, he joined *SCTV* in 1980 after hitting it off with Dave Thomas at a party during a time when the show was seeking new faces for the production's move to Edmonton.

"Rick was a savior," Andrew Alexander said in *SCTV: Behind the Scenes*.

"He came in on that third season, all energy, and he respected the show. He was invaluable."

In addition to playing hockey-loving Canuck "Bob McKenzie," Moranis was famous on the show for his dead-on impersonations of celebrities including Woody Allen, Merv Griffin, and—in a sketch that Jimmy Kimmel names as one of his all-time favorites—singer Michael McDonald.

## SCTV Network 90

In 1981, the show moved to a new network with a new name. *SCTV Network 90* on NBC had an hour-and-a-half late-night slot on Fridays after Johnny Carson. NBC figured if it could make *Saturday Night Live* work at eleven thirty p.m., why not try one a.m. on Fridays? The logic was, perhaps, a little fuzzy, but the show was on a US network, so they had a deal. John Candy, Andrea Martin, and Catherine O'Hara rejoined the company, and, at NBC's request, the show now had musical guests, including Tony Bennett, the Boomtown Rats, Natalie Cole, Hall and Oates, John Cougar Mellencamp, and Roy Orbison. The NBC version lasted two seasons. For a while, *SCTV Network 90* ran opposite a similar show on ABC called *Fridays*, which employed former Compass Player and 1963 Second City alum Jack Burns as head writer.

Martin Short joined the cast of *SCTV Network 90* during the second season at NBC. "When Marty joined, it couldn't have come at a better time," said Andrew Alexander. "Marty was a spark; he was new energy; he was terrific. His enthusiasm was contagious, and *SCTV* turned out to be the perfect show for him to mine his comic genius."

During its run, *SCTV* received thirteen Emmy Award nominations, winning two years consecutively for Outstanding Writing in a Variety or Music Program in 1982 and 1983. Joe Flaherty accepted the first award on behalf of the cast and crew, despite Milton Berle's constant interruption of his speech. Apparently, Uncle Miltie was not a fan of the show.

**FACING PAGE:**
Martin Short (right) as "Ed Grimley," Eugene Levy as "Gus Gustofferson," Andrea Martin as "Edith Prickley," Juul Haalmeyer as "Juul Haalmeyer," Catherine O'Hara as "Lola Heatherton," John Candy as "Johnny LaRue," and Joe Flaherty as "Guy Caballero"

# ANDREA MARTIN

Two-time Tony Award winner Andrea Martin began her career as a singing chicken on *Captain Kangaroo*. An American from Maine, she came to Toronto to perform in *Godspell* before joining The Second City cast at the Old Firehall in 1975. "I think the people who came out of Second City in Toronto were personalities," she said on Showtime's 1988 televised Second City anniversary special, "and I think because we were friends, there was a very comfortable, familiar, joyous feeling of celebration when we performed." A trained actress, Martin had no prior experience improvising and never really lost her fear of it, although she was one of Second City's funniest and most outrageous members. "I don't think there was one night in all the years I did Second City that I ever felt comfortable doing improvisation," Martin said.

On *SCTV*, Martin brought to life the all-leopard-clad station manager "Edith Prickley," a character she first did at The Second City as a mother summoned to a meeting with her child's teacher. She also played harsh-voiced, cue-card-reading "Edna Boil," talk show host "Libby Wolfson," and the deeply repressed sexologist "Cheryl Kinsey," who taught women how to fake orgasms.

# MARTIN SHORT

Often called the nicest guy in show business, Martin Short was well established in the Toronto theater scene when he joined The Second City in 1977. After finishing up a run in *Godspell* (along with several other names that have already popped up in this book), he took over for John Candy in the Toronto stage's ninth revue, *The Wizard of Ossington*. Short discussed his style of comedy on Showtime's fifteenth-anniversary show for The Second City Toronto:

*I would not say that my work at Second City had intellectual appeal as much as more of a clown quality. The scenes I did, I would always make sure there was enough time because I would do full costume and hair changes. I would arrive at the theater early, and it was very important that I have my bowl of water and my dippity-do. And I would bring costumes–well, not costumes–I suppose you would call them clothing. You know, shirts from my childhood that I still fit into, tragically enough.*

*I stopped growing at seven. Bad pants and unusual jackets that normally you wouldn't keep. But I thought, maybe someday. So I always figured that if you walked onstage and looked totally insane, you would get a laugh. And then you were halfway there. If I thought of a picture of me in Second City, it would be a picture I actually have. It's the whole cast, and we're in the middle of a scene, and someone has said something, and I've clearly broken up, and I'm truly laughing. And that's my memory of doing Second City stage.*

Among Short's memorable impressions were Jerry Lewis and Katharine Hepburn. His unforgettable original characters included former child star "Jackie Rogers Jr.," defense attorney "Nathan Thurm," songwriter "Irving Cohen," and the bizarrely infantile "Ed Grimley," a character he created at The Second City, brought to *SCTV*, and then made famous on *Saturday Night Live* with his "I must say" catchphrase.

> "We juggled to make sure the show got done, and to keep everybody content. We were always shuffling towards the guillotine."
>
> **–Andrew Alexander**

**UNDERCOVER PRODUCER**

Producers from the networks came and went, but Canadian line producer Patrick Whitley fortunately stayed the course and kept things together in the background while the network-approved people revolved in and out. Andrew Alexander paid Whitley out of his own pocket to bring him to Edmonton, where his undercover producing duties were kept hush-hush. Whitley is married to another former Second City power producer, Sally Cochrane, who was The Second City's general manager beginning in 1978 until she became the theater's producer, a position she held until 1996.

## The Final Season

When the NBC deal came to an end, devoted fans panicked. In a 1983 *Washington Post* article, Tom Shales painted a rather dramatic picture of the show's final resurrection:

> *A band of SCTV fans recently organized themselves into a grassroots "Save SCTV" movement, picketing NBC studios in New York. On Friday, [executive producer Andrew] Alexander appeared before the inflamed throng and reassured them that SCTV "would continue in some form." Yesterday he said officially of the program, "It's alive."*

Cinemax picked up the show for one more season in 1984, this time for forty-five-minute episodes and again with a slightly tweaked moniker: *SCTV Channel*. In the same *Washington Post* article, Alexander told Shales that the Cinemax deal "enables us to do the show we want to do," although he promised the move to premium cable would not mean Joe Flaherty's "Guy Caballero" would start dropping his pants. (No word on whether Flaherty agreed to those terms in advance.) This time around, the cast was composed of longtime stars Flaherty, Eugene Levy, Martin Short, and Andrea Martin, with featured players (and former Toronto Second Citizens) John Hemphill and Mary Charlotte Wilcox rounding out the cast.

Six seasons and eight years after it started, *SCTV* signed off for good. The final episode aired July 17, 1984. Alexander shared his thoughts on the end of the *SCTV* era with Dave Thomas in *SCTV: Behind the Scenes*:

> *In the history of television, I can't recall a show that played as many different venues. It was just pure survival, going first to syndication, then to the network, then back to pay. That in itself was a huge juggling act.... We juggled to make sure the show got done, and to keep everybody content. We were always shuffling towards the guillotine; the execution was always around the corner because the show just had that edge. I think that created a lot of internal strife. The business side of it was always a problem, so when Cinemax canceled us, I think there was kind of a mutual agreement that it was probably time to call an end to SCTV.*

## The Second City Alumni Fund

In May 2008, *SCTV* cast members Joe Flaherty, Eugene Levy, Andrea Martin, Catherine O'Hara, and Martin Short reunited onstage for the first time in twenty-four years. *The Benefit of Laughter*, a one-night-only event at The Second City Toronto, brought the comedy legends back together to raise money for a former member of the *SCTV* production staff who needed financial assistance due to an illness. The sold-out show raised funds that greatly surpassed what was required by that crew member, and the cast agreed to put the balance toward building something even more impactful. Andrew Alexander formally established The Second City Alumni Fund, a resource for performers, technicians, support staff, and other members of the creative and production teams associated with The Second City theaters and *SCTV* experiencing critical health and financial challenges.

At The Second City's star-studded fiftieth-anniversary celebration in 2009, the *SCTV* cast—this time joined by Harold Ramis and Dave Thomas—reunited on Chicago's Mainstage for charity once again, bringing the fund's total to over half a million dollars, an amount that has doubled since The Second City Alumni Fund's inception.

## *SCTV*'s Legacy

Since its first day on the air, *SCTV* has been a pop culture touchstone that has influenced countless comedians and been an endless source of national pride, receiving a star on Canada's Walk of Fame in 2002. In 2019, *Rolling Stone* called an ensemble featuring John Candy, Joe Flaherty, Eugene Levy, Andrea Martin, and Martin Short as fictional punk rockers the Queenhaters "the greatest punk band of all time." *Esquire* claimed in 2018 that "all the comedy that you love today wouldn't even exist without" *SCTV*. One of the show's most noteworthy admirers, the very non-Canadian Martin Scorsese, brought the cast together in 2018 to film a Netflix documentary examining *SCTV*'s enduring legacy. Flaherty, Levy, Martin, Rick Moranis, Catherine O'Hara, and Dave Thomas took the stage at Toronto's historic Elgin Theatre for a lively look back moderated by late-night host and *SCTV* fan Jimmy Kimmel. "Having the whole crew back together for one last hurrah was so much fun," said Alexander. "It was like we were teleported back to 1981—same tensions, laughs, and camaraderie—a reminder of why this was such an extraordinary ensemble."

While the late Harold Ramis and John Candy were both dearly missed that day, we were honored to be joined by Candy's wife, Rosemary, and his children, Jen and Chris—the next generation of "hosers." As an homage to the late star's "Johnny LaRue" character, Scorsese made sure to finally get his much-fretted-over crane shot.

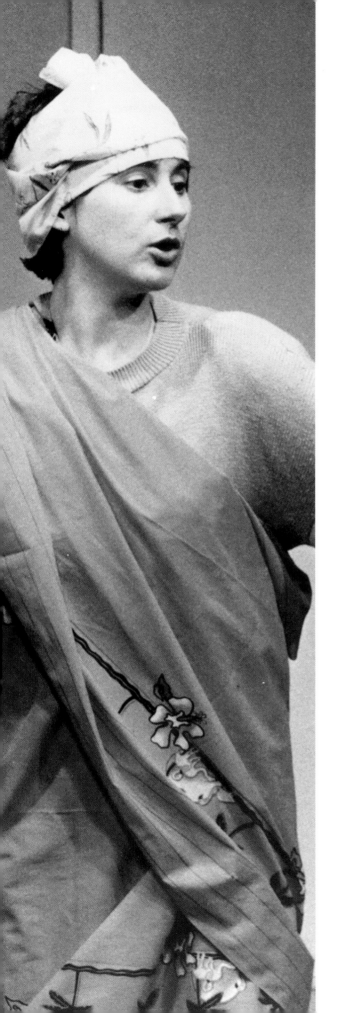

# CHAPTER 6

# THE 1980s

## TRIUMPHS AND TRAGEDIES

By the eighties, The Second City was one of the hottest tickets in town. Hopeful patrons had to call the Chicago box office nearly two months in advance to secure a Saturday night seat. It was no coincidence that the uptick in traffic coincided with the celebrity status achieved by so many Second City alumni in so many one-word titles, including *Caddyshack*, *Ghostbusters*, *Stripes*, *Splash*, and *Cheers*. And then there were the "Blues Brothers," Dan Aykroyd and John Belushi's iconic fedora-and-sunglasses-at-night-wearing *Saturday Night Live* characters who quickly spawned a film, a chart-topping album, and a concert tour. (Belushi warned older folks like Sheldon Patinkin not to see the movie unless they went to a downtown theater on a Saturday night to watch it among the younger urbanite audience it was meant for. He was not wrong.)

In addition to our ever-growing list of alumni blowing up on the big and small screens, two new co-owners saw to it that The Second City was also increasing its comedy footprint all over the map. While there were hits—and certainly plenty of misses—this was the decade that began spreading the gospel of The Second City's collaborative style of creating.

## The Second City e.t.c.

A second theater sat empty within Piper's Alley, the Chicago building The Second City called home. In 1981, the abandoned space, which had long ago been used by Paul Sills to hold workshops, became the short-term location of an unrelated comedy troupe that included Northwestern University student (and one-time Second City Touring Company member) Julia Louis-Dreyfus and recent Northwestern graduate Richard Kind. The Practical Theatre Company certainly gave The Second City a run for its money in terms of improvisational entertainment—and talent—at the time, but its occupancy in Piper's Alley was ultimately short-lived.

**PICTURED ON PREVIOUS PAGE:** Bonnie Hunt (left), Mike Myers, and Barbara Wallace in Chicago's seventieth revue, *Kuwait Until Dark or Bright Lights, Night Baseball*

In 1982, The Second City was suffering from an embarrassment of riches. With plenty of talented people in its orbit, but just one resident stage and a decrease in road gigs, a lot of seasoned, underemployed Touring Company folks were hanging around with nowhere to perform on a regular basis. With the former Practical Theatre space empty, a group of performers, led by Jane Morris and Jeff Michalski, asked Bernie Sahlins and Joyce Sloane if they could put on a Touring Company show there. Sahlins agreed—but *only* if they used it as an overflow theater when the Mainstage show was sold out and *only* if they did archival material, none of their own stuff.

Turns out, no one joins The Second City because they love following rules. In 1983, the cast and crew—Morris, Michalski, Bill Applebaum, Rob Bronstein, Jim Fay, Susan Gauthier, Carey Goldenberg, musical director Ruby Streak, and director Don DePollo—were ready with a full-fledged original show, to be presented to the world in the theater Sloane christened The Second City e.t.c. While Sahlins was out of town, Sloane let them open *Cows on Ice* and invite the critics. Sloane recalled the opening:

Poster art for the e.t.c.'s first show, *Cows on Ice*

I said, "Okay, you can open it, but I don't want to know about it!" The night they opened, I went out of town. They got great reviews; it was really a terrific show. Everything was going just great. Bernie comes back, and would you believe it? On the way from the airport, the driver hands him an old newspaper, and [former Chicago Tribune theater critic] Richard Christiansen's fabulous review for the show is in that paper. So he comes in: "Who did this? I'm going to fire the whole company if you don't tell me who did it! I'm calling Christiansen. You're lucky he's out of town!" Jane Morris comes to me and says, "I'm going to quit because I'll tell Bernie I did it." I said, "Just wait. It'll blow over." He got over it, and they've been doing their own shows back there ever since.

What does e.t.c. stand for, you might ask? Absolutely nothing. "When I gave it the name," Sloane once admitted, "I didn't really have anything in mind. It doesn't really mean anything." (Also, it's always all lowercase, to the inconvenience of critics and copy editors everywhere.)

Although, as Sahlins had envisioned, ticket sales did at first depend on overflow audiences, by the end of the eighties, the e.t.c. had its own following. To date, over forty original revues have been staged in the theater by a list of notable alumni that includes Aidy Bryant, Steve Carell, Stephen Colbert, Keegan-Michael Key, Jack McBrayer, Adam McKay, and Nia Vardalos.

# JULIA LOUIS-DREYFUS AND JANE LYNCH

They are two of the world's most accomplished and adored names in comedy, and though neither were members of The Second City's resident company, Julia Louis-Dreyfus and Jane Lynch both hit the road with The Second City Touring Company in the 1980s.

**Julia Louis-Dreyfus:** On a 2016 episode of *The Late Show with Stephen Colbert*, the award-winning actress and producer reminisced with host and fellow Touring Company veteran Colbert about the less-than-ideal performing conditions they had both experienced on the road. Louis-Dreyfus, who received the 2018 Mark Twain Prize for American Humor, described their usual audience demographic as folks "who might be either asleep or pass-out drunk. It was very glamorous."

**Jane Lynch:** The Emmy and Golden Globe winner graciously shared her less-than-memorable Second City audition for a group of Training Center students in 2016. "I can't say that I did great," Lynch admitted. "When they called, I was shocked." The classically

trained performer was cast in the Touring Company, and she said that's when everything changed. "Once I started doing sketch [comedy], everything blew open," the actress, singer, and author said. And as for Lynch's time on the road? "There's no better training. Nothing throws you."

Julia Louis-Dreyfus (center) in a Touring Company publicity photo, with (clockwise left) Carey Goldenberg, Bill Wronski, Jeff Michalski, Bill Applebaum, and Petrea Burchard

The National Touring Company

Richard Kind (left), Dan Castellaneta, and Isabella Hofmann in 1986

# DAN CASTELLANETA

The e.t.c.'s first show, *Cows on Ice*, was followed up a little over a year later by *Mirrors at the Border*. The show featured Dan Castellaneta, who moved to the Mainstage the following year and was discovered there in 1987 by Tracey Ullman. He left Chicago for a job on *The Tracey Ullman Show*, where he developed the voice of "Homer Simpson" for some animated shorts that popped up on the show now and then before spinning off to their own show. *The Simpsons* began airing in 1989, and, over thirty seasons later, it is the longest-running US prime-time scripted television series in history. D'oh.

## the Second City 63rd revue

### Pursued by a Bear

**EATS**

**SANDWICHES  2.75**

PRICE INCLUDES SHOESTRING POTATOES, DILL PICKLE
AND A CHOICE OF POTATO SALAD OR COLE SLAW

| BREADS | MEATS | CHEESES |
|---|---|---|
| onion roll | corned beef | swiss |
| rye bread | turkey | cheddar |
| kaiser roll | pastrami | american |
| | salami | |
| | roast beef | |
| | ham | |

**CHEESE BASKET...2.25**
Cheese spread with a variety of crackers

**ICE CREAM SPECIALTIES**

VANILLA • CHOCOLATE • BUTTER PECAN • CHOCOLATE CHIP

large  **1.25**          gigantic  **1.50**

VANILLA ICE CREAM TOPPED
WITH YOUR FAVORITE LIQUEUR

**RASPBERRY BRANDY**

**CHOCOLATE MINT          GREEN CREME DE MENTHE**

**CHOCOLATE ALMOND**

large  **2.50**          gigantic  **3.00**

Playbill from Chicago's sixty-third revue, directed by Bernie Sahlins

London, Ontario, cast members David Talbot (left), Kevin Frank, Mark Wilson, and Deborah Theaker in 1986

## Edmonton and London (Ontario) Calling

Not every attempt at expansion has been as successful as the e.t.c. In 1980, Second City opened a location in Edmonton, Alberta, at a glitzy nightclub called Lucifer's, where the cast had to work in front of a wall of amplifiers and a drum kit. It lasted fewer than three years. However, from 1983 to 1992, The Second City had a home in the three-hundred-seat Corner Stage Theatre in London, Ontario. Lyn Okkerse, Andrew Alexander's sister, and her husband, Peter, were producers for The Second City there. While they were still around, both the Edmonton and London stages served as stepping-stones between the Canadian Touring Company and The Second City Toronto, where the Old Firehall was still going strong.

**FROM TOP:** John Hemphill (left) and Don Lake in Toronto's *I've Got a Sequel Part II*, 1983; Jane Morris (left), Chris Barnes, and Jeff Michalski in the e.t.c.'s fourth revue, *Kukla, Fawn and Ollie, or Contra Hear Me Knocking*

## Dead, Gone, Dead

Despite the geographical gains Second City experienced during the eighties, the personal losses were unimaginable. It's hard for anyone to describe the shock and horror that the death of John Belushi created in The Second City. Not only is it difficult to lose a loved one, but when the circumstances lend themselves to a media feeding frenzy, the fallout is immediate, uncontrollable, and devastating. We learned this—for the first time, but not the last, unfortunately—in 1982, when Belushi succumbed to his addiction on March 5 in Los Angeles.

Joyce Sloane was sitting in her office when she received a call from a friend in the press notifying her of Belushi's death. Within minutes, the phone began ringing off the hook, and journalists started arriving at the theater. Sloane, still in shock, posted two staff members at the foot of the stairs to stop the influx of reporters from entering the building.

Several funerals and memorial services followed. Sloane flew to Martha's Vineyard with Bernie and Jane Sahlins for the private Albanian Orthodox funeral. When they arrived, no rental cars were available. Apparently, the media had reserved all the inventory on the tiny island. Sloane, in her inimitable fashion, found a restaurant on the grounds of the airport and convinced the short-order cook to let them borrow his car. The service took place in a stark white New England church, where the shutters were kept closed so the press couldn't see in. Dan Aykroyd and Belushi's brothers, Jim and Billy, were pallbearers; James Taylor sang "That Lonesome Road" at the graveside as news helicopters swarmed overhead.

After a memorial service at St. John the Divine Cathedral in New York City, the Sahlinses took Jim Belushi and his wife at the time, Sandra, to dinner in Greenwich Village. On the way back, Belushi asked the driver to stop for a moment at the White Horse Tavern. He and fellow Chicago alum Will Aldis were known for a scene they had created in the 1978 Mainstage show *Sexual Perversity Among the Buffalo*. In it, they played two brothers drinking at the historic Greenwich Village watering hole while discussing life, family, and death. After knocking several back, the two characters begin talking about poets, which the younger brother (Aldis) wants to be one day:

**Jim:** I'll tell ya what's important. A degree's not important, man. Alright? Livin' right and dyin' right's important. Understand?

**Will:** Yeah.

**Jim:** See this bar here, Mr. Lit?

**Will:** Sorta.

**Jim:** You see it. You know who Dylan Thomas is?

**Will:** Yeah, I know—

**Jim:** Hunh?

**Will:** Yeah, sure!

**Jim:** See that stool right on the end there?

**Will:** Yeah?

**Jim:** Dylan Thomas died right there, man.

**Will:** Really?

**Jim:** Yeah.

**Will:** What happened?

**Jim:** He came here in 1953, right? To do a tour.

**Will:** Yeah.

**Jim:** An, ah, he was an alcoholic. You knew that.

**Will:** He was a poet.

**Jim:** He was a poet, right. You gotta be an alcoholic, sure. Right. So he was sick, right? So he came here—he was sick, right—and he went to the doctor. The doctor told him, "Dylan, you drink any more, you're gonna die." So he came right here, man. Sat right there. Piled twenty-seven shots of white grain alcohol like this—like a Christmas tree, right? Sat there—boomp, boomp, boomp, boomp, boomp, right? His head hit the bar. Went into a coma. Went over to the hospital across the street. Died, man. Sheet over the head. Dead, gone, dead. Right fucking there, man.

Jim Belushi and Bernie Sahlins entered the White Horse that night and ordered a couple of beers. They sat in silence until Belushi spoke softly. "Dead, gone, dead." They finished their beers, and they left.

John Belushi had been just thirty-three years old.

## Anniversaries Galore

In December 1984, The Second City celebrated twenty-five years of existence. Alumni from Playwrights Theatre Club, the Compass, and The Second City—a list that included Alan Arkin, Ed Asner, Shelley Berman, Severn Darden, Barbara Harris, Robert Klein, Harold Ramis, David Shepherd, Martin Short, Paul Sills, David Steinberg, Betty Thomas, Dave Thomas, George Wendt, and Fred Willard—descended upon Chicago (on private chartered jets, no less). A private show took place on the Mainstage with a mixture of performances by alumni and what was at the time the resident cast—Mindy Bell, Jim Fay, Mike Hagerty, John Kapelos, Richard Kind, and Mona Lyden. No one wanted the evening to end, but it finally did, at around two in the morning.

To help further the celebration (and pay for those jets), HBO shot a live television special the following night at Chicago's Vic Theatre. The show was a deep dive into old scenes performed by revered alumni and young talent working side by side. The special aired on HBO and Canada's CBC, which partnered with Showtime in 1988 on a similar celebration of The Second City Toronto's fifteenth anniversary at the Old Firehall. Filmed at the Toronto theater, Eugene Levy produced and directed the one-hour special.

**CRAIG TAYLOR**

Craig Taylor was continuously employed longer than any other person at The Second City, where he was the stoic captain of the Mainstage for over forty years before retiring in 2019. As stage manager, he has been asked to provide the impossible for numerous Second City directors, and he delivers. From setting the stage to running the lights in the booth night after night, Taylor is one of the stalwart constants that makes The Second City feel like a family. He's also, as many professional and celebrated comedians will attest, always the funniest one in the room.

Illustrated Second City cast members commemorate Second City's twenty-fifth anniversary

Richard Kind (left) and Jim Fay in 1984's *Catch 27*

# RICHARD KIND

Richard Kind joined The Second City in 1983 after spending time as a member of the Practical Theatre Company with Julia Louis-Dreyfus. Kind's specialty was playing loudmouthed, intrusive characters made funnier by his ultra-flexible face. (One of his many talents is the ability to stick his entire fist into his mouth.) In 2015 Kind told the *A.V. Club*, "I often call [The Second City] the Harvard of theater. You go on stage every night, and you find out exactly who you are and what you can do. . . . I've never been smarter, and I don't think I've ever been better."

"Richard Kind had this terrific ability to play sympathetic, sweet, frightened, and not-caring—all at the same time," said Andrew Alexander, who hired Kind for a 1987 CBS pilot called 110 Lombard (after the address of the Old Firehall) along with Bonnie Hunt, Don Lake, Mike Myers, and Ryan Stiles. The time slot eventually went to Pat Sajak.

Kind returned to the Mainstage in 2019 to play the set with the cast of *Algorithm Nation or The Static Quo*. Cast member Ryan Asher reported afterward that the versatile character actor "truly couldn't be kinder, funnier, or more lovely."

Utterback illustration
for the Chicago
Mainstage's sixty-
sixth revue, *True
Midwest or No, But I
Saw the Movie*

**FROM TOP:** Harry Murphy (left), Dan Castellaneta, Maureen Kelly, Richard Kind, Craig Taylor, Isabella Hofmann, and Jim Fay celebrate Second City's twenty-sixth anniversary in 1985; Deborah Theaker (left) and Mike Myers as "Hockey Parents" in Toronto's 1987 revue, *Bob Has Seen the Wind*

## Under New Ownership

Len Stuart (left) and Andrew Alexander in front of Second City's original 1959 wooden sign

Just a year after the twenty-fifth anniversary, *Time* magazine hailed The Second City as the "capital of comedy." That capital was about to experience an intense transfer of power, as co-founder Bernie Sahlins sold his remaining interest in the company to Andrew Alexander and Len Stuart. The terms kept Sahlins on as a director, made Alexander executive producer, and moved Joyce Sloane from associate producer to producer and partner. It was the end of one Second City regime and the start of a new era.

## The Second City Training Center

As the new co-owners, Andrew Alexander and Len Stuart immediately began to expand The Second City's nontheatrical business ventures. There had been a noticeable increase in the number of young people moving to Chicago and Toronto to try to make it to a Second City stage, so Alexander decided it was time to establish a formal training program. In 1985, The Second City Training Center opened in Chicago, led by artistic director Martin de Maat, Sheldon Patinkin, and Cheryl Sloane, Joyce Sloane's daughter.

Since launching, The Second City Training Center has grown into the largest school of improvisational arts in the world. Initially designed as a new revenue and talent stream, Alexander told the *Wall Street Journal* in 2016 that "it became clear over time that people were taking classes for different reasons, lifestyle reasons." An expansion in the nineties, led by then–executive artistic director Anne Libera, saw an immediate profit and increase in enrollment.

Today, The Second City Training Centers in Chicago, Toronto, and Hollywood teach over eleven thousand students annually. While the core programming remains centered around improvisation, writing, stand-up, storytelling, directing, and acting, the Training Center has exploded in recent years, discovering ways to bring the many benefits of improv to all types of students. Specialty programs for people with anxiety, autism, or Parkinson's disease, or who are cancer survivors, have made a tremendous impact. Classes for caregivers, teachers, and clinicians have aided professionals in strengthening skills like active listening, patience, and being able to adapt to new situations in real time. Vice president of The Second City Training Centers, Abby Wagner, explained:

> *What everyone who has taught a class here knows is that the art of improv has limitless opportunities to make people's lives better. In our classes, we'll see a painfully shy kid finally open up in a comedy camp or a military veteran adjust back to civilian life by finding their new support ensemble in an improv class. No doubt, we're still working with aspiring professional entertainers that are hoping to make comedy their career, but the work we do at The Second City Training Center is no longer only about getting a laugh; it's also about making a human connection.*

### AN IMPROVISED EDUCATION

For the duration of his association with The Second City, co-founder Paul Sills and his mother, Viola Spolin, taught improv workshops to the eager and uninitiated. The tradition of teaching continued with Sheldon Patinkin and Josephine Raciti Forsberg, a former Playwrights Theatre Club member who became a disciple of Spolin's. Forsberg, whose students included Bill Murray, Harold Ramis, Betty Thomas, and Bonnie Hunt, began teaching workshops at The Second City in the mid-1960s before creating the Players Workshop at Second City, one of the first formal schools of improvisation in the world. "She really was the first person to teach improv in any organized kind of way," Andrew Alexander said to the *Chicago Tribune* in 2011, after Forsberg's death.

# MARTIN DE MAAT

Having been introduced to improvisation as a child by his aunt, improv pioneer Jo Forsberg, Martin de Maat grew up at The Second City, starting out as a dishwasher before moving on to teach classes and even spending a short stint in the early seventies as stage manager. In 1985, de Maat became the first artistic director of The Second City Training Center and led the development of its acting, writing, and improvisation programs for the next fifteen years. Throughout the eighties and nineties, he was one of the central figures of Chicago's improv comedy scene, and certainly the one considered to be the most kindhearted. Among his students, of which he had thousands, were Rachel Dratch, Chris Farley, Tina Fey, Sean Hayes, David Mamet, and Tim Meadows. In *The Second City Almanac of Improvisation*, a book by de Maat's successor, Anne Libera, Second City alum Brian Stack expounded on de Maat's pedagogical gifts:

> I will always remember Martin as a great teacher, but his pure love of teaching process sticks with me the most. He clearly saw all students as individuals, and he wanted to draw out the best from every one of them, surprising the students and himself in doing so.

After de Maat's death in 2009, The Second City opened the de Maat Studio Theater, named in his honor.

## The Second Coming of the Canadians

Though *SCTV* went off the air in 1984, the decade was not at a loss for new Canadian comedians. The eighties saw an influx of fresh faces, including Colin Mochrie, Ryan Stiles, and Mike Myers, who debuted a character at The Second City that he had been playing around with since high school. "Wayne Campbell" appeared in the Toronto Mainstage revue *Not Based on Anything by Stephen King* in a sketch that shows him trying to patch up a fight with his girlfriend (played by Deborah Theaker) by playing Gary Wright's 1975 hit "Dream Weaver" on air guitar. Wright would wind up rerecording the song for the *Wayne's World* film soundtrack in 1992.

Another important comedy connection was forged when Dave Foley enrolled in a class at the Toronto Training Centre. "At my first class, I met Kevin McDonald," he recounted in a 2013 story for Toronto's *NOW* magazine. "We were paired up by our teacher to do the mirror exercise, which is lame. But he made me laugh all the way through class." McDonald invited Foley to join his sketch group, "The Kids in the Hall," which would find fame once Bruce McCulloch, Mark McKinney, and Scott Thompson were added to the lineup. For a brief period, McDonald and Thompson were also in the Toronto Touring Company, though Thompson said he was fired "because I'd take my clothes off a lot. They didn't like that." We can neither confirm nor deny his claims.

# COLIN MOCHRIE AND DEBRA MCGRATH

Improv upstart Colin Mochrie met Toronto Touring Company director Deb McGrath at a Second City audition in 1987. "After hours of auditions, she came up and said, 'It was between you and the cute guy, and you got it.' So based on that I immediately fell in love with her," the *Whose Line Is It Anyway?* star said in a 2016 interview. "About a year later, we started going out. Thank god the cute guy didn't make it." The two have now been married for over thirty years and have a daughter, Kinley. In addition to being brilliantly funny entertainers, Mochrie and McGrath are both outspoken advocates for trans rights.

Together, Mochrie and McGrath headlined a tribute (complete with a military chorus line!) to The Second City and Andrew Alexander during a star-studded gala at Ottawa's National Arts Centre. The festivities were part of the 2018 Governor General's Performing Arts Awards, Canada's most prestigious recognition for the performing arts, where Alexander was a recipient of a Lifetime Artistic Achievement Award.

**FROM TOP:** Colin Mochrie (left) and Neil Crone in Toronto's twenty-eighth revue, *A Nightmare on Sussex Drive*; Debra McGrath (left), Sandra Balcovske, and Kathleen Laskey in Toronto's *Waiting for John Doe*, 1984

FROM TOP: Kathleen Laskey (left), John Hemphill, and Derek McGrath in Toronto's *Little Hostile on the Prairie*; Rick Thomas (left), Nonie Newton-Breen, Meagan Fay, Danny Breen, and Lance Kinsey in 1982

FACING PAGE: Top row: Mike Hagerty (left), Meagen Fay, and Richard Kind; bottom row: Mindy Bell (left), John Kapelos, and Jim Fay in 1984

Mike Myers as "Wayne" in 1987

# MIKE MYERS

Mike Myers had dreamed of joining The Second City since he was four years old, and the day he was hired was momentous for two reasons. "On my last day of high school," he told *Entertainment Tonight* while filming the first *Wayne's World* movie, "my last exam was at nine, my audition for Second City was at twelve, and I was hired at three."

Myers became one of the youngest Touring Company members in our history. He graduated to the Toronto Mainstage a year and a half later, where he worked until Andrew Alexander asked him to come to the Chicago theater in 1988 so Betty Thomas could direct him and Bonnie Hunt in the theater's seventieth revue, *Kuwait Until Dark or Bright Lights, Night Baseball*.

The story goes that Joyce Sloane gave Myers the night off from performing on the Chicago Mainstage so that he could attend The Second City Toronto's fifteenth-anniversary show. During that performance, Myers had the opportunity to work with Martin Short, who promptly called *Saturday Night Live* producer Lorne Michaels to tell him, "You've gotta hire this guy." Shortly thereafter, Myers, who received the prestigious Order of Canada in 2018, joined the long list of Second City performers who have made the transition to *SNL*.

## The Second City Northwest

Back on Illinois soil, the Chicago suburb of Rolling Meadows had a lot of things going for it in 1987. It was conveniently located near O'Hare International Airport. It was the home of one of the state's largest defense contractors. It also had its very own outpost of the world's premier name in comedy. Under the guidance of producer Cheryl Sloane, The Second City Northwest afforded us a third opportunity to create and perform original material in the Chicagoland area, and many times, it served as a place for fresh talent—like Steve Carell, Amy Sedaris, and Stephen Colbert—to bolster their skills before making it to the Mainstage.

The Rolling Meadows theater closed in 1995 when our lease ran out. The Second City Northwest's final show, its fifteenth, was called *The Madness of Curious George*. Directed by Anne Libera, the five-person cast was made up of Matt Dwyer, David Koechner, Theresa Mulligan, Todd Stashwick, and Nancy Walls. Walls and Koechner went right on from Rolling Meadows to *SNL*; the bulk of the rest of the cast went on to make Second City's debut at the Edinburgh Festival Fringe; the Rolling Meadows venue went on to become a cafeteria for Motorola employees.

John Rubano (left) and Steve Carell in Second City Northwest's *Rosebud Was the Sled or Sunday in the Industrial Park with George*, 1989

# BONNIE HUNT

Born and bred Chicagoan Bonnie Hunt made a deal with her dad: she would attend nursing school as something steady to fall back on, but—if she hated it—she could leave. When her father passed away suddenly, a devastated Hunt fought her instincts to quit school, instead opting to honor her promise. During her studies, she was randomly assigned to work with a cancer patient. The man spent a lot of time talking about a coworker who had passed away recently and described how much respect he had for him. Eventually, Hunt figured out the patient was talking about her own father.

Eventually, she finished school and then began her career in comedy (and acting . . . and hosting talk shows . . . and writing . . . and directing . . .) while still working as a nurse, joining The Second City Mainstage in 1986 for three revues: *Catch 27*, *Jean-Paul Sartre & Ringo*, and *Kuwait Until Dark or Bright Lights, Night Baseball*.

Training Center student Bonnie Hunt in 1985

## The Second City Santa Monica

In addition to expanding on Second City's home turf, Andrew Alexander and Len Stuart started looking west. In 1989, the co-owners opened a Second City at the refurbished Mayfair Theatre in Santa Monica, California, on what was then the rather desolate promenade. (Terrible timing—today, that same promenade is one of the busiest shopping and dining destinations in the area.) The West Coast casts were primarily made up of alumni, some now based in Los Angeles, some imported from Toronto and Chicago, including Robin Duke, Mike Hagerty, Bonnie Hunt, Richard Kind, Don Lake, Andrea Martin, and Ryan Stiles. Andy Dick also spent some time there as a member of the Touring Company.

The Second City Santa Monica had two goals: the first was to have a Second City stage in Southern California where our alumni would have a place to showcase their talent to the industry in the best environment possible. "I had no illusions about opening in Los Angeles," said Alexander. "I had seen many of our incredibly talented people leave the stages in Chicago and Toronto, only to fall through the cracks in LA. I knew it was going to be difficult, but I was confident that we could develop a unique creative environment that would work for the performers."

The Second City
Santa Monica,
circa 1989

The second goal was to create a springboard for ideas for new television shows. In association with Ron Howard's Imagine Films, the Santa Monica group developed a parody talk show called *My Talk Show*, which was syndicated in over ninety percent of the country. Despite favorable reviews, it didn't build an audience and was not renewed for a second season. Second City Santa Monica eventually fell victim to apathetic audiences and unrealistic expectations. Alexander reflected on the demise of Santa Monica:

> *I took a group to California including Bonnie Hunt, Don Lake, Jane Morris, John Hemphill, Chris Barnes, and Ryan Stiles. We had a deal with CBS to develop sitcoms. We had offices that we rented in a storefront right next to the theater . . . the whole concept was to come up with ideas for sitcoms. When we had honed those different ideas, we would invite the network to come in and watch them on stage after we'd done the regular show. Well, the conflicts there were pretty severe with everybody. Looking back on it, I can see we were asking them to be satirists by night and prime-time sitcom writers by day. And there was an inherent conflict in that. We were asking them to put away their teeth and aim for the middle.*

Before closing in 1992, comedy icon and all-around good friend to The Second City Robin Williams made a guest appearance, taking audience suggestions like "hell hath no fury like a woman scorned."

# ALISON RILEY AND BETH KLIGERMAN

Alison Riley

Beth Kligerman

Alison Riley and Beth Kligerman are prime examples of how to "yes, and" a career trajectory at The Second City. Hired in 1986 as a member of the bar staff, Riley has held down just about every job title imaginable: dishwasher, server, coat checker, assistant manager, manager, general manager, associate producer, co-producer . . . and, as of 2008, producer of dozens of shows on the Chicago stages. "Alison has always had a keen eye for the material and has done a momentous job nurturing our directors," said Andrew Alexander.

Kligerman began on the customer service front lines as a box office manager in 1993 and soon after added a laundry list of titles to her resume: executive assistant to the executive producer, assistant to the producers, associate producer, casting director, director of talent and talent development, and her current role, director of theatricals casting and alumni relations. She has traveled the globe with Second City; her travels have included no fewer than eighty-seven work-related cruises.

## Losing Gilda

Seven years after losing John Belushi to drugs, The Second City suffered another tragedy when, in 1989, Gilda Radner died three years after being diagnosed with ovarian cancer. Dan Aykroyd, who had shared the struggles at Second City Toronto and the fame and fortune of *Saturday Night Live* with Radner, said, "I loved her like a sister."

"Gilda was possessed of the spirit of the theater," Andrew Alexander said about her passing. "In her short time at Second City, she had a tremendous impact on all of us. She was so good, so human. Her death was devastating for the entire Second City family."

Radner's widower, Gene Wilder, along with some of Radner's friends, opened the first Gilda's Club in New York City in 1995. Other clubs followed, including Gilda's Club Chicago, which opened in 1998. With its distinctive Red Door, Gilda's Club is a place "where men, women, teens, and children whose lives have been impacted by cancer, as well as their families and friends, can feel they are part of a welcoming community of support." Alexander was a co-founder of two of the organization's locations—Chicago and Toronto, where Gilda's Club took over the Old Firehall in a move we think Radner would approve of.

# CHRIS FARLEY

The wild party-boy image didn't always match the real Chris Farley. He was very polite and—when he wasn't "on"—could be extremely shy. He was a devout Catholic, attending mass daily at St. Michael's Church a few blocks behind The Second City in Old Town.

At The Second City, Farley was renowned for throwing himself off the walls, whether it was as a most unpleasant male stripper or the "freak of nature" whale boy who squirted water from his head (enabled by a football helmet covered in pink foam with a straw attached to a hand pump). He liked to compare himself to his idol, John Belushi, despite how hard people like Joyce Sloane tried to steer his behavior elsewhere:

> *Chris liked to compare himself to John Belushi. John was Chris's idol. I tried to explain to him that the character John played in Animal House was just a character. John wasn't like that offstage. I even introduced Chris to John's wife Judy and asked, "Would a lovely woman like this marry him if he were the character from Animal House?" But Chris idolized him. He adored him, as a whole generation did.*

Farley never forgot his roots; he returned often to Second City to perform with the cast during the improv sets. He even attended the company's annual holiday party just days before his untimely death in 1997.

Chris Farley's early headshot (top) and Training Center Polaroid, circa 1987

# JOEL MURRAY

The youngest of nine siblings, Joel Murray was captain of the Loyola Academy football team in high school before following his older brothers Bill and Brian to The Second City, where he co-wrote and performed in two Mainstage revues. In 2015, he gave a candid account of the exact moment he was bitten by the acting bug to the *A.V. Club*:

*When I was in high school, I was trying out for baseball, and I was lacing up my cleats for the second day of the tryout, and I looked across the parking lot, and I was, like, "What are all those girls doing over there?" "Oh, they're trying out for the school musical." I said, "Well, what's that?" They said, "It's West Side Story." I said, "Well, I'm going to put my other shoes back on. See you fuckers later!"*

Joel Murray

## Thirty Years Ago Today

The year 1989 also brought some good memories. Del Close returned to Chicago to direct his final show for The Second City Mainstage, *The Gods Must Be Lazy*, and he hired an extraordinary group of people to be in it: Chris Farley (whom the *Chicago Reader* said "shows considerable promise as a physical comedian"), Tim Meadows, Joel Murray, David Pasquesi, Judith Scott, and Holly Wortell, with Joe Liss remaining from the preceding cast. Not only were they an excellent performing company and a talented group of improvisers, but the show has the distinction of being the first at The Second City to feature two performers of color.

*The Gods Must Be Lazy* wasn't universally admired; like Close himself, it was pretty dark, often misogynistic, and occasionally confusing to the audience. It seemed unfinished, and actually, it was. Close pronounced the show ready to open two weeks prior to opening night, all but blowing off the final two weeks of previews and rehearsals. Creatively, the theater was now facing critics' laments that we had become old hat and formulaic, and Joyce Sloane undertook the difficult task of finding new artistic leaders who

The cast of *It Was Thirty Years Ago Today*, clockwise from left: Chris Farley, Tim Meadows, Judith Scott, David Pasquesi, Joe Liss, Joel Murray, and Holly Wortell

could help regain a bit of the fire that critics felt Second City was lacking. Both she and Andrew Alexander were fans of alumnus Nate Herman, who had expressed an interest in directing. They took a chance and let him direct the next revue. The final Chicago Main-stage show of the decade, which coincided with The Second City's thirtieth anniversary, was appropriately titled *It Was Thirty Years Ago Today*, which the *Chicago Reader* said boasted "one of Second City's sharpest ensembles."

presents its 72nd Revue

**It Was Thirty Years Ago Today**

*Written and Performed by*

**Chris Farley**
**Joe Liss**
**Timothy Meadows**
**Tim O'Malley**
**David Pasquesi**
**Judith Scott**
**Holly Wortell**

*Directed by* Nate Herman
*Produced by* Joyce Sloane
*Executive Producer*—Andrew Alexander
*Musical Director*—Ruby Streak
*Stage Manager*—Craig Taylor

*Due to an arrangement with the Actors' Equity Association, the use of cameras and recording devices is prohibited in this theater.*

10

Playbill from 1989 for Chicago's thirtieth-anniversary show

# TIM MEADOWS

After Michigan native Tim Meadows joined The Second City Mainstage, he soon built a reputation for being soft-spoken, gentlemanly, and a true ensemble player, always eager to make his partner look good. After three revues, *The Gods Must Be Lazy*, *It Was Thirty Years Ago Today*, and *Flag Smoking Permitted in Lobby Only or Censorama*, he was hired by *Saturday Night Live* in 1991, where he had one of the longest runs in the show's history. Throughout his prolific career, Meadows has continued to work with several fellow Second City alums in a multitude of projects and performs regularly as a stand-up, splitting his time between Los Angeles and Chicago.

Tim Meadows
(left) and Chris
Farley in *It Was
Thirty Years Ago
Today*

# CHAPTER 7
# THE 1990s
## CHANGING THE FORMAT

Alumni of The Second City brought the world some of the biggest and most beloved film and television projects of the nineties. Harold Ramis directed Bill Murray in the ever-pertinent *Groundhog Day*. Mike Myers schwinged his character "Wayne Campbell" to the big screen in *Wayne's World*, and Myers's *Austin Powers* franchise became a half-billion-dollar business. Julia Louis-Dreyfus, a Second City Touring Company vet, first appeared as "Elaine Benes" in the second episode of *Seinfeld*. *Saturday Night Live* made Chris Farley a star and Tina Fey its first (and still, only) female head writer. The list goes on . . . but we're getting ahead of ourselves.

## Growing Pains and Gains

**PICTURED ON PREVIOUS PAGE:** Touring Company members Nancy (Walls) Carell (left), Theresa Mulligan, Adam McKay, Mark Levenson (seated), David Koechner, Steve Carell, Jon Glaser, and Tim Meadows

In the early nineties, The Second City Chicago was held together by six full-time employees, two typewriters, and one answering machine that took reservations when no one in the box office was on hand to answer the phone. The company was juggling the stages, the Touring Company (or "TourCo," as we affectionately came to call it), a booming Training Center, television projects, and burgeoning corporate endeavors, thanks to Second City Communications, the company's new venture devoted to bringing comedy and improvisational methods into the workplace.

To better bolster the infrastructure, Andrew Alexander moved to Chicago, entrenching himself in the day-to-day serious business of making people laugh, bringing with him an entrepreneurial spirit and his own brand of leadership. It was Alexander's intention to lift the company out of the rut it had found itself in. Combined with Joyce Sloane's

mother hen approach, it made for a more dynamic—though admittedly contentious—Second City. "'Tourist trap' is not a term we want to be associated with what we do, so we shook things up for a while," the co-owner said about the transitional time. "This is live theater; there's always going to be a certain fragility to it. We made changes that some Second City people didn't like." Alexander promoted Kelly Leonard to the role of associate producer in 1992 and producer in 1995. Sloane was transitioned into the role of producer emeritus, a largely symbolic position, in a move that was met with controversy and even indignation by many.

Leonard, son of Chicago radio and television broadcaster Roy Leonard, had begun climbing the rungs at The Second City right out of college. "I arrived at the front bar of Second City on a Friday night—certain that I'd be put to work in the marketing department or something," remembered Leonard. "I washed glasses for six straight hours. My hands were raw. The only noble thing about the experience was that I found out that David Mamet had been a busboy at Second City."

Leonard was ultimately hired to work in the box office by manager Anne Libera before Alexander brought him on as his assistant in 1991, which led to his producing career. (Another box office employee of note hired by Libera? Her old college roommate, Stephen Colbert.)

The cast of *Economy of Errors*: Ron West (left), Steve Carell, Fran Adams, John Rubano, Michael McCarthy, Jill Talley, and Tim O'Malley

# ANNE LIBERA AND KELLY LEONARD

Anne Libera and Kelly Leonard are one of The Second City's indomitable, resilient ensembles. After meeting at the theater, the two married in 1996 and became parents to two incredible children, Nick, a Skidmore theater student, and Nora, a volleyball player and actress. They were both part of Second City's youth ensembles—a program Libera created during her tenure as executive artistic director of The Second City Training Center. In the summer of 2018, with her family and friends by her side, sixteen-year-old Nora began an unimaginably brave battle against cancer, which she fought with humor and grace until her devastating passing one year later. Everyone at The Second City, as well as supporters around the world, will forever consider themselves indomitably proud and limitlessly loving members of #TeamNora.

Kelly Leonard (left) and Anne Libera at The Second City's fortieth anniversary

## A Van Down by the River

While hard changes may have been happening behind the scenes, onstage, things were nothing less than magical. Long before he lived in a van down by the river on *Saturday Night Live*, Chris Farley's "Matt Foley" character made his first home on the Chicago Mainstage in the 1990 revue *Flag Smoking Permitted in Lobby Only or Censorama*. The show, Farley's fourth at The Second City, also featured Tim Meadows, Tim O'Malley, David Pasquesi, Jill Talley, Holly Wortell, and Bob Odenkirk, who returned to moonlight on the Mainstage during a summer off from his *SNL* writing job. The sad-sack motivational speaker "Foley" turned up in the improv set after the show one night. Brian Stack (who would go on to join the e.t.c. cast before writing for Conan O'Brien and Stephen Colbert) witnessed the moment firsthand:

> *I was in the audience the first time Chris did his Matt Foley character. His friend, Matt Foley, a soft-spoken Catholic priest, was also in the audience, and Chris thought it would be fun to use his name for such an outrageous character. Chris destroyed the place that night. He was, of course, capable of brilliantly subtle performances too, but when he went for pure, raw laughs, I've never seen anyone better.*

Knowing lightning could—and should—strike again, Odenkirk developed a full scene for the character. He brought it in one night to try out and "it slaughtered," he said. "Farley wouldn't get off stage until everyone laughed. . . . It made me laugh every single time just as much as it did the first time." While most Second City scenes are constantly being tweaked in front of the audience until they're just right, that wasn't the case with "Motivation." It stayed pretty much the same from that night on, including its first incarnation on *SNL* in 1993, when the line "I live in a van down by the river" became part of the zeitgeist.

Chris Farley (left), Jill Talley, Bob Odenkirk, Holly Wortell, and Tim Meadows perform "Motivation" in *Flag Smoking Permitted in Lobby Only or Censorama*

# DAVID MAMET

Before he became an award-winning playwright, screenwriter, author, and director, David Mamet spent a summer in high school working as a busboy and soda jerk at The Second City. Soaking up all the short-form comedy night after night had an impact on the budding young writer. In a 1997 interview with the *New Yorker*, Mamet admitted, "For the next ten years, none of my scenes lasted more than eight minutes."

Clockwise from top left: Jill Talley, Bob Odenkirk, Chris Farley, David Pasquesi, Tim Meadows, Holly Wortell, and Tim O'Malley

# BOB ODENKIRK

Bob Odenkirk began his journey at The Second City in 1983 by cold-calling Joyce Sloane and asking if he could come to Old Town to interview her. After the meeting, the college student spotted Del Close at the counter of a neighborhood bookstore, as Odenkirk told a crowd of Second City Training Center students in 2017. "I said, 'Are you Del Close? Can I interview you?'" Close invited Odenkirk to his apartment, right across the street from Second City, and the two talked for hours. It was the day after Close had (most recently) quit the theater—and the day the future *Mr. Show with Bob and David* co-creator decided he wanted to go into show business.

Three years after Odenkirk left Chicago for a writing gig at *Saturday Night Live*, one of his friends,

Second City director Tom Gianas, asked him to join the Mainstage cast. It was "like being asked to pitch for the Cubs," Odenkirk said. However, some talent felt that his hiring was an upheaval of the customary casting system, where most people had to work their way up from the Touring Company, and there was friction. Sloane had to intervene. "She told everybody that Second City is not the post office. You don't just put in your time and automatically move up. There is no guarantee."

Despite his incredible success in comedy and—against all odds—drama (with lauded roles on *Breaking Bad* and *Better Call Saul*), Odenkirk continues to give back to the Second City community. He makes regular visits to the Training Center to offer his sage advice to comedy students.

Clockwise from top left: Jenna Jolovitz, Scott Allman, Jackie Hoffman, Jimmy Doyle, Scott Adsit, and Ian Gomez in the e.t.c.'s *Disgruntled Employee Picnic or The Postman Always Shoots Twice*, 1992

## "John" Carell Plays the e.t.c.

Chris Farley was not the only future star in the building in 1990. After a stint in the Touring Company and four revues for the company's suburban outpost, The Second City Northwest, Steve Carell opened *Northwest by North Wells* that November along with Rose Abdoo, Fran Adams, John Rubano, and Ron West. Directed by Tom Gianas and Kevin Crowley, the retrospective of The Second City Northwest's material on the e.t.c. stage received favorable reviews. The *Chicago Tribune* wrote, "You will rarely see funnier sketches on stage than John Rubano and John Carell as a pair of hit men communing with nature; or the same pair as a pet bird (Rubano) and pet dog (Carell), bedeviling their owner (Fran Adams). Rubano and Carell are certainly the stars of the night." The review was correct in calling Carell a star; it missed the mark (or the "Steve," if you will) by calling him "John."

One scene that never made the cut for Carell at Second City—an improvised game of poker—turned out to be one of the best plays of Carell's career. "The idea that I had," Carell said about the scene (which appeared in the improv set a few times, but didn't wind up making it into a show) on CBS's *60 Minutes* in 2014, "was a group of guys playing poker and just regaling each other with stories of sexual conquest and one guy who clearly didn't have a frame of reference and was trying to keep up with these stories." After pitching writer, producer, and director Judd Apatow the idea years later, the twosome wrote the screenplay for *The 40-Year-Old Virgin*. The 2005 smash-hit film almost didn't finish filming; Carell said the studio wanted to pull the plug on production after less than a week. As he explained to Conan O'Brien in a 2016 interview, the studio representatives told him and Apatow, "'We've been watching footage, and you look like a serial killer.' . . .

Steve Carell (left), Paul Dinello, Stephen Colbert, and David Razowsky sing "The Obvious Song" in 1993's *Take Me Out to the Balkans*

John Rubano (left) and Steve Carell

# STEVE CARELL

Steve Carell spent nearly ten years studying and teaching improvisation at The Second City Training Center. (You can find the grainy video of his graduation performance online.) He has admitted to asking his improv students to do exercises that involved crossing the room as slowly as possible, enabling him to go get a cup of coffee before they made it to the other side. He wrote and performed in multiple revues for the Mainstage and e.t.c., working alongside peers like Jackie Hoffman, Amy Sedaris, Jill Talley, and Stephen Colbert, who was originally Carell's understudy. The two performed a bevy of infamous sketches together, including a scene in which Carell played a blonde, shirtless Fabio, complete with a handheld, mane-blowing fan, and "Maya"—which they revived for The Second City's fiftieth anniversary in 1999. (In "Maya," Carell and Colbert play a pair of friends who have come to visit Colbert's hometown. After the town's residents giddily greet Colbert as "Shirley Wentworth," he explains to his befuddled travel companion Carell that "when I'm home, I'm an old black woman." The scene is still a regular part of

the Touring Company's repertoire.) At Second City, "you have the freedom to fail," Carell said backstage during the celebration. "You can do good work or bad work, but the main idea is you keep trying and refining. . . . The audiences here are fantastic and extremely forgiving. They understand the concept of what Second City's about, and they give you latitude, and they reward you if you've done a good job."

After his tenure at The Second City, Carell conquered the worlds of TV and film. He received an Oscar nomination in 2015 for his work in *Foxcatcher* as well as multiple Emmy and Golden Globe nods for gifting the world with "Michael Scott" on the American adaptation of *The Office* for seven long, hard seasons. (That's what she said.) Carell actually beat out Bob Odenkirk for the role, with the latter admitting, "It was the right choice. I get it."

Carell is married to Second City and *SNL* alumna Nancy (Walls) Carell. In 2018, they brought their children to see Chicago's 106th Mainstage revue, *Dream Freaks Fall from Space*, leading Carell to proclaim on Twitter, "My kids now know what funny is."

I was so bummed out. I thought, 'That's it.' That was the big shot, and it wasn't going to work out." Thankfully, it did work out—and it made Carell a star.

Coincidentally (or not), Carell does have "serial killer" experience onstage. In a 1992 Second City scene called "High Rise," he played a murderous man doing laundry in an apartment building basement while flirting with an overly trusting woman, played by Amy Sedaris:

> **Amy:** Well, don't be mad at me.
>
> **Steve:** I'm not mad. I'm not mad, like, I'm-gonna-kill-you mad. It's just frustrating is all. It's hard to meet people.
>
> **Amy:** Well, how many people have you killed?
>
> **Steve:** Seventeen. But the thing is, I've met thousands of people in my life. I have only killed seventeen.
>
> **Amy:** You're a serial killer!

A pilot for an A&E show called *The Second City's 149 1/2 Edition* includes a filmed version of the scene (another vintage gem you can search for online), this time with Jenna Jolovitz playing Carell's laundry partner.

# AMY SEDARIS

Amy Sedaris joined the Mainstage in 1992 after playing in the Touring Company and The Second City Northwest. From grandmas to squirrels to a dead-on impression of Reform Party founder Ross Perot, her penchant for playing oddball characters (even when the oddball is herself, like on her surreal homemaking show, *At Home with Amy Sedaris*) began at The Second City. "Everything I learned at Second City I still use," Sedaris told *Bustle* in 2019. She holds the distinction of being one of the few actors here that liked to wear wigs for almost all of her huge, obscene, crazy characters.

Touring Company cohorts Sedaris, Paul Dinello, and Stephen Colbert have been collaborators, not to mention thick as thieves, for more than thirty years. They collectively dreamed up the shows *Exit 57* and *Strangers with Candy*, which also spawned a film. On *The Late Show* in 2019, Colbert also credited Sedaris with keeping him fed during their broke years on the road. "When people asked me how you get by in show business, I said, 'Find people like Paul and Amy, 'cause we kept each other alive.'"

Paul Dinello (left), Amy Sedaris, Mitch Rouse, and Stephen Colbert in Northwest's ninth revue, *Destiny and How to Avoid It*

## Stephen Colbert and Nia Vardalos Hit the 'Burbs

In December 1991, former box office employees Stephen Colbert and Nia Vardalos appeared in their first original resident stage show, *Ku Klux Klambake*, at The Second City Northwest. The show was the stage's third in a row directed by Kentucky-born Annoyance Theatre founder (and one-time veterinary student) Mick Napier. "Second City is one of the best places to work as a director because the policy is that those stages are held sacred. . . . It really is the director and the performers, and what you're seeing onstage is the voice of the actor, which I hold sacred as the director," Napier said in a 2015 WGN Radio interview about working on Second City revues.

Roger Lewin/Jennifer Girard Studio

Stephen Colbert (left) and Nia Vardalos in the early nineties

The cast of 1991's *Welcome to the Barn Raising*, Second City Northwest: Nia Vardalos (left), Paul Dinello, Amy Sedaris, Scott Allman, Jackie Hoffman, and Ian Gomez

# NIA VARDALOS

Nia Vardalos took a job in the box office at The Second City Toronto to take classes and watch the show for free. One night, a performer was sick, and, in the era before texting, her understudies couldn't be tracked down. That's when Vardalos confidently declared she knew the whole show and was ready and willing to step in. With fifteen minutes to curtain, there really was no other choice. She was hired for the London, Ontario, Touring Company the next day.

After moving to Chicago, Vardalos spent time on both The Second City Northwest and e.t.c. stages, winning Chicago's prestigious Jeff Award for 1994's *Whitewater for Chocolate*. It was her

one-woman show, however, based on her wedding to then-husband and fellow Second Citizen Ian Gomez, that would change the course of big fat fate. Producer and actress Rita Wilson saw the Los Angeles show one night and was so impressed that she championed the project to her husband, Tom Hanks, who helped Vardalos turn her story into an independent film. The runaway 2002 hit *My Big Fat Greek Wedding*, which Vardalos wrote and starred in, became the highest-grossing independent film of all time and earned her an Oscar nomination for Best Original Screenplay. The sequel was released in 2016, with Second City and *SCTV* legend Andrea Martin reprising the role of "Aunt Voula."

Paul Dinello (left) and Stephen Colbert in 1993

# STEPHEN COLBERT

A young, broke Stephen Colbert took a job at The Second City box office in 1987 answering phones and selling merchandise in exchange for free classes. After coming up the "ratline" (as he has referred to his early employment) as a busboy and server at the theater, Colbert joined The Second City Touring Company before getting bumped up to understudy for another up-and-comer, Steve Carell. Colbert soon got his chance to be part of original shows, performing at The Second City Northwest alongside Paul Dinello, Ian Gomez, Jackie Hoffman, Amy Sedaris, and Nia Vardalos. He moved to the e.t.c. for *Where's Your God Now, Charlie Brown?* and Mainstage in 1993 for *Take Me Out to the Balkans*, which

also featured Sedaris and Carell. The future *The Colbert Report* and *The Late Show with Stephen Colbert* host ended his Second City career again paired up with Carell in Chicago's seventy-eighth revue, *Are You Now, or Have You Ever Been Mellow?*

"It was a great education about what I was able to do and what audiences enjoyed, and the limits of self-indulgence, and the need to please and how you balance those," Colbert said to the *A.V. Club* in 2006 about his time at The Second City. "I found out what my strengths were." Turns out, one of his greatest strengths was selling merch. Colbert held a longtime record at The Second City for the most T-shirts sold in a single day.

## The Second City's Outreach Program

While The Second City and its members did their best to represent the world around them, the ensembles did not always accurately reflect the makeup of America. Andrew Alexander, who was living in Los Angeles in 1992, realized this during a sobering national turning point, the Rodney King riots. "Two days later, I flew back to Chicago, and the cast—all white, no minorities—were struggling with how to deal with this issue," he explained. "It struck home."

The next day, The Second City's Outreach Program launched with the mission of fostering new voices in the improv community. The program was directed by Frances Callier, a Touring Company performer and the director of the Training Center. The initiative took off, offering workshops and scholarships that laid the groundwork for the formation of pioneering improv groups in the LGBTQI, Asian American, African American, and Latinx communities, including GayCo Productions (co-founded by former Training Center director Ed Garza in 1996), Stir Friday Night, and Salsation Theatre Company.

Renamed "Outreach and Diversity" in 2002 and "Diversity and Inclusion" in 2015, the initiative has tremendously expanded under the leadership of Second City Detroit alumna Dionna Griffin-Irons, who has since become the company's director of diversity talent inclusion and development. She explained the importance of passing the torch:

> Every person of color that has performed on a Second City stage has been instrumental in helping another person of color. One of my favorite "passing the torch" stories comes from Angela V. Shelton, who would call herself black in every scene: "As a black woman, I believe . . ." This ensured another black female would get hired in her role after she left. It worked. That's how I became her understudy before I joined a resident stage.

"Every person of color that has performed on a Second City stage has been instrumental in helping another person of color." **–Dionna Griffin-Irons**

**FROM TOP:** Megan Moore Burns (left), Fran Adams, Rose Abdoo, and Peter Burns in the e.t.c.'s *We Made a Mesopotamia, Now You Clean It Up*; Kathryn Greenwood (left) and Ed Sahely in Toronto's *Shopping Off to Buffalo*, 1991

**FROM TOP:** Matt Dwyer (left), Pat Finn, Renee Albert, David Koechner, and Jennifer Estlin in Second City Northwest's 1994 revue *It Ain't Over Until the Fat Lady's Done Watching the OJ Trial*; Top row: Jennifer Irwin (left), Albert Howell, Bob Derkach, Mollie Jacques, Teresa Pavlinek; bottom row: Jack Mosshammer (left), Janet Van De Graaff, and Bob Martin in Toronto's *Tragically OHIP*, 1996

## The Second City Detroit

The company's commitment to championing diverse voices found a new platform in September 1993. The Second City Detroit opened as part of the city's rapid restoration efforts and thanks to a unique business partnership with the Ilitch family. (Mike Ilitch founded Little Caesars Pizza and went on to own both the Detroit Red Wings and Tigers.) In a city where urban renewal is an ever-present theme, creating focused social and political satire was no small thing. Detroit cast member Keegan-Michael Key explained to a local talk show at the time:

> In my opinion, the Detroit Second City's job—what makes us a different animal than Chicago and Toronto—[is that] Chicago has an international fan base. We have a local fan base. And so we try to do material that is indigenous to Detroit. . . . We reflect life, but we reflect life to Detroiters and suburban Detroiters.

The Detroit cast became the company's most diverse from day one. Anne Libera, then the director of the Training Center, held an intensive three-week boot camp with the dozen or so audition finalists, and eight were chosen: Robin Bucci, Colin Ferguson, Jerry Minor, Suzy Nakamura, Andy Newberg, Tim Pryor, Jackie Purtan, and Angela V. Shelton, with pianist and musical director Mark Levenson imported from The Second City Northwest, John Holston as stage manager, and Norm Holly directing. Andrew Alexander brought in Lyn Okkerse from Canada to begin a five-year producing stint in the Motor City.

Over the course of its fourteen-year run, The Second City Detroit called two addresses home (the theater moved to suburban Novi in 2004), put up thirty shows, had its own Touring Company, ran a successful Training Center, and developed talent on the stages and in the classroom that included Larry Joe Campbell, Nyima Funk, Marc Evan Jackson, Keegan-Michael Key, Antoine McKay, Maribeth Monroe, Sam Richardson, and Tim Robinson.

**FACING PAGE:**

The first Second City Detroit cast, clockwise from top left: Colin Ferguson, Jackie Purtan, Andrew Newberg, Robin Bucci, Angela V. Shelton, Suzy Nakamura, Jerry C. Minor, and Tim Pryor

# ANGELA V. SHELTON

Angela V. Shelton holds the distinction of being The Second City's only alum to have been a member of the Chicago Mainstage, e.t.c., Toronto, and Detroit Second City resident ensembles. She is also one-half of the comedy duo "Frangela" along with Frances Callier. The comedy partners and best friends met at The Second City.

Brian Stack (left), Horatio Sanz, Jerry C. Minor, and a dummy in the e.t.c.'s seventeenth revue, *40 Ounces and a Mule*

Nyima Funk (left), Keegan-Michael Key, Samantha Albert (behind Keegan-Michael Key), Peter Grosz, Andy Cobb, and Jean Villepique in *Curious George Goes to War*, the e.t.c.'s twenty-fourth revue

# KEEGAN-MICHAEL KEY

Nobody takes their comedy more seriously than Peabody and Emmy winner Keegan-Michael Key. Long before he co-starred with Barack Obama as the president's "anger translator," the classically trained actor was a mainstay of Second City's Detroit theater, where he co-wrote and performed in eight revues. Key moved to the Chicago e.t.c. in 2001, taking home Jeff Awards for two of his three shows on that stage, *Holy War, Batman! or The Yellow Cab of Courage* and *Curious George Goes to War*. "It's kind of the place where I cut my comedy teeth, and it felt more like I was getting . . . a master's degree in comedy, and learning on the job," Key said in a 2016 Michigan Radio interview. "That's kind of the beginning of my comedic career."

Key met his future *MADtv* co-star and *Key & Peele* collaborator, Jordan Peele, while at The Second City, where the duo fell in comedy love at first bit. The *Get Out* Oscar winner told the *Hollywood Reporter*:

*All of a sudden, I am performing in the next room from Keegan-Michael Key, who I had heard about, but I had never met. And all I heard is you have to see this guy. . . . He just has this energy like no one I had ever seen and since in all of comedy. It's like, you know, there's a couple people who have that kinetic energy that somehow still feels true. And he had that. And, I was just in awe, and you know, maybe a little bit of like, "Oh, this motherfucker is good."*

## Tina and Amy Are Hired

Tina Fey and Amy Poehler auditioned in Chicago for The Second City Touring Company within hours of each other, Poehler at 12:45 p.m. on August 30, 1994, and Fey the following day at 3:45. (Yes, we pulled the casting receipts.) The two had met the year prior in classes at another Chicago improv theater, iO. In her book, *Yes Please,* Poehler described their common ground: "She was sharp, shy, and hilarious. . . . Her name was Tina and she was like me but with brown hair."

After attending callbacks together and both landing the gig, their life on the road in "BlueCo" began. (Joyce Sloane named the Blue and Red Touring Companies after the Ringling Bros. traveling troupes; when we needed another one, Green was added.) "I still feel affection for the members of BlueCo like we served in the military together," Fey wrote in her book, *Bossypants.* "Specifically the French military, because we were lazy and a little bit sneaky."

Amy Poehler (bottom center) and some of her Touring Company castmates, clockwise from top left: Bill Chott, Rachel Hamilton, Pat McCartney, and Frances Callier

# AMY POEHLER

Amy Poehler moved to Chicago after graduating from college to immerse herself in the Chicago improv scene. She enrolled in classes at The Second City and studied with Del Close, about whom she said, "He was a comedy genius who had taught all of my heroes." In 1995, Poehler and Close shot an Andrew Alexander–produced pilot about hackers in an RV called *RVTV.* The show also featured Matt Dwyer, who told comedy blog *Splitsider* shortly after the tape was unearthed, "It was a great deal of fun, and I remember both Amy and I were thrilled to be working with Del. Del was an icon to all of us." Do yourself a favor and look it up online.

Poehler "dressed like an eighth-grade boy back then, in Converse sneakers and band T-shirts, but made it a girly thing," wrote Poehler's peer and friend Rachel Dratch in a 2010 *Bust* profile. "She was a pioneer. Instead of waiting around to be moved up the ranks of Second City, like most of us were doing, Amy and her three cohorts from the Upright Citizens Brigade—Matt Besser, Matt Walsh, and Ian Roberts—moved to N.Y.C. to start a theater in 1996."

## Farewell to John Candy

Tragedy befell the Second City family once again on March 4, 1994. John Candy passed away after suffering a heart attack at age forty-three, leaving behind his wife, Rosemary, and his two young children, Christopher and Jennifer.

Kelly Leonard remembered hearing the news:

> I was at a hotel in the suburbs looking at a new potential location when a hotel employee came in and said there was an emergency call for me. My wife was at the theater and said, "John Candy just died. The press is calling. They're at the front desk, and Andrew [Alexander]'s locked himself in his office." I hustled back to the theater and could barely enter through the front door, as it was blocked by camera crews and newsmen. John was one of Andrew's very best friends, and Andrew was more distraught than I have ever seen him. We created a short statement for the press and decided to say nothing more.

Memorial services were held in Los Angeles and Toronto. Both were attended by throngs of friends, family, and fans. "I was privileged to be asked by Rose Candy to deliver one of the eulogies given at John's funeral," Alexander said. "John and I—like many others—had gone through some rough periods when he was not happy with me, nor I with him. So I was thankful that three years before John died, we were able to put all of the rough times behind us and continue the wonderful friendship."

The funeral procession left the church on Sunset Boulevard and proceeded south on one of the city's busiest thoroughfares, but the California Highway Patrol and LAPD actually closed the highway traveling south to accommodate the cortege to the cemetery. The police held their hands to their chests while blocking all the exit ramps in an emotional and stirring tribute to the lovable, wonderful Canadian. It was an unheard-of gesture in Los Angeles, and one that none who witnessed it will ever forget.

Candy's generosity of spirit and immense talent are still felt in the work we do every day at The Second City. After a renovation to the Toronto campus in 2015, a ribbon-cutting ceremony was held to commemorate the grand opening of the John Candy Box Theatre. The new Training Centre space became home to more than just Candy's name—embedded in the stage is a fragment of the original stage from the Old Firehall on Lombard Street, where Candy and so many other comedy legends got their starts. "We like to say it's still supporting emerging artists some forty years after it was first installed," said Toronto's Training Centre artistic director, Kevin Frank, about the piece of our shared history.

Candy's legacy received another great honor in late 2018 when his first grandchild and namesake, Finley John William Sullivan, was born to Jennifer Candy and her husband, Bryan Sullivan. On his nursery wall hangs a framed picture of an animated albatross named "Wilbur," the character Candy voiced in Disney's *The Rescuers Down Under*.

## Smash the *Piñata*

In 1995, The Second City shook up the company's format in a new revue, challenging the structure and content of all Second City shows that came before or after it. Chicago's *Piñata Full of Bees*, directed by Tom Gianas, boasted a cast consisting of veterans Scott Adsit, Scott Allman, and Jenna Jolovitz along with newcomers Rachel Dratch, Jon Glaser, and Adam McKay. As the group began to create and stage new material, Gianas had the set from the last revue completely dismantled, leaving only a bare stage. Props and costumes were hung in full view of the audience, and cast members sat onstage and watched while their fellow performers played out their scenes. Music director Ruby Streak brought in sampled music to augment the scenes and blast during transitions. She also worked with the actors to score scenes themselves, putting a bass guitar, drums, and even a cello onstage.

*Piñata* was a show that not only looked different than any Second City revue in history but that also had an anarchistic political edge that hadn't been seen on the Mainstage since the late sixties and early seventies. A particularly divisive moment went down in the set one night when Adsit soberly told the audience, "I'm sorry; we have to stop the show. The president [Bill Clinton] has been shot. We don't know the details, but there are monitors out in the lobby, and we can watch the coverage. You're welcome to stay." Take a guess how that stunt went over with the crowd:

> **Dratch:** The audience totally believed it and gasped, then went silent.
> **Adsit:** I brought a TV out onstage so they could stay and watch live coverage on the news. Instead of that, the TV showed sports bloopers. The cast all came out and were each won over by the hilarious sports bloopers. We laughed at the TV while the audience watched us. About ten percent of them got it and laughed, sixty percent were bewildered, and thirty percent got it and were furious. We stayed onstage laughing at sports bloopers until the entire audience had left.
> **Dratch:** They hated us. As Scott Allman said of their response, "You could hear a mouse shit."

The cast of *Piñata Full of Bees*: Jon Glaser (left, in pig mask), Adam McKay, Jenna Jolovitz, Scott Allman, Scott Adsit, and Rachel Dratch

Afterward, show producer Kelly Leonard "had to write many letters to customers rightfully outraged by the material." One of the show's most unifying moments, however, is an all-time favorite of Adam McKay's, as he told Jimmy Carrane in an *Improv Nerd* podcast:

> It was at the time that Blockbuster was editing their movies 'cause they were
> owned by right-wing Christians, and we, in the midst of some big rant, told the
> audience this was going on, and fuck Blockbuster, throw your Blockbuster cards
> up there. And every night, I would just see it rain Blockbuster cards, and we'd be
> running around with scissors cutting them in half. And it was just incredible. It
> was just like this little moment of activism in the midst of a comedy show that
> I'll kind of never forget. I mean, there's a lot of amazing things in that show. But
> that image of those Blockbuster cards raining down is so cool.

> "The whole revue is fresher, feistier, more invigorating and scarier–a leap forward in style that manages miraculously to breathe new life into some of the troupe's cherished themes from the past." —*Chicago Tribune*

Leonard still has the jar of cut-up cards in his possession. It was one of the few salvage-able items saved by Tyler Alexander from the ashes of The Second City's 2015 extra-alarm blaze. The jar, pictured at right, is still sooty from the fire.

Reviews for *Piñata Full of Bees* were glowing, with *Chicago Tribune* arts critic Sid Smith writing, "The whole revue is fresher, feistier, more invigorating and scarier—a leap forward in style that manages miraculously to breathe new life into some of the troupe's cherished themes from the past." Within a few months, both McKay and Gianas joined the *SNL* writing staff, and when Glaser was hired away to work on *The Dana Carvey Show*, a Touring Company member named Tina Fey got bumped up and took over.

## Equal Representation

*Piñata Full of Bees* was a tough act to follow, but Mick Napier was hell-bent on undoing a longtime proclivity at The Second City: the lopsided gender ratio. While historically, Second City shows had mostly used more male than female performers, that didn't sit right with the director. "It was always difficult to find a scene with women in it, let alone a scene that represented a female point of view," Napier told the *Chicago Tribune*. "So that became important to me."

In 1996, *Citizen Gates* opened in Chicago, featuring the Chicago Mainstage's first gender-equal cast. The trio of Rachel Dratch, Tina Fey, and Jenna Jolovitz was one of The Second City's most notable equal casts, but it was not the first. The e.t.c.'s *Channel This or Die Yuppie Scum* upended the ratio in 1988 when director Jane Morris cast three men and four women: herself, Judith Scott, Jill Talley, and Holly Wortell. Toronto also broke the typically disproportionate male mold in 1989 with *When Bush Comes to Shove*. Director Sandra Balcovske featured three women—Wendy Hopkins, Lindsay Leese, and Alana Shields—and three men—Patrick McKenna, Colin Mochrie, and Tim Sims. The e.t.c. tipped the scales again in 2017 with *Fantastic Super Great Nation Numero Uno*. The show featured three men and four women: Sayjal Joshi, Katie Klein, Julie Marchiano, and Tien Tran.

# ADAM MCKAY

Academy Award winner Adam McKay spent two years in the Touring Company before joining the e.t.c. cast in 1995 and the Mainstage in 1996 for *Piñata Full of Bees*. "Everyone knew Adam was a special talent back then, super smart, super funny, clearly the head of his class," Steve Carell said to the *Los Angeles Times* in 2015. Onstage at The Second City, McKay specialized in bizarre juxtapositions between his characters and their environments, like white-bread, suburban gang members or zombies who run into old friends from high school.

McKay became the head writer of *Saturday Night Live* in 1997, going on to write and direct some of comedy's biggest hits, many of which saw him team him up with fellow Second City alums like Carell. He launched the website Funny or Die in 2007 with Will Ferrell, but his most recent work has taken a turn toward the dramatic. *The Big Short*, released in 2015, earned him an Oscar for Best Adapted Screenplay, as well as a nomination for Best Director, an honor he also received in 2018 for *Vice*. To The Second City, he will always hold the title of "Best Ensemble Member Portraying Noam Chomsky as a Public School Substitute Teacher."

Adam McKay (lower left) and (clockwise from top left) Jim Zulevic, Jimmy Doyle, Dee Ryan, Jenna Jolovitz, and John Hildreth in the e.t.c.'s *One Nation, Under Fraud*, 1995

> "Rachel's humor is so joyful and never at anyone's expense. It's always just silliness and joyfulness." **–Tina Fey**

# RACHEL DRATCH

Some Second City performers have an enviable advantage over their fellow ensemble members: the audience is in love with them. Rachel Dratch continuously had the audience eating out of her hand and is the reason so many others who have seen her perform become improvisers. "Rachel's humor is so joyful and never at anyone's expense," said Tina Fey, her former *Paradigm Lost* castmate and the other half of the two-woman show *Dratch & Fey*. "It's always just silliness and joyfulness."

After spending several years in the Touring Company, Dratch was ready to quit when she was cast in the Mainstage's revolutionary *Piñata Full of Bees* in 1995. During her time at The Second City, she co-wrote and performed in four revues, twice winning Jeff Awards for Actress in a Revue before joining the cast of *Saturday Night Live*, a job she had dreamed about since third grade.

A couple of years ago, Dratch was slapped with a sobering reminder of her time spent in Chicago: the city sent her a parking ticket for fines dating back to 1997. "Chicago does not f around. I received this parking ticket in the mail today. Look at the date. It's from TWENTY years ago," she tweeted. The Second City gladly offered to pony up the $73.20 fine.

Stephnie Weir (left) and Rachel Dratch in *Promise Keepers, Losers Weepers*, 1998

"I THINK IT WAS THE BEST JOB I EVER HAD. THE HAPPIEST TIME OF MY LIFE, IN A LOT OF WAYS. . . . TO BE LIVING IN CHICAGO, TO BE PAID TO IMPROVISE ON A NIGHTLY BASIS AND BE A PART OF THAT INSTITUTION WAS A GREAT JOY."

–Tina Fey

Scott Adsit (left), Jenna Jolovitz, Tina Fey, and Kevin Dorff in the *Paradigm Lost* scene "Gargoyle"

# TINA FEY

Tina Fey took a job working at the front desk at a suburban YMCA in the mornings and took classes at The Second City at night, cementing her dedication to the art form of improv. "The first time I went to see a Second City show, I was in awe of everything. I just wanted to touch the same stage that Gilda Radner had walked on. It was sacred ground," she told *Believer* in 2003. "But my perspective changed pretty radically when I finally got into the Training Center. I became immersed in the cult of improvisation. . . . I was so sure that I was doing exactly what I'd been put on this earth to do, and I would have done anything to make it onto that stage."

In 1996, the Touring Company member moved to the Mainstage as an understudy for Jon Glaser in *Piñata Full of Bees* before going on to co-write and perform in two original revues, *Citizen Gates* and *Paradigm Lost*. In a 1999 documentary called *Second to None*, which captured the creation of

*Paradigm Lost*, director Mick Napier said about the future star, "She's very, very smart. She has a very innocent, childlike quality about her that she knows how to deal with, and it gives her a lot of power on-stage. All of her characters are so dimensional and fresh. She's constantly surprising me with stuff."

No one at The Second City is surprised by the incredible amount Fey has achieved in front of the camera, behind the scenes, and even on Broadway, where she and Jeff Richmond, the fellow Second City alum to whom she is married, opened *Mean Girls* as a musical based on the iconic film. In an interview with Brian Williams, she summed up how The Second City set her up to succeed by explaining, "You learn to not be afraid to fail. And you learn to support other actors onstage. . . . You can put Second City people in a scene, and they'll make the other people look good, as opposed to trying to show off themselves."

## *Paradigm Lost* and Found

Mick Napier cemented his status as one of comedy's most thrilling directors with *Paradigm Lost*, a show centered around the dreams, nightmares, and shifting realities of a corporate executive (Jim Zulevic) who is in a coma. The show won Jeff Awards for Best Director, Best Production, Scott Adsit for Best Actor, and Rachel Dratch for Best Actress. The rest of the ensemble—Kevin Dorff, Tina Fey, Jenna Jolovitz, and Zulevic—weren't too shabby, either. "It was just a really perfect harmony," Napier told WGN Radio about the comedy dream team.

Years before anyone would learn how to break the internet, Napier also accomplished another Second City first during the process of the show: "I was able to do a journal on the internet at a time when no one in the cast was on the internet." As one of the web's first bloggers, Napier captured his experience in journal entries like this, which he published in book form for the second edition of his improvisation bible, *Improvise: Scene from the Inside Out*:

> *February 13th, 1997*
>
> *This is the day of the opening night. Today, for me, will be like the last scene of Goodfellas. . . . But I'm hoping it doesn't end the same way. For the last two days, we have been working non-stop. While Craig [Taylor] has been learning a new programmable light board and hanging lights (which change, God bless him, every five minutes on a whim), Lyn [Pusztai] has been coordinating the set, room, and costumes. The cast and I have been working furiously on the show.*
>
> *I am very happy with the show.*

Critics were happy with it, too. The *Chicago Tribune* warned us, "The only thing that should be gnawing at the collective conscience of the current generation of Mainstage performers at Second City is that their latest revue, *Paradigm Lost*, sets a new standard of troupe-oriented comedy to which successive ensembles will be held."

*Paradigm Lost* was significant for one more reason. For the very first (and only) time, cameras were allowed inside The Second City's creative process for the 1999 documentary *Second to None*. Produced by HMS Media and hosted by Jim Belushi, the film followed the show's creative time line. In the footage, an inexperienced Fey revealed, "If you're improvising, it's not like a straight play. If you don't initiate and get out there, you just won't be out there. And I'm not in the current show quite that much, probably because it's my first show. So this time, I'm gonna do more." By the time *Second to None* aired, Fey had, in fact, done "more" by becoming *SNL*'s first female head writer, succeeding Adam McKay in the job. Dratch had also joined the cast, along with three-time e.t.c. player Horatio Sanz.

Utterback illustration
for the Chicago
Mainstage's eighty-
second revue,
*Paradigm Lost*

Jim Zulevic (left) and (clockwise) Jeff Richmond, Michael Broh, Neil Flynn, Pete Gardner (a.k.a. Pete Zahradnick), Jerry C. Minor, Miriam Tolan, Dee Ryan, and Brian Stack in 1996

# JIM ZULEVIC

Of all the people to grace a Second City stage, none were as hilarious, angry, and lovable as Jim Zulevic. A tremendous comedic force from Chicago's South Side, he came to the theater as a student before joining the Touring Company in 1992 and later performing five revues on the e.t.c. and Mainstage. Zulevic was adored by audiences and his fellow ensemble members alike, and as Kelly Leonard remarked after Zulevic's untimely death in 2006 at age forty, "His talent was so huge, it was barely controllable."

After his passing, Andrew Alexander established the Jim Zulevic Award in his honor. The annual grant, given out every year at the holiday party, is awarded to a Second City staff member or performer whose drive and creative spirit are infused with the same spark that made Zulevic one of a kind. "I was lucky enough to work with Jim every night for a year," Tina Fey told the *Chicago Tribune*. "Jim loved Chicago and The Second City, and he loved old-school improv."

## Toronto Re-Roosts

Just before the theater's twenty-fifth anniversary in 1997, The Second City Toronto moved into an overly ambitious new state-of-the-art facility at Fifty-Six Blue Jays Way. While longtime home the Old Firehall had plenty of bohemian charm, it was small, technically underequipped, and too far from where the action in the city had moved. Alumna and former Second City Toronto artistic director Sandra Balcovske recalled saying farewell to the Firehall on its last night:

> *There was a half-dozen of us who stayed later than anyone else, probably five or six in the morning. We thought about writing something on the wall, and we started to write down people's names, couples who had met there, who had kids, people who'd had relationships inside the company. It turned into an incredible family tree.*

Unfortunately, the Toronto expansion was a bust (bad acoustics, just for starters), and a move across the street took place a few years later.

The Second City Toronto's complex at Fifty-Six Blue Jays Way

## Goodbye, Chris

As we began to look ahead to the turn of the century, The Second City had plenty to celebrate, and the annual holiday party seemed especially happy in 1997. We even welcomed back Chris Farley, who was by then a bona fide superstar, to celebrate right alongside staff and talent. Just two days later, on December 18, Farley was found dead in his apartment. Kelly Leonard described the moment he learned the tragic news:

> *Chris's brother John was in the Touring Company at the time, and he was late for an important rehearsal. I was a little pissed, and I knew he'd been staying at the John Hancock building. When I called the apartment, Ted, Chris's assistant, answered the phone. I asked for John, and Ted said in a rushed and strange voice, "The police are here. I can't talk. John will call you." And he hung up. I actually didn't think too much about it, but not two minutes later, a local radio station called me looking for confirmation that Chris was dead. I spun around in my chair to see two news vans pull up in front of the theater. Having been through this with John Candy, I had some idea of what to do. I called Andrew [Alexander], and we worked on a statement to the press.*

After the performance that evening, as camera crews and morbid curiosity seekers still surrounded the building, Kevin Dorff, a Mainstage cast member and Farley's good friend, addressed the audience:

> *At this time, we would like to say on behalf of The Second City how saddened we were today by the news of the death of our friend Chris Farley. Shakespeare said, "Brevity is the soul of wit." Chris Farley had the soul of a comedian, and sadly, his life was too brief. As someone who knew him, worked with him, and learned a lot from him, I can tell you that while he was here, he made a lot of people laugh, right here on this stage and on others, and I know that this was his greatest joy, and he had a very happy life for that reason. While we here at The Second City family will miss him, our sympathies and our best wishes go to his family in Wisconsin and here in Chicago, to whom he is irreplaceable and always will be, of course. Now that being said, I should tell you that there will be a brief break before we do Chris's favorite part of the show, the improv set.*

Farley was only thirty-three years old, the same age his idol, John Belushi, had been at his death.

## Can We Get a Suggestion for a Thirteenth-Century Scottish Warrior?

Chris Farley was not the only one who relished the improv set. It is often the best part of the show for both the actors and the audience. While the "third act" is no stranger to celebrity guests, one of our favorites was a not yet publicly unhinged Mel Gibson, who came to the theater one night in 1998 while filming in Chicago. He had hidden unrecognized in the audience, but after the show Kevin Dorff and Jim Zulevic talked the *Braveheart* star and two-time Oscar winner into playing the set. "People in the audience could tell something special was going to happen," recounted Beth Kligerman, who was an associate producer at the time. "The lights fluttered, and all of a sudden—in a wig and wearing a flannel shirt tied around his waist like a kilt—Mel was up on a bentwood chair in full William Wallace mode. The audience didn't quite first understand, and then they went bonkers. It was deafening. Totally electric."

## "Acrobatics All the Way Out"

As the decade came to a close, we lost one more iconic name. From his fabled "living wake" to his alleged final words ("I'm tired of being the funniest person in the room") to his (again, alleged) skull donation, there are many legends surrounding the death of Del Close in March 1999. Here is one more unique perspective.

Many years ago, Andrew Alexander had Close and Toronto alum and director Bruce Pirrie create a series of monologues that would interrupt the show as it was in progress. They called Close's character "Ozzie Mandius," and his monologue on death has particular resonance:

> *I was reading in a newspaper the other day about a skydiver who dived out of an airplane and did aerial acrobatics for several thousand feet. When he pulled the rip cord, the main chute did not open. Then he pulled the emergency chute cord, and that did not open. And then what did he do? He did flips and acrobatics head over heels at the top of his ability all the way into the ground. Splat. Now that's my kind of guy. That's kind of a metaphor for life, isn't it? I mean, we're all going to hit the ground—splat—eventually, aren't we? So what I'm going to do is follow that guy's example and do acrobatics all the way out.*

**FROM TOP:** Larry Joe Campbell (left), Joshua Funk, and Grant Kraus at The Second City Detroit, 1996; The cast of Toronto's forty-fifth revue, *Y2K: The Chip Hits the Fan*: Gina Sorell (left), Marypat Farrell, Gavin Crawford, Lee Smart, Tracy Dawson, and Doug Morency

**FACING PAGE:** The cast and crew of the e.t.c.'s 1999 revue *History Repaints Itself* on the Piper's Alley escalators, clockwise from top left: Craig Cackowski, Sue Gillan, Klaus Schuller, Jack McBrayer, Angela V. Shelton, Trey Stone, Martin Garcia, Jeff Richmond, and David Pompeii

## The Second City Turns Forty

December 1999 saw a tremendous milestone: The Second City celebrated its fortieth anniversary in Chicago. Alumni were invited back for four days of seminars and film festivals showing old material. Second Citizens from every generation came in, including Alan Arkin, Tina Fey, Joe Flaherty, Jo Forsberg, Tom Gianas, Mike Hagerty, Barbara Harris, Fred Kaz, Tim Kazurinsky, Richard Kind, Robert Klein, Mina Kolb, Tim Meadows, Joyce Piven, Harold Ramis, Tony Rosato, Avery Schreiber, David Shepherd, and Ron West. Sheldon Patinkin was overwhelmed by the experience, reflecting:

> The first night of the four-day weekend, the opening of the Mainstage show, I walked into the theater and saw people from the last forty-eight years of my professional (and personal) life—all the way back to when I was a sixteen-year-old student at the University of Chicago—as well as my brother and sister-in-law, all in one room. That's a lot of years, a lot of memories, all crashing in at once. It was exhilarating and terrifying at the same time, and it was one of the only times in my life that I can remember having a full-out anxiety attack.

As part of the festivities, both stages opened new revues on consecutive nights. The Mainstage's *Second City 4.0*, directed by Mick Napier with music direction by Ruby Streak, had a cast that included Kevin Dorff, Susan Messing, Tami Sagher, Rich Talarico, Stephnie Weir, and Ed Furman, who said the cast got quite a surprise at the end of the performance:

> Nobody told us there was going to be an alumni photo op after the show. It ends, and I see people starting to stand up. I think, "Okay, maybe a standing ovation?" Then, I see audience members slowly start walking towards us, but the light's in my eye, so I can't see faces. One shadow gets closer—and it's Alan Arkin. Then it's Avery Schreiber and some SCTV folks. It was crazy, kind of like a zombie thing, but benign. Nobody got killed.

**TORONTO'S SILVER ANNIVERSARY**

A year prior to Chicago's fortieth anniversary, The Second City Toronto feted its twenty-fifth year with a one-hour special for the CBC. Produced by Andrew Alexander, the 1998 show was filmed at the Toronto theater, capturing the cast's backstage shenanigans and kicking off with Joe Flaherty and Eugene Levy reprising their *SCTV* news anchor characters, "Floyd Robertson" and "Earl Camembert." The special also featured Canadian comedians Robin Duke, Jennifer Irwin, Patrick McKenna, Jenny Parsons, Martin Short, Dave Thomas, and Dave Foley, playing a libidinous God who laughs at the Bible, saying, "Guess you had to be there."

# SUSAN MESSING

With accolades like "Improviser of the Year" and "Funniest Woman in Chicago," Susan Messing is an award-winning improviser, comedian, and teacher. An alumna of The Second City, she is also a founding member of Chicago's Annoyance Theatre and was a director for The Second City Touring Company.

"Passionate, smart, and very, very funny, Susan Messing is the Switzerland of our Chicago improv community—always there to help connect the improv institutions and remind us all that we are one. She's a remarkable woman that I love to call my friend," says Andrew Alexander.

Susan Messing (left) and Rich Talarico in the scene "Break-In" from Second City's fortieth-anniversary show

Next door, Jeff Richmond took on directing duties for *History Repaints Itself*, featuring Craig Cackowski, Martin Garcia, Sue Gillan, Jack McBrayer, David Pompeii, and Angela V. Shelton, with Michael Thomas heading up the music.

The final day of celebrating wrapped up with a brunch to honor Patinkin, Bernie Sahlins, and Joyce Sloane. Sahlins took the opportunity to wax poetic on all that The Second City had accomplished in its first four decades:

> *Look at the world today, how we've improved it. Because of The Second City, there is no racism. War is a thing of the past, and we've eliminated poverty. But seriously, folks, and do let me turn serious for a moment to assure you that it's not comedy's role to change the world. The fact is, man is the only animal that laughs, and comedy's major role is to evoke the laughter that celebrates our unity as mortal creatures—we who were born into this world without our consent and must leave it the same way; we who must eat and drink, defecate and break wind in order to live and procreate. Comedy informs us that in this respect, we are not alone, that as kings and peasants, priests and penitents, we are all in the same boat, moved to find ways to deal with our fate. Our laughter is at once a protest and an acceptance of our common destiny.*

# CHAPTER 8
# THE
# 2000s
## LAUGHTER BY
## LAND AND BY SEA

As a new century began, The Second City remained true to its origins, thrilling audiences—even in the face of a national tragedy and a changing world—with the kind of satire and laugh-out-loud humor for which it had become world-famous. Like the improv pioneers who had broken new artistic ground in decades prior, the comedy company again sought to experiment in uncharted waters. In addition to forming new artistic partnerships, The Second City expanded to two new cities and one new, decidedly wetter, frontier—the sea—before commemorating a golden anniversary.

## Second City Theatricals

In 2000, The Second City's blossoming new Theatricals division began channeling the company's talent and collaborative sensibilities into new kinds of projects that lived apart from the tried-and-true revue format. "We never said, 'Let's create a theatricals division,'" Kelly Leonard said. "We had good ideas for stuff and no stages to put them on. A lot of the work we were doing, like *Dratch & Fey* or Jeff Garlin's one-man show, was going up on off nights in the e.t.c."

Beginning a tradition of partnering with prominent arts organizations to create unlikely productions, The Second City opened *Hamlet! The Musical* that summer at the Chicago Shakespeare Theater. With music and book by Second City's Jeff Richmond (who also directed and played "Hamlet" opposite Alexandra Billings as "Queen Gertrude") and Michael Thomas, the satirical twist on the Bard moved off-Broadway two years later with a new name, *Melancholy Baby*, and became the first show to run in Hell's Kitchen hub the Ars Nova theater.

**PICTURED ON PREVIOUS PAGE:** The cast of the e.t.c.'s *Holy War, Batman! or The Yellow Cab of Courage* in 2001: Samantha Albert (left), Andy Cobb, TJ Jagodowski, Jack McBrayer, Abby Sher, and Keegan-Michael Key

Second City took on Shakespeare again for a *Romeo and Juliet* musical parody in 2004. The anything but epigrammatic *The Second City's Romeo and Juliet Musical: The People vs. Friar Laurence, The Man Who Killed Romeo and Juliet* featured Second City Detroit and e.t.c. alumnus Keegan-Michael Key and *MADtv's* Nicole Parker as the star-crossed lovers. The show, co-written by Ron West and Phil Swann (with West also directing and performing as "Lord Capulet") was again staged at Navy Pier's "Chicago Shakes" and was a critical success, with *Chicago Tribune* critic Chris Jones writing, "Oodles of clever material and a truly remarkably impressive ability to make fresh satiric hay out of the most hackneyed iconography in all of dramatic literature, [director] West's show somehow avoids every pothole. In short, it's a blast."

By building on The Second City's creative process and commissioning original scripts from Second City talent, Second City Theatricals has gradually but steadily built a robust catalog of dynamic projects. "Second City Theatricals has created some extraordinary shows," said Andrew Alexander. "From those early Shakespeare projects to our captivating 2014 collaboration with Hubbard Street Dance Chicago and the wildly smart, funny *She the People*, we have expanded our creative reach, inspiring a whole new generation of writers and directors to approach comedy in entirely new ways."

**FROM LEFT:** Nicole Parker (left) as "Juliet" and Keegan-Michael Key as "Romeo" in 2004; Mick Napier (left) as "Hamlet" and Alexandra Billings as "Queen Gertrude" in 2001

## The Second City Las Vegas

Chicago was not the only place where new undertakings were getting off the ground. Forming a Second City in Sin City was something of a no-brainer, and in 2001, a Las Vegas run was officially announced by Andrew Alexander at a press conference, with help from alums Richard Kind, George Wendt, and Fred Willard.

The Second City Las Vegas opened at the Flamingo Las Vegas Hotel and Casino in March in partnership with Jam Theatricals. Initially directed by Mick Napier, the first show, *The Best of The Second City*, did not connect right away with audiences. As new Vegas residents, the cast lacked knowledge of the city's culture, infrastructure, or locals, and the unfamiliarity went both ways. "In Chicago, we didn't have to pay to advertise. Everyone knew us," said Robin Hammond, who transitioned from her job producing Second City corporate events to become the Vegas show's supervising producer. "In Vegas, where the population changed every four days, it was all about billboards, magazines. It was a high roller mentality."

The September 11, 2001, terrorist attacks occurred just six months after the show's opening at the Flamingo. The Vegas Strip was unsettlingly quiet that day, and it seemed that canceling the show that night was the only appropriate decision. But, "I checked the numbers," Hammond explained, "and we had actually started *selling* tickets. All these people were stranded in Las Vegas [due to the cancellation of all flights in and out]. I kept checking the numbers. We made the decision to do the show that night. People were clearly wanting and needing an escape from the grief."

Creatively, Las Vegas was a different animal for the trained improvisers. While Second City artists typically create original material during the after-show improv sets, "in Vegas, it's a transient town. People want to see a show real quick and then go back to gambling," director, writer, and actress Kay Cannon explained to *Fast Company* in 2005. "So we didn't have that third act where you try things out. We wrote an original show." In a meaty nod to *Saturday Night Live*, that show was called *The Not Ready for $3.99 Prime Rib Players*. Ultimately, Second City's comedy crapshoot didn't pay off long-term, and in 2008, we left Las Vegas.

During The Second City Las Vegas's seven-year run, the Bugsy's Celebrity Theatre stage at the Flamingo showcased a rotating cast that included Dan Bakkedahl, Rob Belushi, Kay Cannon, Martin Garcia, Shelly Gossman, Michael Lehrer, Jean Villepique, Holly Walker and Jason Sudeikis, who told the *Las Vegas Sun* that "working for The Second City is like playing football for a big-time school. Based upon our alumni, we are a fertile recruiting ground."

The cast of The Second City Las Vegas in 2002: Jason Sudeikis (left), Karen Graci, Seamus McCarthy, Ed Goodman, and Kay Cannon

# JASON SUDEIKIS

At Jason Sudeikis's audition for The Second City Touring Company, director Mick Napier paired the Kansas transplant with a woefully underprepared scene partner—a guy whose mother had somehow talked the casting team into letting her son have a shot. Despite the handicap, "Jason lifted him up and carried him through the scene, just cool as a cucumber," said longtime casting executive Beth Kligerman. "In our hearts and minds, he won that audition right there." After his time at The Second City Las Vegas, Sudeikis was hired by *Saturday Night Live* as a writer before he joined the cast in 2005.

In 2017, Sudeikis, who happens to be the nephew of George Wendt, served as roast master at The Second City's all-star benefit *I Can't Believe They Wendt There: The Roast of George Wendt*, the "very first, and possibly the very last, Second City celebrity roast," he warned the crowd.

## Tragedy and Comedy

Unlike The Second City Las Vegas, the Chicago theater did cancel performances on September 11, 2001. The following night, an audience mostly made up of stranded out-of-towners watched the Mainstage performance. After the show, ensemble member Ed Furman addressed the house, sincerely thanking them for being there. "It was so powerful," remembered Beth Kligerman. "It was really kind of magic. A lot of the people there were stuck in Chicago and couldn't get home."

Nearly three thousand miles west, The Second City Touring Company was also stranded. The night before a USO show at a military base on Kodiak Island, Alaska, BlueCo "went out partying like mad," recounted former Touring Company member Rachael Mason, now the head of advanced improvisation for The Second City Training Center. They returned to the base in the early-morning hours and went searching for pancakes in the common area—where the news was always on. Mason described what unfolded next:

> We walk in to see Tower One smoking, and we're watching it just in time for the second plane to hit. . . . Base alarms start going off. We thought it was World War III. . . . We were supposed to do a show that night, and they asked us not to, because the base was on lockdown. That meant from building to building, not just if you wanted to leave. A day or two later, the base commander finally comes to us and asks, "Will you please do a show for our troops?" Now, USO contracts were very specific about what kind of things we can and cannot do and say. He says to us, "Just make them laugh." We put together a new running order and wrote a couple of custom scenes. When it's time to do the show, our audience is holding live firearms, not pointed at us or anything, but it was a whole new level of "we better do real good." They loved it. Going into it, nobody had felt like laughing or being funny, but we were all healing together.

The group was held on the island for a week longer than their scheduled two-day trip before being evacuated "in an *Indiana Jones*–style, C-130 military cargo plane" to a mainland base in Anchorage for another week. From there, they were moved to Salt Lake City before making their way home to Chicago. "I'd never experienced bonding on that level," native New Yorker Mason said. "I'd never experienced comedy saving the day on that level. For comedians, there's no better way to serve your country than doing a fucking show for the USO. It was life changing."

### Embryos on Ice! and Holy War, Batman!

Chicago's new Mainstage revue was scheduled to open on September 12. There was no time for the revue to respond to the tragedy, which would require scrapping the old show and restarting the entire creative process—which usually takes eight to ten weeks. "We were fried," said cast member Ed Furman. "Everyone was in shock. We were not in the place to start over after the world was changed." Behind the scenes, the show had already been fraught with creative issues. Furman explained:

> We spent all summer in the dark theater in process. The director was not a fit to direct a show there. At all. Things were not going well, and rehearsals were not fun, so he left, and [director] Jeff Richmond stepped in. We were already way behind, and when September 11 happened, Jeff left to go be with Tina [Fey].

Fey, Richmond's wife, was working at *Saturday Night Live*, and he quite understandably left to join her in New York, requiring Mick Napier to come to the rescue as the show's third (and final) director. *Embryos on Ice! or Fetus Don't Fail Me Now* opened just eight days after the attacks, with a note tucked into the program explaining that the revue "was essentially written under a different set of rules than now exists in our nation." At least one critic lambasted it for not addressing the tragedy. In her review, *Newcity* critic Nina Metz wrote, "It is baffling why this nimble-witted group of writers and performers did not adapt their show to reflect this. . . . Hopefully, the members of Second City will reconsider their show and take this opportunity to sharpen and rediscover their comedic passion."

Meanwhile, the e.t.c. ensemble was in the early stages of creating its new show, and director Joshua Funk was given a clear directive by management. "Kelly [Leonard] and Andrew [Alexander] called me into their office and said, 'Your show needs to be ALL about September 11th.' I said, 'All right, let's get to work.'" The cast, composed of Samantha Albert, Andy Cobb, TJ Jagodowski, Keegan-Michael Key, Jack McBrayer, and Abby Sher, with musical director Trey Stone and stage manager Klaus Schuller, started to experiment immediately, and Funk duly prepared each audience. As he explained:

> I would go out there and say, "Tonight in the improv set, we're going to do material that is entirely based on what happened last week. If you're up for it, please stay. If it's too raw, too much to handle, we understand, and you are welcome to leave." We would take a break, and absolutely no one would leave. Everyone stayed, every time, and we learned very quickly what people were—and were not—ready to laugh at. . . . It was truly an experiment in human behavior.

**FROM TOP:** The cast of Chicago Mainstage's 2000 revue, *Slaughterhouse 5, Cattle 0*, clockwise from top left: Sue Gillan, Ed Furman, Rich Talarico, Steve Lund, Tami Sagher, Jeff Richmond, Craig Cackowski, and Angela V. Shelton; Jamillah Ross (left), Naomi Snieckus, Matt Baram, Jennifer Goodhue, Sandy Jobin-Bevans, and Paul Constable in Toronto's 2003 revue *Armaget-It-On!*

Jagodowski said:

> *It was impossible for 9/11 not to be the backdrop for it all. It was the context within which all the scenes took place. . . . It was still relationship scenes, scenes that weren't hitting it on the political head. What do you do with the fear? With what it means to be American? How do you go on with your daily life? We still tried to make it humanly relatable in light of a horrible event.*

*Holy War, Batman! or The Yellow Cab of Courage* opened on November 11, receiving critical acclaim for its adroit handling of raw emotions, racial inequality, and patriotism. The show managed to fulfill "the same function that Bob Hope and Abbott and Costello movies did during World War II," wrote the *Chicago Reader*. "Making life more bearable simply by making us laugh long and loud."

Chicago audiences were not the only ones finding respite in comedy. New York City first responders were being sent to Chicago to decompress and see the show. "Every week, we would have firefighters from Ground Zero come," Funk said. "After the shows, they would come backstage and cry with us and laugh with us and tell us how much they needed this. . . . It was the first time I understood the importance of what we do. All of a sudden, comedy became vitally important."

# TJ JAGODOWSKI

After seeing Steve Carell, Stephen Colbert, and Amy Sedaris in *Take Me Out to the Balkans*, Holyoke, Massachusetts, native TJ Jagodowski enrolled in improv classes. He began his professional career at The Second City answering the phone before joining the Touring Company, then the Mainstage and e.t.c. casts. Jagodowski has a long, storied history as a prolific improviser, and his "TJ & Dave" collaboration with fellow Second City alum David Pasquesi has been called "the premier improv duo working today" by the *New York Times*.

Once a year, Jagodowski performs for twenty-four hours straight as the ringmaster of The Second City's annual improv and music marathon, which has been raising money for disadvantaged Chicago families for nearly twenty years. He has participated since the event's inception.

Samantha Albert (left), Keegan-
Michael Key, TJ Jagodowski, Jack
McBrayer, and Abby Sher in 2001

Jack McBrayer in the e.t.c.'s twenty-second revue, *Better Late Than Nader*

# JACK MCBRAYER

After graduating from the University of Evansville in Indiana with a degree in theater management, Jack McBrayer came to Chicago in 1999. That summer, the city experienced a heat wave, and The Second City had free air-conditioning. It also had people like Rachel Dratch and Scott Adsit onstage. McBrayer was sold. As part of the e.t.c. cast, where he co-wrote and performed in three revues, his southern charm and insanely funny character work made him a crowd favorite. McBrayer's likability also charmed Tina Fey and Jeff Richmond, who created the role of "Kenneth the Page" on *30 Rock* with him in mind. "Every entertainment job I've had has been because of Second City," McBrayer told the *Wall Street Journal* on the eve of the company's fiftieth anniversary. "It's very incestuous—and thank God. Otherwise I'd be starving."

## The Second City That Never Sleeps

Some of The Second City's most significant moments have come in the wee hours of the night—or the predawn morning. "Andy [Cobb] and I were backstage once talking about how, goddamn, we love to improvise," said TJ Jagodowski. "I was like, 'We should improvise for twenty-four hours straight.'" In the summer of 2002, Cobb put together a one-time show featuring twenty-four hours of improv, with the proceeds from the show going to a Chicago homeless shelter.

That winter, the idea evolved when Cobb combined efforts with then–theater manager Heather Whinna. For several years prior, she and Steve Albini (the recording engineer and musician to whom she is married) had been fulfilling letters to Santa sent to the post office, humbly answering requests for help from Chicago families during an especially tough time of the year. Cobb asked her to help him pull off another event, and they would donate all the money to her "Letters to Santa" efforts. A new holiday-time tradition was born.

Since 2002, the name has changed a few times—*The Second City That Never Sleeps*, *Letters to Santa*, *24 Hour*—but the mission has remained the same. Every year, a dedicated group of improvisers commits to spending twenty-four hours onstage. "In a field of endeavor where you can be incredibly selfish, everyone is there that night for the right reason," said Jagodowski. "For someone else. For someone they're more than likely never gonna meet or see the impact their efforts have on their lives."

The show is broken up by a smorgasbord of special guests (from rock star statistician Nate Silver to the internet's most famous cat, Lil Bub) and performances from marching bands, mariachi bands, and music icons. (Bob Mould! Billy Corgan! J Mascis!) Alumni who have moved on to other life and career phases look forward to

Poster art for the 2006 staging of The Second City's annual twenty-four-hour benefit

returning for the annual event, and The Second City has even added new friends to the mix over the years, including Fred Armisen and Wilco front man Jeff Tweedy, who auctions off private concerts at the homes of winning bidders. "The generosity of the people involved in this event cannot be overstated," said Whinna. "Friends pitch in with what they've got to offer for one full day, and the future of a dozen families who are desperate for any assistance is changed literally overnight."

During the holiday season, our Chicago actors also collect donations after the shows, and The Second City matches the amount raised. "Second City is proud to give this event—and this community of inspirational, funny, sweaty artists—a home. It's always wonderful to see our alumni come back to Chicago, and it's even better when it's for a such an uplifting grassroots cause," said Andrew Alexander. In a 2015 essay for the *Huffington Post*, Albini summed up how the money changes lives:

> *Over the years, we have distributed over a million dollars directly into their hands. Families have been able to move into better housing and safer living conditions, solve health crises, relocate and reunite family members, and otherwise stabilize precarious lives in a way that enabled them to flourish. . . . The extent of poverty in the city makes it inevitable that we are missing some families, families who are outside the reach of an aid organization, doubtless still addressing their need and fear to Santa Claus at the North Pole, but if the nature of need is that it is all around us, then reaching in any direction allows us to make a dent in it.*

Every Christmas morning, Whinna, Albini, and a group of friends hand deliver gifts, necessities, and some cash to as many letter writers as possible. The tradition is well worth losing sleep over.

## *WORDS* about Black History

The Second City's ongoing efforts to use humor as a bridge led to the theater's first Black History Month show in 2002. Curated by Dionna Griffin-Irons and directed by Claudia Michelle Wallace, *WORDS* featured a lineup of twenty-four African American poets, comedians, improvisers, musicians, and dancers from both Chicago's North Side and South Side neighborhoods. "I wanted to increase African-American presence at Second City," Griffin-Irons told the *Chicago Tribune* at the time, "but I also thought that it would be wonderful to do a collective work, featuring alumni, instructors and even novice spoken word artists."

*WORDS* became one of the early playing spaces in Chicago for young comedians of color, including writer and talk show host Robin Thede, actor Lamorne Morris, Lookingglass playwright, director, and actor Kevin Douglas, and several more. An annual hit, the show ran in Donny's Skybox Theater (named for the late, universally admired Second City alumnus and director Don DePollo) for five years before branching out into a festival format.

In 2018, Griffin-Irons brought a new iteration, *The Second City's Black History Month Show*, to The Second City for a limited run in the e.t.c. in response to a suggestion from original *WORDS* cast member Seth Thomas, who also directed the subsequent 2019 staging of the show at UP Comedy Club. The show pulled scenes and material written and originally performed by Second City's black alumni, including Frances Callier, Nyima Funk, Shantira Jackson, Keegan-Michael Key, Tim Meadows, Jerry Minor, Sam Richardson, Amber Ruffin, and Angela V. Shelton. Griffin-Irons explained that audiences would be surprised to discover that the archival material dealing with race, class, and gentrification "is even more relevant and topical now."

The cast of *WORDS* in 2002

The cast of Chicago's *Thank Heaven It Wasn't 7/11*: David Pompeii (left), Martin Garcia, Brian Boland, Al Samuels, Debra Downing, and Abby Sher

Utterback illustration for the e.t.c's twenty-eighth revue, *Immaculate Deception*

## Touring the Middle East

After September 11, The Second City committed to supporting US troops stationed around the world. The Touring Company, which had gone on its first USO tour in August 2011, headed out to military bases in Kosovo, Bosnia, and Germany. They performed for "some of the best audiences we've ever had," said 2002 tour director Joshua Funk, despite the fact that the soldiers were "on pins and needles, because they were about to be deployed to Iraq. . . . We were on the brink of war."

In 2004, RedCo went to the Middle East for an intense eleven-day tour that set out on Election Day. Once they landed in Kuwait, the members of the comedy company—director Jimmy Carlson, music director Chad Krueger, and ensemble members Rebecca Sage Allen, Alex Fendrich, Nicky Margolis, Lori McClain, Andy St. Clair, and Craig Uhlir—immediately realized they were in another world. "The soldiers were either on their way into Iraq for their first tour or on their way back. There were a lot of wide-eyed, scared kids," Carlson, who hails from a long line of veterans, said. "We were there to take their minds off war for forty-five minutes to an hour." The director explained how the cast was transported out after two shows in Kuwait:

> They gave us body armor and Kevlar helmets and put us on a C-130 military cargo plane to Iraq. . . . From the green zone in Baghdad to the bases, we had to take military helicopters. There was no way they were transporting us on the ground. . . . We didn't know until afterward that everything in Baghdad was going to hell in a handbasket while we were there.

As two Black Hawks swooped down to evacuate the Touring Company members, the brigade commander who had been tasked with their security addressed Carlson, who was heading the wrong way to board one of the four-bladed helicopters. "He said, 'Hey, thanks for making me smile for the first time in six months—or laugh in nine months. Don't run the other way, or you'll get your head chopped off.' And then he slapped me on the butt. The scariest guy I have ever seen."

## The Second City Cleveland

The Second City replanted its roots closer to home (and far removed from active combat) in 2002. The Second City Cleveland opened in Cleveland's Playhouse Square, the country's second-largest performing arts center (after New York City's Lincoln Center). Audiences in the custom-built 14th Street Theatre tended to be working-class, suburbanite Ohioans who did not quite spark to the Second City brand of humor, and filling the house proved to

Alex Fendrich (left), Craig Uhlir, Andy St. Clair, and Jimmy Carlson in Iraq, 2004

be a challenge. Joe Ruffner, who came on as a stage manager for the last two shows, remembered an especially slow night before the theater closed in 2004:

> *The Friday eleven p.m. shows gave us trouble. No one wanted to come out that late after a long work week. One night, there was only one table of five people in the audience. The cast asked if we were going to do the show because there's an [Actors'] Equity [Association] adage about not having to do a show for fewer people in the audience than there are in the cast. Backstage, the cast—Katie Caussin, Nate Cockerill, Cody Dove, Lauren Dowden, Randall Harr, and Kiff VandenHeuvel—took a vote. They unanimously voted to do the show. That's the kind of people I work with.*

It was starting to become pretty clear that building brick-and-mortar permanent homes in annexed cities might not be the best business move. Second City Theatricals began a new creative formula—sending casts to soak up the local flavor of a city and then write and perform a city-centric show for a six- to twelve-week run at a regional theater there. 2006's *How I Lost My Denverginity* at Denver's Garner Galleria Theatre "endeared us to a market," said Kelly Leonard. "We built up a great relationship with an artistic company that shared our creative and ethical points of view, and it was a success."

"There were a lot of theaters looking to bring in the ever-elusive younger audience," said former managing producer Jenna Deja. "We found a real niche." In addition to Denver, Second City casts have been dispatched to cities all across the United States, from San Diego (*The Good, the Bad, and the I-5*), Dallas (*The Second City Does Dallas*), Louisville (*It Takes a 'Ville*), Cincinnati (*Pride and Porkopolis*), and Orange County (*Can You Be More Pacific?*).

## The Second City Ships Out

While The Second City had already conquered many locations, there was one place that remained virgin territory for the comedy vets: open waters. Kelly Leonard explained how The Second City and Norwegian Cruise Line's partnership came about:

> I was in my office, and Andrew [Alexander] walked in with a USA Today. He puts it on my desk and says, "Look at this." It was an article about cruise lines working with different brands and shaking up the cruise ship entertainment. He was like, "We should do this." And I was like, "Okay." I pulled up AOL, looked up the biggest cruise lines, and put together a pitch. Within three weeks, I had two major companies seriously interested. [Former Norwegian Cruise Line vice president of entertainment] Keith Cox and I flew to Las Vegas to meet. He saw our show there and said, "I really want to do this. Let's talk terms."

The Second City shipped out its first cast and crew in January 2005 on the *Norwegian Dawn*. That first show "went over okay," said director Jimmy Carlson, "but what we thought would have worked for this specific audience just didn't. It was a misfire. We could make fun of the *experience*, as long as we didn't make fun of the *people* who had all signed up to be on this cruise." After navigating the right content fit (something "highly bespoke" to cruisers, explained Leonard), The Second City found its sea legs. "We were contracted to be on one vessel," said Beth Kligerman, "and it became many more, very quickly."

Andel Sudik, an alumna of the e.t.c. who performed with and directed "The Second City at Sea" (and has admitted to once wearing seasickness bracelets for four months straight), tried to explain the lifestyle onboard:

Second City cast members aboard the *Norwegian Dawn*: Molly Erdman (left), Andy St. Clair, Brian Morris, Paul Grondy, Sue Salvi, and Kevin McGeehan, circa 2005

> *It's wild living on a floating hotel. It gets really easy to take for granted the gorgeous locales you're visiting when you have a curfew like a twelve-year-old and have not walked on land at night for months. That said, to quote an old friend, "It was the best of times; it was the worst of times; it was ship times."*

As Sudik and her castmates once boarded a half-built ship in advance of its inaugural run, "workmen saw us approaching with our suitcases. One took the cigarette out of his mouth and, in a gorgeous French accent, said, 'Welcome to hell,'" Sudik recalled. "He was right—the ship was behind schedule. . . . The only working toilet was backstage, and it didn't have a light, so there was piss everywhere."

Over the course of the thirteen-year partnership, which came to a close in 2018, Second City talent entertained travelers en route to ports in the Caribbean, Hawaii, Alaska, Istanbul, Italy, Egypt, France, and more. While the perception at first was that the ship gigs would provide further employment to retired resident stage performers, the growing need for floating talent created an endless pipeline for emerging stars. Getting cast in "BoatCo" became the entry-level performing gig for aspiring Mainstage talent, and familiar faces who once performed aboard Norwegian ships include Vanessa Bayer, Aidy Bryant, Jordan Klepper, Thomas Middleditch, Alex Moffat, Sam Richardson, Cecily Strong, and Steven Yeun.

Close quarters, unpredictable audiences, and exotic locales led to a lifetime of memories both good and bad (let's be real—Strong described the experience as "half vacation, half prison" in *Vanity Fair*) for the dozens of Second Citizens who shipped out with Norwegian over the years. "The number of people who met their now spouse or significant other out there? It's wild," said Kligerman. "It's such a different world. A different culture. It wasn't our culture, but we certainly adapted to it."

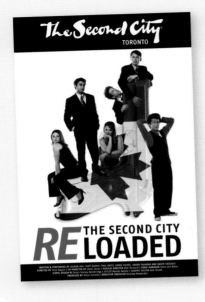

### The Second City: Reloaded

The Second City Toronto was on the move again in 2005, exiting the cavernous complex that had nearly put the company in financial ruin and finding a new home directly across the street in a vacated television soundstage attached to Wayne Gretzky's restaurant. "I had been staring at Ninety-Nine Blue Jays Way for years," Andrew Alexander said. "Little did I know that it would be our savior. We would have saved ourselves a lot of heartache if we had found that location eight years earlier."

Klaus Schuller, producer and executive director of The Second City Toronto from 2005 to 2017, had a specific litmus test for the new theater:

*As soon as they poured the new stage and the concrete dried, I jumped up there to look at where the audience would be seated. I thought, "Okay, this feels right. This is gonna work." During the first preview, Andrew [Alexander] was standing next to me on the balcony, and we could both feel the laughter in that room. It was like the moment when we knew everything was going to be okay.*

The new venue opened with a new show, *The Second City: Reloaded*, directed by Mick Napier. A review in the *Toronto Star* noted that the vibe of the building gave off "the cozy feel" of the Old Firehall on Lombard Street.

## The Second City Goes to College

As The Second City Toronto settled into its new address, at home in Chicago, Andrew Alexander had another kind of evolution on his mind. He asked Anne Libera, then the Training Center's executive artistic director and an adjunct professor at Columbia College Chicago, "Why don't we have a college program at the Training Center?" Libera replied, "Because we don't want to teach science and math."

Galvanized by the goal of becoming "the Juilliard of comedy," The Second City Training Center joined forces with Columbia College Chicago, and the Comedy Studies program launched in the spring of 2007. The groundbreaking program offered juniors and seniors college credit and a "semester abroad" at Second City, where they were immersed in the worlds of comedy theory, history, writing, acting, improvisation, and more. "In creating the program, we wanted to provide more than improvisation training; we wanted to offer coursework that would support comedians of all types," Libera said in a 2012 *Vulture* feature on Comedy Studies. "It seemed clear that a large element of that success was a kind of comedy 'cross training.'"

Before long, Comedy Studies had its own spin-off. A full-fledged undergraduate bachelor's degree in theater with a concentration in comedy writing and performance was announced in 2013, also at Columbia and also overseen by Libera. "If you're funny, I can make you funnier," she said on an episode of fellow Second City executive (and her husband) Kelly Leonard's podcast, *Getting to Yes, And*. "People get better at comedy through practice."

Since its inception, Second City's partnership with Columbia has helped develop a broad range of diverse new voices in comedy that have found professional success across several platforms. "My theory is that there's a Comedy Studies mafia that is slowly taking over.... We've got people writing on shows, we've got people performing, there's an enormous number of stand-ups," Libera said. "It's a really intense, amazing thing."

Lauren Ash (left) and Andy St. Clair in *Taming of the Flu*, Chicago's ninety-seventh Mainstage revue

# LAUREN ASH

Having trained at Toronto's Second City Training Centre as a teenager, Toronto and Chicago Mainstage alumna Lauren Ash has the distinction (along with Mike Myers) of being one of the youngest hires ever at The Second City. The multiple Canadian Comedy Award winner and *Superstore* star once summed up her Second City experience with the following five words: "Joyous. Difficult. Consuming. Fulfilling. Drunk."

Mary Sohn (left), Aidy Bryant, and Jessica Joy in the e.t.c.'s thirty-fifth revue, *Sky's the Limit (Weather Permitting)*

# AIDY BRYANT

"The dream of working in comedy felt so far away to me when I first entered the program. . . . Doing Comedy Studies really let me step into that world," said comedian, actress, writer, and producer Aidy Bryant, who went from being a 2009 Comedy Studies program graduate to performing with The Second City on a cruise ship to joining the cast of the e.t.c. before being hired by *Saturday Night Live* in 2012. "It felt really attainable, and like something I could work hard [for] and achieve, and I did."

## Bye-Bye, Novi

The Second City Detroit wrapped up its downtown run at the theater inside the Hockey-town Cafe with a ten-year-anniversary show, *Ten*, in March 2004. A year and a half later, Second City Detroit reopened in suburban Novi (that's no-*vye*, not no-*vee*), Michigan. The new space, the site of a former brewing company, allowed for renovations including a larger theater and several Training Center classrooms to accommodate the increasing number of students.

The Novi location's final revue, *Night of the Living Debt*, opened in August 2007. The Second City Detroit closed for good that December, having put on a number of Michigan-centric shows, with titles like *Michigan Impossible: All Laid Off & No Place to Go*, *Gratiot Happens*, *Kevorkian Unplugged*, *Power to the People Mover*, and *Less Talk, Motown*.

Tandem celebrations were held in 2018 to commemorate the twenty-fifth anniversary of the groundbreaking work and close-knit connections forged by The Second City Detroit, with alumni gathering in both Detroit and Los Angeles.

# SAM RICHARDSON AND TIM ROBINSON

Twenty-one-year-old Detroit Training Center teacher Tim Robinson met eighteen-year-old improv student Sam Richardson in an improv class, and the two became fast friends. Robinson even sneaked the underage Richardson into bars. After working together in two revues on the Chicago Mainstage, and after urging from Jason Sudeikis, the duo co-created Comedy Central's *Detroiters,* based on their shared time in the Motor City. "At one point we made friends with Jason in our time at Second City," Richardson told *Uproxx* in 2017. "And he said, 'You two should do a show together.' Then, boom, off to the races."

Tim Robinson (left) and Sam Richardson in
*South Side of Heaven*

**FROM TOP:** The cast of Toronto's sixty-fourth revue, *Barack to the Future*: Marty Adams (left), Leslie Seiler, Reid Janisse, Darryl Hinds, Karen Parker, and Kerry Griffin; The cast of Chicago's ninety-fourth Mainstage revue, *America: All Better!*: Mike O'Brien (left), Anthony LeBlanc, Joe Canale, Brad Morris, Lauren Ash, Shelly Gossman, and Emily Wilson

**FACING PAGE:** The cast of Chicago's ninety-third Mainstage revue, *War! Now in Its Fourth Smash Year!*, clockwise from top left: Joe Canale, Ithamar Enriquez, Claudia Michelle Wallace, Molly Erdman, Maribeth Monroe, and Brian Gallivan

The cast of *Between Barack and a Hard Place*: Amber Ruffin (left), Brian Gallivan, Ithamar Enriquez, Molly Erdman, Brad Morris, and Joe Canale

## Mr. Obama Goes to Second City

Accolades in 2007 for Chicago's ninety-fourth Mainstage revue, *Between Barack and a Hard Place*, meant Obama staffers descended upon the show in droves. "The title of the show timed up perfectly when his popularity locally and nationally was starting to build," said cast member Brad Morris. "It was an extra-exciting time." One December night, the senator himself—with the Secret Service in tow—made a visit to The Second City as part of a campaign fundraiser at the theater. "Obama was on the stage delivering a short speech, and the mic was crackling," remembered Andrew Alexander. "I ran backstage to get him a new one, which turned out not to be a smart move. The Secret Service quickly descended upon me and stopped me from traipsing out onstage."

Barack Obama visits with the cast and crew of *Between Barack and a Hard Place*.

Morris recalled doing his best to facilitate a special moment between himself and the future president after the show:

> *As a native Chicagoan, I felt unrealistically close to Barack. As he was leaving, I said, "Hey." All the Secret Service guys turned around. I remember saying, "Keep doing what you're doing." Immediately after it came out of my mouth, I realized that was the dumbest thing I could have possibly said. It doesn't mean anything. He says back to me, "That was the plan. That's what we're gonna do.". . . He shook my hand, and he disappeared down the back steps of the theater. I thought, "Does Barack have any idea how many drugs and cigarettes and drinks have been consumed in that staircase?"*

The cast of *Between Barack and a Hard Place* was one of Second City's most diverse to date. *Chicago Tribune* critic Sid Smith noted:

> *The cast of this revue is a remarkable ethnic rainbow: one African-American [Amber Ruffin], one Latino [Ithamar Enriquez], a white woman who's one-eighth Mexican [Molly Erdman], a Jew [Brad Morris], a gay [Brian Gallivan] and an Irish-Italian Catholic who happens to be left-handed [Joe Canale]. There's not a right-handed white Anglo-Saxon heterosexual male Protestant in the bunch.*

Among the show's many memorable moments was a song by Ruffin called "Good to be Black," where she sang about how being black in Obama's America was better than being

Utterback illustration of the cast of the Chicago Mainstage's ninety-fourth revue, *Between Barack and a Hard Place*

# "DOES BARACK HAVE ANY IDEA HOW MANY DRUGS AND CIGARETTES AND DRINKS HAVE BEEN CONSUMED IN THAT STAIRCASE?"

–Brad Morris

an immigrant or "other" of any kind. ("Things aren't like they were before; terrorism and immigration opened a whole new door.") Ruffin calls the sketch her all-time favorite during her time at The Second City, because "it would never fly anymore."

Two years later, The Second City brought back Barack (actually, Sam Richardson as "Barack") for the all-new show *Barack Stars*, the company's first world premiere in Washington, DC, which was staged at the Woolly Mammoth Theatre Company. "I started talking with Second City about bringing a show to Woolly Mammoth shortly after we moved into our new home in 2005," the theater's then–artistic director, Howard Shalwitz, stated in 2009. "But with the election of Obama—and the arrival of numerous Chicagoans as part of the new administration—it became inescapable."

"To get to do a whole show of Second City social and political satire, in our nation's capital, in a great theater just blocks from the National Mall, is a real honor and privilege and thrill for all of us," director Marc Warzecha told NPR in an interview prior to the show's opening.

Second City had made its DC debut thirteen years earlier at the Kennedy Center with *Truth, Justice, or the American Way*, a transplanted Chicago Mainstage show directed by Tom Gianas and featuring Steve Carell, Jon Glaser, David Koechner, Adam McKay, Tim Meadows, Theresa Mulligan, and Nancy Walls. In the next decade, both the Kennedy Center and Woolly Mammoth stages would become artistic homes away from home for The Second City.

Amber Ruffin (right) and Emily Wilson in a scene from *No Country for Old White Men*

# AMBER RUFFIN

Nebraska native Amber Ruffin got her start doing community theater and improv in Omaha, but her talent soon earned her spots on bigger stages, including Boom Chicago in Amsterdam and The Second City, where she was a member of the Touring Company before joining the Mainstage for the ninety-fourth and ninety-fifth revues, *Between Barack and a Hard Place* and *No Country for Old White Men*. In 2014, Ruffin joined the inaugural writing staff NBC's *Late Night with Seth Meyers*, becoming the first African American woman on the writing staff of a late-night network talk show.

## Rod Blagojevich Superstar!

For a company whose currency is political satire, doubling down on a gubernatorial scandal was a sure thing. In 2008, Chicago Mainstage alum Ed Furman and Second City Touring Company musical director T.J. Shanoff were approached by Kelly Leonard to take on the recent rise and fall of Illinois governor Rod Blagojevich, who had just been charged with corruption by federal prosecutors. The two got to work immediately. Furman banged out a ripped-from-the-absurdist-headlines script in two days, "with Wikipedia open," he admitted. "Everything was out there. You just had to turn it into dialogue." Shanoff quickly composed the songs.

On the heels of Blagojevich's impeachment in January, the rock opera parody sold out a limited engagement at the e.t.c. in early 2009. *Rod Blagojevich Superstar!* was updated (to account for the nonstop breaking news in the saga) and then brought to the Chicago Shakespeare's Upstairs theater, where its run was soon extended. Early in the production's life span, a *Variety* review astutely asked the question "With his craving for cash undiluted, and his need for attention so craven, is it really out of the realm of reality to imagine Blago deciding that maybe he'd like to play himself?" The answer was no, much to Shanoff's consternation, as he explained in a blog post for *Oy!Chicago*:

> *The cast, crew, and creative team were in disbelief once [Blago's] appearance was confirmed. Could this really be happening? Would he actually show up? Would one of us get punched in the face once he heard the lyrics ascribed to his wife in her tender ballad, "I Don't Know How to F\*\*king Love Him"?*

One surreal Saturday night, Blagojevich and his signature mane of jet-black hair showed up in the flesh, accepting an invitation from The Second City. "When he came out, the audience went crazy," Furman said. Joey Bland, the actor who portrayed Blago, explained how strangely the night unfolded:

**"ANOTHER SATISFIED VICTIM"**
While audiences look to satirists like The Second City to comment on recent headlines and the current pop culture landscape, we are also known for blurring the lines of reality in the name of comedy—and sometimes, love. In a modern classic from the 2009 Chicago Mainstage revue *America: All Better!*, Mike O'Brien would interrupt an Old West saloon scene to "propose" to fellow ensemble member Shelly Gossman. Night after night, things would unravel quickly after she turned him down . . . and the crowd would fall for it. "The actors had to sell that one hundred percent," said revue director Matt Hovde. "And every night, the audience thought it was real."

"The expression we used was, 'another satisfied victim'—to see if you could mess with the audience, but have them come away saying that it was a blast," O'Brien told the *Chicago Tribune*'s Nina Metz in 2015. "It's one of my favorite things."

*We had him come up onstage at the end so I could interview him.... One of the first things I asked him was whether or not he hated us and the show. He said no, he'd enjoyed it, but he did have one problem with it: the prop brush we used was too small. We needed one more like what he used. I told him he should send me one, and he said he would, and we all laughed that he better keep that promise. The whole audience had heard it. He sent it to me at Navy Pier a couple of weeks later with a note that said something like, "Dear Joey, this is what I meant. Big, not small. Sincerely, Rod." I still have the note somewhere, and my son uses the brush regularly.*

Blagojevich, who was paid an undisclosed amount for the good-natured and, by all accounts, gracious special appearance, also told the media he would donate to Gilda's Club after the performance. Gilda's Club chief executive officer LauraJane Hyde reported to us that "Blago never made good on that promise, and he didn't offer me a Senate seat, either."

After that epic night, the show was briefly sent on the road. Blagojevich was sent to jail for fourteen years.

## The Second City on TV

The runaway success of *Rod Blagojevich Superstar!* again gave credence to the adage that truth is stranger than fiction. In the aughts, The Second City leaned into nonscripted television with projects involving both a behind-the-scenes docuseries and—wait for it— a reality competition show.

In 2006, Second City and *SCTV* alum Dave Thomas worked with documentary filmmaker Sharon Bartlett on a three-part television endeavor called *The Second City: First Family of Comedy*. Co-hosted by Thomas, one-time Touring Company member (and "Kids in the Hall" member) Scott Thompson, and Joe Flaherty, the series focused on Second City's Chicago origin story, the history of *SCTV*, and the career paths of some of our most celebrated and notable alumni, with candid interviews from Andrew Alexander, Alan Arkin, Dan Aykroyd, Jim Belushi, Tina Fey, Mike Myers, Catherine O'Hara, Harold Ramis, and Martin Short.

The competition show *The Second City's Next Comedy Legend* premiered on CBC in 2007 with a warning that stated, "The following program contains coarse language, satire and a lot of people acting like idiots. Viewer discretion is always a good idea." Co–executive produced by Alexander and hosted by WWE diva (and one-time Second City Toronto student) Trish Stratus, the show saw eight hopefuls from all across Canada vie for a spot in the Canadian Touring Company. "We were looking for ways to educate a national audience on who we were and give the Touring Company prime exposure. This show was the answer," said

Alexander. With a judging panel composed of Mick Napier, Joe Flaherty, and London, Ontario, alumna Elvira Kurt, the eight contestants were eliminated one by one. Megan McDowell, who had never done improv before entering the competition, came out on top, winning a chance to go out on the road. McDowell is now a working stand-up based in Halifax.

Improv on TV hit a high note in 2007: Oprah Winfrey did a segment on her show in which Second City alumni Nyima Funk and Maribeth Monroe performed alongside the queen herself in a ("fun, but weird," recalled Monroe) segment promoting a short-lived NBC improvisational sketch comedy show.

## Fifty Years of Funny

The Second City pulled out all the stops (and a behemoth cheesecake topped with a signature bentwood chair) in December 1999 to mark its fiftieth anniversary. After a year of planning, the three-day celebration kicked off with a chartered Southwest flight full of alumni heading to Chicago from Los Angeles. Producer Alison Riley described the scene:

> *I flew to LA to get everyone on the plane. As I'm checking everyone in, it's like a wedding reception line. People who I hadn't seen in years are walking up to me and hugging me. By the end of the line, I was just shaking. Shaking. We get everyone onboard, and it's a full plane. Not five minutes after takeoff, everyone leaps to their feet and starts talking on the microphone, doing bits. Nobody sits down the whole flight, and we got to Chicago in what seemed like minutes.*

As the plane door opened at Midway Airport, Andrew Alexander, his wife, Diane, and Joyce Sloane greeted the guests—Second City expats of every generation—with a red-carpet runway and a champagne toast in the hangar. "To Second City, and to you," Alexander said, raised glass in hand. Robin Hammond, part of the team who ensured the weekend was a once-in-a-lifetime experience, explained why every detail had to be just right:

> *It was important to Andrew; it was important to everyone. We still had Bernie [Sahlins], Sheldon [Patinkin], and Joyce, and we knew this was a chance to honor the first generation. We looked at other, larger theaters around the city that could better fit everyone, but it was not home. Our prime concern was making sure all the alums felt welcome. No matter what year you were from or how famous you'd gotten—we wanted everyone to feel honored and like they were coming home. It had to be at North and Wells.*

Over the next three days, a series of star-studded panel discussions, performances, and parties lit up Piper's Alley, with students and ticket buyers mingling right alongside the

celebrities. "I can't believe this is happening," Sloane said, essentially speaking on behalf of every person in attendance, with Mick Napier correctly observing that "seeing all these people come back is like tripping on acid."

Friday's festivities were dedicated to an *SCTV* reunion, while Saturday and Sunday featured a lineup of panels and performances. "It's like they weren't talking to the audience; they were talking to each other, and the audience just got to listen in, which I thought was more special," said Jenna Deja, who produced the panel discussions that featured everyone from original 1959 cast member Mina Kolb and Compass co-founder David Shepherd to relative neophytes like Kay Cannon, Stephen Colbert, Keegan-Michael Key, and Jack McBrayer.

Saturday night culminated with *The Second City Alumni: One Night Only*, concurrently running in both the Mainstage and e.t.c. theaters. (The performers switched stages at the act break so they could perform in both rooms for both crowds). Directed by Napier and Matt Hovde, the show was a salute to classic scenes from The Second City archives, brought back to life by alumni from every decade, including Rose Abdoo, Scott Adsit, Jim Belushi, Danny Breen, Frank Caeti, Larry Joe Campbell, Steve Carell, Dan Castellaneta, Stephen Colbert, Kevin Dorff, Robin Duke, Brian Gallivan, Martin Garcia, Jeff Garlin, Ian Gomez, Peter Grosz, Mike Hagerty, Isabella Hofmann, TJ Jagodowski, Bruce Jarchow, Fred Kaz, Tim Kazurinsky, Keegan-Michael Key, Richard Kind, Robert Klein, David Koechner, Mina Kolb, Bob Martin, Jack McBrayer, Tim Meadows, Beth Melewski, Susan Messing, Colin Mochrie, Maribeth Monroe, Jane Morris, Bob Odenkirk, David Pasquesi, Harold Ramis, David Rasche, Horatio Sanz, Rebecca Sohn, Jim Staahl, Brian Stack, Betty Thomas, Miriam Tolan, Nia Vardalos, George Wendt, Fred Willard, and many, many more.

"Everyone went on and crushed their scene," said Riley, "because Second City actors all speak the same language. They had been only running these scenes beforehand for twenty minutes, and had one walk-through, but it was seamless."

"I got to interact with people I'd always looked up to," said Hovde, who first knew he wanted to be a part of The Second City after seeing a kid's show at the theater when he was ten years old. "One of the great things about Second City is that [the work] exists in that moment only. . . . It's meant to be live, in front of an audience, and just a little chaotic. It was pretty awe-inspiring to be in the room." To make sure as many people as possible could witness what was happening onstage, monitors were set up to run a simulcast feed in the

**FACING PAGE:**
Andrea Martin (left) and Martin Short at the *SCTV* reunion held during Second City's fiftieth-anniversary celebration

Andrew Alexander (left) and Bernie Sahlins at the fiftieth anniversary

just-unveiled new Training Center space (formerly home of the Black Orchid Theatre) on the fourth floor, which was transformed into a pop-up lounge for the occasion.

"At one point during the festivities, I said to the assembled crowd, 'This is three days of joy, remembrance, and an opportunity to erase any hard feelings or battle scars.' For me, that was the success of the weekend," Alexander said about the "yearlong organizational feat" that was brought together by Second City staff and creative leaders Diana Martinez, Robin Hammond, Jenna Deja, Kelly Leonard, Beth Kligerman, Alison Riley, Chris Pagnozzi, Monica Wilson, Bob Knuth, Keith Karem, Mike Conway, Kerry Sheehan, Mick Napier, Matt Hovde, and the legion of ever-dedicated staff members who power The Second City. Hammond, who handled the weekend's marketing and communications duties, summed up the intention behind the monumental, all-hands-on-deck efforts:

> At the heart of it, it was about connection. We wanted alumni to connect with their old friends and the different generations to talk and get to know each other. It was also a chance for the audience to connect with alumni and see their favorite performers. For us, we got to reconnect with the city of Chicago. We had Second City fiftieth-anniversary banners lining Michigan Avenue. The whole nation knew about it. We were everywhere.

Andrew Alexander (second from left) addresses the audience during the fiftieth-anniversary weekend as Len Stuart (left), Joyce Sloane, and Sheldon Patinkin look on.

Former Training Center student turned superstar Carell unpacked how the celebration affected him with the *Chicago Tribune* a few years later:

> *It was unexpectedly emotional for me, that whole weekend. I thought it would be fun. We'd drop in. I hadn't been to Chicago in a while. Nancy [his wife] and I could go back to where we used to live and check out some of our old haunts and have some good meals. And it was so much more than that. It affected me on a personal level, to reconnect with friends I hadn't seen in years. And it is that common thread. There's a bond there that I guess I didn't anticipate feeling so strongly—and a bond to the place and what it represented to all of us.*

Stephen Colbert (left) and Steve Carell perform the scene "Maya" during Second City's fiftieth-anniversary celebration.

# CHAPTER 9
## THE 2010s
### THE SECOND CITY ON FIRE

**A**FTER ALL THE hoopla surrounding The Second City's fiftieth anniversary subsided, the company was left with a half-century hangover, the cure for which was more celebration and recognition. In 2010, The Second City was awarded a Lifetime Achievement Award from Just for Laughs Montreal, the biggest international comedy festival in the world. A few years later, Second City earned Chicago's Fifth Star Award "for significant contributions to the city's arts and culture scene. (And let the record show that one Mr. Fred Willard was on hand for ceremonies in Montreal and Chicago's Millennium Park.) With nearly forty Jeff Awards in Chicago and multiple Canadian Comedy Awards racked up for Second City Toronto and its talent, we had a lot to be proud of.

Despite the onslaught of accolades, The Second City fought any instinct to slow down or become complacent. Despite the loss of some of the people who had been the heart and soul of The Second City since our earliest days through the present—Bernie Sahlins, Joyce Sloane, Sheldon Patinkin, Harold Ramis, Training Center writing program head Mary Scruggs, and Len Stuart—this decade would bring some of the most thrilling art in our history, revolutionize the ways our unique style of collaborative creation is taught and studied, build gainful new business endeavors, and survive one hell of a fire.

## The Second City Hollywood

Andrew Alexander never gave up on his California dreams for a West Coast home for The Second City, despite the previous disappointments in Pasadena and Santa Monica. "Having a Los Angeles outpost is a way to have a home for our alumni when they land in Hollywood, which so many of them eventually do," maintained Alexander. To provide improv training for especially industry-savvy students, Second City had been holding improv classes at the Hollywood Improv Lab since 2000. Eventually, additional classroom space was rented at 6560 Hollywood Boulevard to accommodate the growing program, which took over the second floor of the building in 2006 to set up shop full time as the third Second City Training Center. In 2010, The Second City Hollywood held a grand "reopening" weekend to show off a major makeover. The open house brought out alumni and friends including Larry Joe Campbell, Keegan-Michael Key, Tim Meadows, Joel Murray, Horatio Sanz, Fred Willard, and Chris Farley's brothers Kevin and John, who, along with Norm Macdonald and David Spade, hosted a special performance benefiting the Chris Farley House, a residential and outpatient treatment for addiction in the Farleys' hometown of Madison, Wisconsin.

Since the venue's overhaul, it has been a home away from home for transplanted Second Citizens, offering them a studio theater stage to play on, a sea of familiar faces, and a direct connection to the city's casting directors. "On a weekly basis, the industry reaches out asking for talent, and I'm happy to say we can deliver," said Carrie-ann Pishnak, director of marketing and associate producer for The Second City Hollywood.

For a brief time, the Hollywood location also served as headquarters for The Second City Network, a digital extension that had online hits with original web series like Brian Gallivan's *Sassy Gay Friend* and parodies of viral videos ("World's First Live Lip-Dub Divorce Proposal," "Help Obama Kickstart World War III!") that amassed millions of views. The call for Second City Network pitches also prompted Keegan-Michael Key and Jordan Peele to create some popular digital shorts, which then inspired the duo to approach Comedy Central about a potential TV project. After the cable network encouraged them to put together a show to workshop, Key and Peele got busy at The Second City Hollywood, testing scenes and getting audience feedback to hone their work in advance of their showcase at the Comedy Central Stage, where their performance got them a green light for *Key & Peele*.

## SCHOOLED AT THE SECOND CITY HOLLYWOOD

**Bill Hader:** When Bill Hader accepted the 2018 Emmy for Outstanding Lead Actor in a Comedy Series, he credited his time at The Second City in his acceptance speech, saying, "I took classes at Second City LA. I was taught there that you should always make the other people look good, so I hired other great actors who made me look good."

**Kiernan Shipka:** Already several seasons into playing Jon Hamm and January Jones's daughter on *Mad Men*, Kiernan Shipka joined the youth program at twelve years old and said her improv training has "helped me with pretty much every aspect of my life. . . . I think that Second City improv teaches you to not take yourself too seriously."

**Masi Oka:** In 2012, Second City Hollywood grad Masi Oka helped announce The Second City's international partnership with Yoshimoto Kogyo, one of Japan's largest entertainment entities, to bring improv training and performances to Japan. "In Japan, satire has long been looked down upon," he explained to the *Chicago Tribune*. "Attacking politicians and politics has been considered taboo. . . . This should be both a catalyst and a great jolt in Japan."

Edgar Blackmon
in Chicago's one
hundredth Mainstage
revue, *Who Do We
Think We Are?*

LEFT: The cast of Toronto's seventieth revue, *We've Totally (Probably) Got This!*: Stacey McGunnigle (left), Carly Heffernan, Jason DeRosse, Alastair Forbes, Nigel Downer, and Ashley Comeau in 2012

ABOVE: Holly Laurent (left) and Katie Rich in the *Who Do We Think We Are?* scene "Sporty and Fishy"

LEFT: Steve Waltien (left), Holly Laurent, Edgar Blackmon, Ross Bryant, Tawny Newsome, and Katie Rich perform "Cute" in *Let Them Eat Chaos*, 2013

Jen Candy grew up with comedy's elite as her extended family. In 2015, Candy brought candid conversations with the greats who had worked with or been influenced by her father, John Candy, to the stage. *Couch Candy* was a show directed by Holly Wortell at The Second City Hollywood. Alumni like Andrea Martin, Eugene Levy, Andrew Alexander, Ann Ryerson, Robin Duke, Dick Blasucci, Fred Willard, Martin Short, and more of Candy's "crazy aunts and uncles" chatted and, of course, discussed their favorite candy. (How does Short satisfy his chocolate cravings? With the Canadian delicacy Crispy Crunch, "a Butterfinger with attitude.") "It was one of those shows where the old guard liked coming to watch, even when they weren't on it," Candy said. "They like supporting each other. *Couch Candy* brought together old and new friends who all share the same love for comedy, for Second City, and for my dad."

# UP Comedy Club

Hollywood was not the only location to receive a swanky makeover. In 2012, UP Comedy Club opened on the third floor of Piper's Alley in the space formerly occupied by *Tony n' Tina's Wedding*. The upscale cabaret-style theater became the new home of "Booth One," the city's most storied seat. Originally a fixture at golden age Chicago hot spot the Pump Room, the original booth famously sat the likes of Frank Sinatra, Judy Garland, David Bowie, Josephine Baker, Audrey Hepburn, and Ronald Reagan. Andrew Alexander purchased the restaurant's updated version in 2011 in a private auction.

The new space was designated as a place to highlight the vast Chicago comedy landscape with improv shows, new theatrical productions, family programming, and the increasing number of names breathing new life into the stand-up comedy scene. "We saw UP Comedy Club as a great opportunity to incubate new works as well as have a place to showcase some of the country's funniest stand-up comedians," said Alexander. UP quickly proved to be a player on the stand-up scene, but, ultimately, stand-up dates were reduced in the club's regular programming. According to Alexander, "The great discovery was that the demand for our own stories and sketch-driven shows was greater than we expected."

Today, UP Comedy Club features some of The Second City's most exciting projects to date. *Chicago Live!* saw Second City partner with the *Chicago Tribune* for a weekly live radio and stage show that blended news and comedy. *#DateMe: An OkCupid Experiment* began development at The Second City Hollywood, where it was called *Undateable*. Written, directed, and performed entirely by the fearlessly funny women of The Second City, the popularity of *She the People* also necessitated multiple Chicago remounts, in addition to engagements at The Second City Toronto and the Woolly Mammoth in Washington, DC. *The Second City's Sunday, Bloody Mary Sunday* improv brunch, holiday shows like *The Second City's Nut-Cracking Holiday Revue*, the improvisational master class *Improv All-Stars*, and *Slate* and The Second City's politically charged *Unelectable You* have all found a home on the UP stage. The theater has even hosted heads of state. When Canadian icon Margaret Trudeau staged her "fearless, vulnerable and determinedly transparent" (according to *Chicago Tribune* critic Chris Jones) *Certain Woman of an Age*, her eldest son, Canadian prime minister Justin Trudeau, sat in the audience, beaming with pride.

**FROM TOP:** The cast of *#DateMe: An OkCupid Experiment*: Beth Melewski (left), Robyn Lynne Norris, Sam Super, Robyn Scott, Kevin Sciretta, and Chris Redd; Margaret Trudeau (second from left) is congratulated onstage at UP Comedy Club by her children, Canadian Prime Minister Justin Trudeau (left), Kyle and Alicia Kemper, and Alexandre Trudeau.

**LOIS KAZ**

Hired in 1968, Lois Kaz just about held the entire building together with her no-nonsense demeanor (and the enormous, jangly stash of keys she always carried) until her retirement in 2012. "She's been in a general state of irritation, aggravation, and general pissed offedness for forty years," ribbed producer Alison Riley at Kaz's bon voyage. "And despite all that, she really cares about us, she really loves us, she really takes care of us." In 1994, a group of Second City performers named their weekly long-form show (where improvisers take a single suggestion and create a lengthier piece out of it) in the e.t.c. "Lois Kaz" in tribute. "I was honored," Kaz said during her farewell remarks, "and when the reviews came out, it said, 'Lois Kaz can do no wrong.'"

## Celebrating Diversity

The Second City's mission is to entertain, inspire, and transform through fearless comedy. This mission found its way to sixteen talented upstarts in 2014 with the genesis of the Bob Curry Fellowship. Named for The Second City's first African American resident stage performer, Bob Curry, the program gives actors and improvisers from diverse multicultural backgrounds the opportunity to train and study at all three Second City locations. Program co-founder Dionna Griffin-Irons explained how the initiative first took off in Chicago:

> We knew there was this need in the community. I pitched an emerging-voices intensive for people of color that would take away the financial burden and get more people exposed to the improv art form. . . . I collaborated with my colleague [Second City Training Center artistic director] Matt Hovde, and we developed a curriculum that would not only hone sketch comedy and improv skills, but also taught the history of Second City, the business of comedy, and how to get hired.

Around the same time, *Saturday Night Live* was facing public criticism for the lack of diversity in its cast, giving Griffin-Irons an idea. "It was a good time to call NBC and tell them about this program to see if they'd support it," she said. "It was a win-win." NBC has sponsored the Bob Curry Fellowship every year in Chicago, with the first group of fellows knocking it out of the park. "They set the bar, and every group thereafter has had to match or exceed the talent that preceded them," Griffin-Irons said about the trailblazers.

Many graduates of the program have found a place in The Second City's talent pool and beyond. E. J. Cameron, a 2016 recipient of the fellowship, moved from Georgia to Chicago to pursue comedy "like a smart adult—with two hundred dollars and two duffle bags," he said. The day after he graduated from The Second City Training Center Conservatory, the school's prestigious cornerstone program for aspiring professional comedians, he began the Bob Curry program. "It's a super crash-course intensive. . . . You get what most people learn in years concentrated into this vitamin." After performing on a cruise ship and landing a spot in the Touring Company, Cameron joined the e.t.c. company for its forty-third revue, *Grinning from Fear to Fear*. Other Bob Curry fellows have gone on to find success on Second City's resident stages, in Second City Theatricals productions, and in Hollywood, both in front of and behind the camera.

The year 2015 saw the kickoff of two more banner events for The Second City. First, Second City Hollywood staff found themselves wondering "if we were missing an opportunity to be involved in the community," said Jen Hoyt, vice president of production. Realizing the city lacked a formal diversity festival, the Los Angeles Diversity in Comedy Festival was created, finding support over the years from 3 Arts Entertainment,

Nickelodeon, Thruline Entertainment, and NBC. Second City Hollywood artistic director Joshua Funk said:

> The LADCF is an opportunity for performers and audiences to socialize, take classes, attend panels, and watch some of the best diverse talent in the country. It's also a chance for the LA film and television industry to connect with the community. We feel it's important for us to not only shine a light on diversity during these four days, but to thread it through everything we do at Second City Hollywood throughout the year.

Also launching in 2015, The Second City and NBC's Break Out Comedy Festival has showcased some of the most dynamic emerging and seasoned comedic acts in stand-up, sketch, and improv. Providing a much-needed annual platform for stand-ups of color from all over the country to have their voices heard, the annual fest in UP Comedy Club has welcomed hosts including Second City alumni Tim Meadows, Christina Anthony, and David Pompeii, Touring Company vet Chris Redd, former Training Center student Danny Pudi, Azhar Usman, and Felonious Munk.

The 2014 Bob Curry fellows and faculty; top row: Patrick Rowland (left), Shantira Jackson, Torian Miller, Peter Kim, Damian Jason White, Travis Turner; middle row: Matt Hovde (left), Saliha Muttalib, Niccole Thurman, Rashawn Nadine Scott, Kimberly Michelle Vaughn, Sam Bailey, Lisa Beasley, Julie Nichols, Lauren Malara, Ali Barthwell; bottom row: Dionna Griffin-Irons (left), Chucho Pérez, and Dewayne Perkins

## The Second City Hits a High Note

As the decade got underway, the ensemble work at The Second City had never been stronger. Toronto's 2010 Mainstage revue *Something Wicked Awesome This Way Comes* set new box office records and nabbed a Canadian Comedy Award, and *South Side of Heaven*, the Chicago Mainstage's ninety-ninth revue, was hailed by the *Chicago Tribune* as "groundbreaking, richly textured and deliciously dark." Director Billy Bungeroth said the cast of that show, Edgar Blackmon, Holly Laurent, Timothy Edward Mason, Katie Rich, Sam Richardson, and Tim Robinson, went into the creative process with an attitude of "Let's figure out how to make the audience part of our weird club." Rich added, "There was no time to be scared. It was time to be fearless and raw and personal. . . . And here's the thing— we failed. A lot. We failed loudly and gloriously. But that's how we got the product we got." Some of that "pretty bonkers" product involved Richardson playing a stripper in a pink Speedo, a scene he called the most terrifying thing he has ever done in front of an audience. As he told the *Los Angeles Times* in 2017, "I do all these spins, kicks and toe touches. I pour water on myself. . . . It was the most terrifying because I didn't use padding in my pants, so depending on how good a day it was, it was in front of 350 people—sometimes it's cold, you never know."

The cast of *South Side of Heaven*: Timothy Edward Mason (left), Tim Robinson, Edgar Blackmon, Katie Rich, Holly Laurent, and Sam Richardson

SOUTH SIDE of HEAVEN

EDGAR BLACKMON   HOLLY LAURENT   TIM MASON
KATIE RICH   SAM RICHARDSON   TIM ROBINSON
DIRECTOR BILLY BUNGEROTH   MUSICAL DIRECTOR JULIE NICHOLS
assistant director JESSICA MITOLO   stage manager MEGHAN TEAL   producer ALISON RILEY & KELLY LEONARD
executive producer ANDREW ALEXANDER   THE SECOND CITY 1616 N WELLS ST CHICAGO IL
ScotWWarrenDesign.com

The Second City e.t.c.
SKY'S THE LIMIT
(Weather Permitting)
THURSDAY @ 8PM • FRI & SAT @ 8 & 11PM • SUN @ 7PM
312-337-3992 • WWW.SECONDCITY.COM

SOMETHING WICKED AWESOME THIS WAY COMES...

Things got even more fearless when renowned soprano Renée Fleming heard her voice played during the 2011 e.t.c. revue *Sky's the Limit (Weather Permitting)*. The serendipitous moment (we're still thankful she didn't sue us) sparked one of The Second City's most ambitious undertakings, a 2013 collaboration with the Lyric Opera of Chicago titled *The Second City Guide to the Opera*. "Opera is so stuffy; opportunities to poke fun were rife," said director Bungeroth. Written by Kate James, Tim Sniffen, and music director Jesse Case, the production found an unlikely comedic star in Sir Patrick Stewart, a friend of Fleming's. "One day at rehearsal, [Stewart] asks us, 'Don't you guys ever go up there and just wanna freak out and run out the back door, like, *I can't do this*?'" recalled Bungeroth, who won Chicago's top theater recognition, a Jeff Award, for directing the project. "We were like, 'Yeah,' and he goes, 'Me, too.'" (The Second City worked with the Lyric again for the emphatically titled collaboration *Longer! Louder! Wagner! The Second City Wagner Companion*.)

Aidy Bryant (left), Michael Lehrer, Tawny Newsome, and Chris Witaske pull the strings for Andel Sudik (left) and Mike Kosinski in 2012's *We're All in This Room Together*

Pairing comedy with more "highbrow" art forms birthed another artistic coup, this time with the Toronto Symphony Orchestra. *The Second City's Guide to the Symphony*, directed by Chris Earle, conducted by TSO music director Peter Oundjian, and hosted by Colin Mochrie, was a satirical symphony send-up that was originally scheduled to run for only two performances at Roy Thomson Hall in 2014. "Peter Oundjian had gotten wind of *The Second City Guide to the Opera* and thought there *has* to be something like this for symphonic music," said Carly Heffernan, one of the show's performers and co-writers. A tour was inevitable. "Next, we got to play the Kennedy Center with the National Symphony Orchestra, which was unreal. We've been all over the States, all over Canada. . . . To sing in some of these beautiful orchestra halls with a full orchestra accompanying you is so powerful."

Conquering the world of dance was next, which The Second City took on with Hubbard Street Dance Chicago in 2014. "We wanted to see what we could do on a grand scale," said Bungeroth, who helmed the end result, *The Art of Falling*. "Second City had always been about minimalism. We wanted to see what would happen if we went spectacle. We had five choreographers working in five different rooms at one time. . . . It was incredible. [Hubbard Street artistic director] Glenn Edgerton was a complete joy. There were never any limits." The surprising blend of comedy and dance, with a script written by Bungeroth, James, Mason, and Chris Redd, with music direction from Julie B. Nichols, connected with audiences and critics on a visceral level, with Andrew Alexander calling it "one of the finest pieces of theater I have had the chance to witness."

"It was about how comedy and dance serve this larger theme," Bungeroth said. "To love is to fall—to take a risk." *Chicago Tribune* critic Chris Jones wrote after the show's 2016 remount:

> *"The Art of Falling" is an exceptionally artful and life-affirming show. . . . It is rare to see the fusion of modern dance and the style of sketch comedy that was invented in Chicago. At this level, it is unprecedented. It is revelatory in all kinds of ways—not to mention mercifully irreverent and a whole lot of fun.*

"To love is to fall—to take a risk."

—**Billy Bungeroth**

**FROM TOP:** Cast of the e.t.c.'s 2014 revue, *Apes of Wrath*: Eddie Mujica (left), Brooke Breit, Asher Perlman (in back), Punam Patel, Carisa Barreca, and Tim Ryder; Tawny Newsome (left) and Mike Kosinski in the Chicago Mainstage's *Depraved New World*

## ABOUT LAST NIGHTS

When Second City actors are about to move on, they partake in a very special rite of passage. Co-artistic director of The Second City Chicago Matt Hovde explained:

*We try to honor each performer's time here by giving them complete control over the improv set on their last night, so they get to choose what their last moments onstage will be. Last nights can be incredibly moving . . . and sometimes incredibly long. Some actors choose to just improvise and play with their friends. Some perform their favorite scenes that they've been a part of, doing a little retrospective of their Second City career. And some just wave and get a pie in the face—part of the tradition is that during the last scene of the night, someone sneaks up and smashes a pie in their face so they have to say their farewells covered in whipped cream. Last nights are a messy tradition that can be very sweet.*

One particularly memorable last night was Keegan-Michael Key's, a "sprawling, two-hour set filled with amazing scenes and testimonials," recalled Hovde. "It felt like part celebration, part revival." Michael Lehrer, an alum of the e.t.c., got a tattoo live onstage during his last night. "I was abusing Adderall and too full of ideas, so I decided to get a gigantic permanent picture of Chicago on my back, even though I'm from Queens," said Lehrer.

Claudia Michelle Wallace said what made her last night meaningful was that it was "the first time my father ever saw me perform in a Second City show, but what I remember the most was the speech—and at the end of it, looking at my kids in the audience and telling them to follow their dreams."

**FROM TOP:** Nyima Funk pies David Pompeii in 2003 as Keegan-Michael Key looks on; Debra Downing gets her just desserts, also in 2003.

## Where There's Smoke, There's Satire

With a string of hits and a blitz of new talent, you could say The Second City was on fire . . . and then it actually was. Just around lunchtime on Wednesday, August 26, 2015, black smoke could be seen billowing out of The Second City Chicago's headquarters. The staff quickly realized that a fire had broken out—and would later discover the extra-alarm blaze was the result of a kitchen mishap at Adobo Grill, the restaurant on the first floor of the Piper's Alley building. A grease fire had traveled up the vent, all the way to the roof. In true Second City form, staff members alerting each other to the imminent danger first had to signify their sincerity with the universal comedian code for serious business: "This is not a bit."

As it was a summer afternoon, the first concern was safely evacuating the many children on-site for the Training Center comedy camps. "It was just a matter of physically checking every space, every office, every classroom and running through the building, forcibly telling people to get the f out," recalled Second City's vice president of operations, Mike Conway, who did not swear at any children on-site but *did* suffer from a small amount of smoke inhalation. He would never quite live down the subsequent news footage of being wheeled in a gurney (he was fine), but his capacity for calm under pressure was to be commended.

**OWNERS AND OPERATORS**

Since Andrew Alexander and Len Stuart took over The Second City in 1985, it has remained a family-run business. As CEO and executive producer, Andrew divides his time among Chicago, Los Angeles, and Toronto. Writer and producer Diane Alexander, Andrew's wife, developed and produced *#DateMe: An OkCupid Experiment* in UP Comedy Club for two years before bringing it to New York for an off-Broadway run in 2019. Her longtime professional relationship with Margaret Trudeau, the former wife of Canada's fifteenth prime minister, Pierre Elliott Trudeau, and the mother of the twenty-third, Prime Minister Justin Trudeau, inspired Alexander to create and produce Ms. Trudeau's one-woman show, *Certain Woman of an Age*, which premiered in 2019. Andrew and Diane's son, Tyler, is a former Marine who was vice president of brand and marketing and oversaw The Second City Network until leaving the company in 2016 to pursue a degree at DePaul University. After missing the camaraderie of the Marine Corps, Tyler was accepted into the Los Angeles Police Department and also hopes to stay involved in Second City's digital and television development opportunities.

After the passing of Len Stuart in 2016, his son, D'Arcy, became the company's chief operating officer, a role that has allowed him to create a vision for the future of Second City as an entertainment juggernaut. In 2018, D'Arcy and his wife, Amanda Hamilton, became the parents of future comedy magnate Kennedy Isla Stuart.

Steve Johnston joined the company in 2004 and served as president and managing partner of Second City Works before being appointed president of The Second City in 2017. "Over time, Steve had absorbed and learned the importance of what makes Second City tick," said Andrew Alexander. "He embodies the 'yes, and' philosophy. We are very lucky to have him on the team."

Andrew Alexander was in Los Angeles when the fire broke out, receiving the news in a call from his son, Tyler. "Tyler called me and said, 'The building's on fire.' I went online and saw the live feed, and it felt like I was watching my whole life go up in flames in real time." Kelly Leonard, who had moved offices two weeks earlier to a prime location in the Queen Anne–style building's turret, said, "I lost everything. Every memory, every photo . . . gone." Andrew flew back to Chicago that night. The next morning, he, Tyler, D'Arcy Stuart, Conway, and general manager Tim Christoffersen went in to survey the damage. "It was pretty devastating," Tyler recalled. "I knew the fire was bad, but to go through and see the extent of the damage was pretty shocking." As Andrew described, "The roof was caved in and my office was completely gone. Two entire floors of offices were obliterated. But amazingly, when I went into the theaters, they were in nearly pristine shape."

Despite the incineration of the administrative offices, it was as good an outcome as could be hoped for. Andrew's personal mementos had been photographed and preserved by Second City's archivist, Chris Pagnozzi, a year earlier. The stages and the historic exterior arches were safe, although, Tyler explained, "Once we started to get into the cleanup, we started to see that although the structure of the theaters and the stages had been preserved, there was a huge amount of smoke damage, and that's no joke." There was much to clean up, and the show must go on.

The company was prepared to forge ahead, catastrophe be damned. Just the day prior, the cast of the 104th Chicago Mainstage revue—Chelsea Devantez, Paul Jurewicz, Rashawn Nadine Scott, Sarah Shook, Daniel Strauss, and Jamison Webb—had begun work on their new show with director Ryan Bernier and musical director Jacob Shuda. The day of the fire, Scott was at work on a pitch in the Piper's Alley Starbucks when she was told to evacuate:

> *I watched fire truck after fire truck park and get to work. The number of people there made it feel like the whole building was going to burn down. . . . It was wild and ominous. After a little while, [producer] Alison Riley rallied us to the nearest bar to explain what was going on.*

At first, Webb feared the worst:

> *Every Second City revue has some hiccups along the way, I'm sure, but there was no precedent for this. . . . We had smudged the theater on the first day to rid it of bad vibes, so there was a moment of, ". . . we did extinguish the smudge sticks, right?" And I can safely say that we had. We did not want to be known as the cast that burned The Second City down.*

Devantez said it was a double punch to the gut:

> *When you're a comedian and there's a real emergency, it becomes clear instantly just how worthless your job is. We started cracking jokes immediately—"too soon" is an understatement. . . . It was hard to process what was going to happen to this building I loved so much. . . . It had been my home away from home for many years at that point.*

Faced with an unexpected hiatus, the cast moved across North Avenue to the Old Town Ale House where, Scott said, "in the midst of drinking, we decided to go to Boston for the weekend because there was no show. The next morning, we were at the airport. Shots make people bold." A few days later, rehearsals resumed in the nearby Chicago History Museum, but performances were canceled for at least three weeks, the longest period in the theater's history. (The odd show has been called off over the years due to extreme blizzard and/or polar vortex conditions.)

It was a different can of worms for the Training Center, where thousands of students were enrolled in classes—classes that had to be "re-homed" for an indefinite period of time. The vice president of The Second City Training Center, Abby Wagner, recounted the ensuing chaos:

> *We decided to try to get as many classes rescheduled as we could. . . . People and theaters who were supposedly our competitors started reaching out, saying, "We're here for you, whatever you need." We went straight to Walgreens and bought a ton of poster board and Post-its, bunkered down at [neighboring Old Town bar] Corcoran's, and got to work. . . . We'd meet in the morning and make sure all that day's classes had a space to meet and that the teacher and students knew where they were going. Then, we'd disperse across the city—everywhere from theaters like the Annoyance and A Red Orchid to places like Lincoln Park Zoo and Cards Against Humanity. We worked from eight a.m. to midnight every day for weeks. We had to.*

The remote operation went on for four weeks. "The students were truly blown away when they found out they still had classrooms to report to," said Alexander. "The encamped Training Center staff pulled off the miracle of miracles under the leadership of Kerry Sheehan, Abby Wagner, and Rosie Chevalier, who were the very definition of the term *ensemble*." When classes returned to Piper's Alley, the staff members who had given so much of themselves were left with something in return: matching flame tattoos. "We all got flames on our bodies, high on adrenaline. In hindsight, should we have gotten a permanent insignia on our bodies? Probably not," admitted Wagner. "But we did."

Tyler Alexander (left), Andrew Alexander, and D'Arcy Stuart at the Second City Training Center's reopening in 2016

Remarkably, The Second City Mainstage was ready to reopen just three weeks and one day after the disaster. Thanks to the tremendous efforts of (and improvisation by) the Chicago Fire Department, all three of The Second City's historic theaters had been spared, and a reopening event was planned for September 18. "Our first show was for the firemen who really went above and beyond their call of duty," said Jurewicz, a member of that Mainstage cast. (The 104th revue, *Fool Me Twice, Déjà Vu*, did eventually officially open in December.) "They literally risked their lives to sort of channel the water away from where the stages were," Conway said of the hundreds of thousands of gallons used to put out the flames. "You can still see the water lines outside the doors of UP Comedy Club on the third floor. I'll never clean those off." After an all-night effort to get things ready, Christoffersen opened the doors to the Mainstage. "I said, 'Ladies and gentlemen, the house is open,' and I locked eyes with Alison Riley," he remembered. "Her eyes were welling up. I thought something *else* had just gone wrong."

Bit by bit, the building has (mostly) recovered, thanks to the efforts of many, including Conway, Christoffersen, Stuart, then–facilities manager Jackie Anderson, creative director of marketing Bob Knuth, and Tyler Alexander. While it took more than a year for the escalators to get back up and running, the infamous backstage walls of the theaters—with their scrawled messages by countless alumni and noteworthy visitors—are just as grimy and profane as they have been for decades. And to prove that The Second City never lost its sense of humor for even a moment, T-shirts commemorating the fire were distributed to all employees, emblazoned with the mantra "Where there's smoke, there's satire."

**WALLS OF FAME**

One of the (many) perks of being a member of the Chicago Mainstage or e.t.c. casts has nothing to do with being applauded by an audience. Rather, true infamy lives on the backstage walls, where cast members immortalize each other's quotes from the improv sets. Alum Brad Morris broke down the significance of the tradition:

*The whole time you're part of Second City, you're pinching yourself that you're part of this club. There is no way more momentous to prove it to yourself–or to future cast members– than by being on the wall. And if [longtime stage manager] Craig Taylor writes down something funny or dumb you said, that's the top of the mountain. . . . Those quotes really capture how weird and spontaneous this place and its thinking truly is.*

Part of Second City's 2016 expansion saw the opening of 1959 Kitchen & Bar, where audience members, comedy students, and Second City talent all mingle. Designed by Bob Knuth, the restaurant's decor pays homage to The Second City of yesteryear. In fact, the history lesson begins before you even enter. The red front doors are replicas of those that graced the original Second City location, of which very few photographs exist. The hardware on the doors is notable, too. "When you come into 1959, you're grabbing the same handles John Belushi did to come into work," said Mike Conway about the circa early-1970s hardware, discovered in storage.

Inside, you will also find a bust of Harold Ramis in the corner, a prop from Harold Ramis Film School advisory board member Paul Feig's 2016 *Ghostbusters* reboot. It was graciously gifted to The Second City by Erica Mann Ramis, the late alum's widow.

## A Comedy Explosion

The Second City came back bigger and better than ever. On the heels of 2015's remodel of the Toronto Training Centre, the Chicago Training Center found itself ready to grow exponentially. "After the fiftieth anniversary, we really started to build momentum and tap into new people that hadn't been to Second City before," said Chicago Training Center artistic director Matt Hovde. "We got a lot of press coverage. We were seeing growth every year."

In 2016, a twenty-five-thousand-square-foot expansion doubled the size of the Chicago Training Center. "The myth is that the expansion happened because of the fire," Abby Wagner said. "It only ended up putting us back one term. It didn't hurt us. If anything, the fire weirdly kind of nudged construction along." Kerry Sheehan, who was president of The Second City Training Center from 2007 to 2017, explained how the project added not only to the building, but to the community:

> *It was super exciting to build two additional student theaters [the Blackout Cabaret and Judy's Beat Lounge] to give everyone the stage time necessary to fine-tune their skills, but I was most excited about building a space that could become a home away from home for our students, a creative space where students could learn, convene, collaborate, and create amazing things.*

The entrance to 1959 Kitchen & Bar on the second floor of Piper's Alley

As part of the build, the Harold Ramis Film School (HRFS) toasted its grand opening at a ribbon-cutting event on March 18, 2016. "My friend and colleague Harold Ramis lived the very ethos of 'yes, and,'" Andrew Alexander said. "He was a true collaborator and a true creative genius, and that's why, when the idea of opening a film school came about, his was the only name it made sense to put on the sign." The school was opened with the full support of Erica Mann Ramis, the late filmmaker's wife.

The first and only film school of its kind, the yearlong program exposes students to comedy theory, storytelling, screenwriting, and, naturally, improv. "I loved the possibility of helping start a school that would celebrate the serious business of comedy," said HRFS chair and Ramis's longtime producing partner, Trevor Albert. "And Harold's unique talents would be passed on to a new generation of comedic storytellers." Students are also invited to attend master seminars with comedy legends and Harold Ramis Film School advisory board members. These sessions have welcomed (just to name a few) Judd Apatow, Martin Short, Betty Thomas, and Eugene Levy, who emotionally ended his talk by saying, "Being able to talk to the students who are here now at the Harold Ramis Film School is just one of the honors of my life."

Not all efforts met with success, however, as a disturbing shift began to take place in Chicago following the 2016 presidential election. Cast members citing a frightening uptick in racist, misogynistic, and homophobic slurs from the audience led the company to post signs outside the theater doors declaring a zero-tolerance policy for hate speech. The signs read, "Second City has a zero-tolerance policy and does not allow hate speech of any kind whether it's directed toward our artists, employees or patrons. Those verbalizing any homophobic, misogynistic, xenophobic, racist or prejudiced comments will be asked to leave."

The move was met with mixed reviews from critics and audience members alike, and the signs certainly did not solve the problem. Half the cast of the e.t.c.'s *A Red Line Runs Through It* departed abruptly as a result of the pervasive negative atmosphere in front of and behind the curtain. Alexander admitted things could have been handled differently, and there was much to be learned:

> We didn't do the best job of protecting the cast and that, combined with some internal cast strife, caused this wonderful show to come to an abrupt end. The Red Line cast was an extremely talented, funny, and provocative ensemble. They created a truly edgy show on the heels of a very toxic political environment that bled into the theater on a nightly basis. The outgrowth of that environment produced the signage that was to express our zero-tolerance policy. We will be better prepared for the 2020 environment, which I am sure will be equally unpleasant.

**THE BENCH**
The wooden bench tucked away along the east wall of the Chicago Mainstage room, right behind the piano, is arguably the best seat in the house. "When I first started working as the box office manager, it was referred to as the director's or the producers' bench," said Beth Kligerman. "That was their domain. That was the place where Joyce [Sloane] would sit down to watch the show." In our modern era, when alumni come back to see a show, they will usually decline VIP treatment, instead opting to "just sit on the bench."

**JOHN KRAMER**

John Kramer is the bar supervisor at The Second City and has been an integral part of the company since he started here in 1981, and he has seen more than his fair share of changes in the building. "The front bar outside of Mainstage was the heart of the theater," he explained. "That was where you would hang out after the show and the audience had cleared out. Joyce [Sloane]'s office was right off the bar. We used to be extremely liberal with the liquor. . . . And as long as there was a manager there, they would keep the bar open, sometimes until four a.m." Kramer famously makes a point of connecting with every new member of the night staff by saying, "Welcome to show business."

There was offstage friction unfolding as well. Members of the night staff—the bartenders, servers, cooks, hosts, and dishwashers—felt increasingly bitter toward management, and there was a move in 2017 to unionize in order to address the many concerns about pay, communication with management, and overall treatment. "It was very emotional and heated," said Mike Conway. "In many ways, it didn't seem like Second City was practicing what they preached with their staff."

"Once upon a time, everything happened at night here. The producers, managers, everyone was here at night. With the classes and the rest of the business growing over the years, a lot of staff works regular daytime hours now. A connection had been lost," said John Kramer, a member of Second City's night staff since 1981.

Ownership, management, and many of the company's longtime employees were concerned that unionization would change the culture of The Second City. In an effort to make progress toward a resolution, Alexander said, "[Second City president] Steve Johnston, [co-owner] D'Arcy Stuart, and I met with the staff over several nights and days to listen and learn. It was a tense environment, but we asked them to give us twelve months to solve the problems." Ultimately, forming a union was voted against, but the effect of the efforts has been ongoing, Alexander explained:

> Many of our employees are struggling artists, and it's our job to help as much as possible to support and nurture their career goals. As management, it became apparent we had taken our team for granted and badly neglected their multiple hot-button issues. We now meet with night staff representatives on a regular basis to problem solve in the moment. I'm extremely proud of the improved state of our relationship.

Kramer reported, "I can happily say they really did everything they said they would, and more."

## A Comedy Force to Be Reckoned With

Building on the cornerstone philosophy of "yes, and," The Second City and the Kennedy Center unveiled plans in 2018 to bring several new sketch comedy revues and original scripted plays to Washington, DC. No stranger to the Kennedy Center since our first run there in 1996, The Second City has found several successes there with productions like the politically infused *The Second City's Almost Accurate Guide to America*, twisted Twain-wreck *When Life Gives You Clemens*, and holiday merriment like *Love, Factually* and *Twist Your Dickens*.

At Woolly Mammoth Theatre Company, where we have been staging work since 2009, shows like *Nothing to Lose (But Our Chains)*, *She the People*, and the box office

The Second City returned to television with specials in 2012 and 2015. *I, Martin Short, Goes Home*, which aired in 2012, featured Robin Duke, Joe Flaherty, Eugene Levy, Andrea Martin, and Fred Willard alongside Martin Short himself. *The Second City Project* on Global Television Network re-envisioned *SCTV* for the 2015 world. More TV is in the works, as The Second City announced a development deal with Insight Productions to partner on scripted and unscripted comedic projects in the coming years.

**FROM TOP:** The cast of *She the People* in 2018: Alex Bellisle (left), Emma Pope, Carisa Barreca, Kaye Winks, Katie Caussin, and (seated) Kimberly Michelle Vaughn; Eugene Levy addresses Harold Ramis Film School students in 2019.

record–smashing *Black Side of the Moon* (which opened four days after the 2016 election, requiring some unanticipated last-minute rewrites) have made Second City a comedy force to be reckoned with in DC. "It's apt for the pinnacle of sociopolitical satire to find a satellite home in the nation's capital, although most would agree Washington is already overrun with elected comedians," said Andrew Alexander.

In addition to making things official with the Kennedy Center, The Second City joined forces in 2018 with another equally formidable institution. In conjunction with DePaul University's School of Cinematic Arts, an unprecedented program was announced in May 2018. After the success of the Harold Ramis Film School, co-owners Alexander and D'Arcy Stuart found themselves asking, "How do we make this a program for people who want a college degree?" After reaching out to the director of DePaul's School of Cinematic Arts, Gary Novak, the plan was hatched quickly, with the university fully embracing the "yes, and" rule of improv—they suggested creating the first-ever master's degree in comedy.

Beginning with the fall 2019 semester, DePaul's offerings included a master of fine arts in screenwriting with a concentration in comedy, a bachelor of fine arts in film and television with a concentration in comedy filmmaking, and a minor in comedy filmmaking. Program director Jack C. Newell maintains that the long-term value of these first-of-their-kind programs will go well beyond the walls of either Second City or DePaul:

> No other film school offers the kind of program that we've developed with DePaul. Being able to get advanced degrees in comedy will create a whole new generation of filmmakers coming out of Chicago. My hope is that these students will then go on to become teachers at other institutions and that, years down the road, the future generations of filmmakers they teach will be exposed to and taught Second City's philosophies and sensibilities.

Less than four months after news broke of The Second City and DePaul University's collaboration, DePaul received a coveted spot on the prestigious *Hollywood Reporter* annual "Top 25 American Film Schools" list. "So rarely do you meet a goal so quickly," said Abby Wagner. "We hoped to eke ourselves out a position in three years. We were number thirteen, right out of the gate."

## "BE IN THIS MOMENT"

When Dick Costolo graduated from the University of Michigan with a degree in computer science, he took the only logical next step in his career: he moved to Chicago to take classes at The Second City. (He also eventually became COO and CEO of Twitter.) In a 2013 commencement speech at his alma mater, Costolo shared this story, and the takeaways have deep implications in life, in business, and, of course, in comedy:

*I was studying at Second City with [a] legendary director there, Martin de Maat. And Steve Carell was out onstage. Steve and I were in the same group, and he was improvising something . . . and I was backstage, and I thought of this amazing line. I thought, "I've got to go out there and get into this scene, and I'm going to get this line out." So I enter the stage, and I try to start moving the scene in the direction of what I wanted to say, and Martin stops the scene. Says, "Stop, stop." And he says to the whole class—but really he's talking to me—he says, "You can't plan a script. The beauty of improvisation is you're experiencing it in the moment. If you try to plan what the next line is supposed to be, you're just going to be disappointed when the other people onstage with you don't do or say what you want them to do. And you'll stand there frozen. Be in this moment."*

## "Yes, And" at Work

The equally goal-driven Second City Communications debuted a brand-new name in 2015. As Second City Works, the business arm of the company held true to its mission: to bring Second City's award-winning improvisation and comedy techniques to businesses and clients around the globe. That year, Kelly Leonard and Tom Yorton, the former CEO of Second City Works, published *Yes, And* with Harper Business. The book is an essential read for those seeking to become better leaders and more collaborative followers by employing these seven elements of improv:

1. **Yes, and,** by which you give every idea a chance to be acted on;

2. **Ensemble,** reconciling the needs of individuals with those of the broader team;

3. **Co-creation,** which highlights the importance of dialogue;

4. **Authenticity,** or being unafraid to speak truth to power and break the rules;

5. **Failure,** which is a good thing (really);

6. **Follow the follower,** which gives any member of the group the chance to assume a leadership role; and

7. **Listening,** in which you stay in the moment and know the difference between listening to understand and listening merely to respond.

*Yes, And* also delves into the valuable lessons that can be mined from some of the biggest successes—and failures—of high-profile business leaders, two of whom were once students of The Second City Training Center: former Twitter CEO Dick Costolo and Groupon's founder and ex-CEO, Andrew Mason.

**CLOCKWISE FROM TOP:** The cast of *Dream Freaks Fall from Space*: Ryan Asher (left), Jeffrey Murdoch, Kelsey Kinney, Tien Tran, Tyler Davis, and Nate Varrone; Martin Morrow (left), Rashawn Nadine Scott, and Jamison Webb in Chicago's 104th Mainstage revue, *Fool Me Twice, Déjà Vu*; Emily Fightmaster performs "Gender Alien" in the e.t.c.'s 42nd revue, *Gaslight District*.

## Comedy for a Cause and Effect

By all financial accounts, The Second City's businesses were booming in the 2010s, but the most important kind of prosperity was the kind that changed lives. Inspired by 2008's immensely successful *SCTV* reunion, *The Benefit of Laughter*, The Second City produced three philanthropic shows over the course of the decade, in addition to Chicago's annual *24 Hour* holiday-time marathon. In 2014, *The Second City All-Star Comedy Benefit* brought alumni including Scott Adsit, Aidy Bryant, Jack McBrayer, Tim Meadows, George Wendt, and Fred Willard back to the Chicago Mainstage for a night of fun and fundraising for Gilda's Club Chicago and The Second City Alumni Fund.

Three years later, *Take Off, Eh* made magic—and three hundred twenty-five thousand dollars—in Toronto. The benefit was put together to aid Spinal Cord Injury Ontario and Jake Thomas, the nephew of Dave Thomas, who had been recently paralyzed in a snowmobiling accident. Martin Short was the impetus for the sold-out event. His former *SCTV* co-star Thomas told the CBC, "Marty said, 'Let's do a show,' and I said, 'Well, I don't want to impose,' and he said, 'Nonsense! If it was my kid, I would impose on everybody, starting with you!'"

The night, which Short (and sometimes "Jiminy Glick") hosted, featured a once-in-a-lifetime lineup of the biggest Canadian names in comedy and music: Dan Aykroyd; Catherine O'Hara; Eugene Levy; "Kids in the Hall" members Dave Foley, Kevin McDonald, and Scott Thompson; comic Rick Mercer; Paul Shaffer; Rush's Geddy Lee; and musicians Murray McLauchlan and Ian Thomas, Jake's father, who told the CBC, "I'm deeply touched by all this love and kindness." Rick Moranis also agreed to bring his and Dave Thomas's iconic "McKenzie brothers" back to life, inspiring not only the evening's name but also some additional generosity. The "Great White North" hosts auctioned off the opportunity to join them (and their parkas) onstage to help reprise the famous *SCTV* segment.

"When Dave Thomas approached Andrew [Alexander] about *Take Off*, it was like putting the band back together," said the show's producer, Klaus Schuller, who also admitted, "I don't get starstruck often, but backstage I got into a conversation with Geddy Lee and Paul Shaffer about life and music, and I lost what was left of my mind."

More minds were lost during the 2017 benefit *I Can't Believe They Wendt There: The Roast of George Wendt*. With Wendt's nephew (and fellow Second City alum) Jason Sudeikis on roast master duty, the Chicago event saw Bob Odenkirk, Betty Thomas, Dave Koechner, Keegan-Michael Key, Tim Kazurinsky, Julia Sweeney, and Wilco lead singer Jeff Tweedy hurl their finest insults at one of the nicest people in show business. Undeserving target Wendt, who was even verbally assaulted by his wife, fellow Second City alum Bernadette Birkett, did get a chance to retaliate, but not before *Conan* regular

"Triumph the Insult Comic Dog" said his foulmouthed piece (thanks to the hand up the puppet, which belonged to Robert Smigel).

The epic four-hour show's many highlights included a video message from Wendt's former *Cheers* co-star Ted Danson, an original song performed by 1972 Second City alum David Rasche, a live resurrection of the "Super Fans" (*SNL*'s famous mustache-wearing, Mike Ditka–loving "Da Bears" guys), and a show-ending surprise guest even the producers had no clue was coming. Backstage, as event producer Liz Kozak and director Billy Bungeroth frantically looked over the running order to see if there was anything they could cut from the show—which was already running two hours over schedule—Chris Rock waltzed in with a couple of bodyguards and said, "I'm gonna fuck shit up." He headed right out onto the stage, and the crowd erupted.

"We were acutely aware there was another audience waiting outside to get into the theater for the regular eleven p.m. Saturday night Mainstage show," Kozak said about the unexpected addition. Sudeikis (who we later found out had been the one to invite Rock) and Koechner kindly went downstairs to glad-hand the crowd and thank them for their patience, but no one seemed upset—the whole building was just buzzing.

The roast raised more than two hundred thousand dollars for Gilda's Club Chicago and The Second City Alumni Fund. The eleven p.m. (now one a.m.) audience who waited those extra two hours forgave us.

## The Second Science Project

In improvisation, there's a comedic device known as the "callback," a moment in a scene or a show that brings back something mentioned earlier in a new context. It's the improv version of a full-circle moment.

Nearly six decades after Bernie Sahlins, Paul Sills, and Howard Alk opened our doors, The Second City headed back to the University of Chicago, where it all began, to explore the science of funny. In a truly full-circle partnership with the University of Chicago and its Center for Decision Research at the Booth School of Business, layers of laughter are being peeled back to examine behavioral sciences through the lens of improvisation.

When the idea sparked for Kelly Leonard, who now holds the title of executive director of insights and applied improvisation, he was given the green light by Second City president, Steve Johnston, to pursue it. "I was curious about the infinite applications that an academic research partner could help us to identify, verify, and bring to life," said Johnston, "in the spirit of reigniting and connecting all our realms at Second City—artistic, personal, and business performance improvement."

In an initial meeting with the Booth School's behavioral scientists and professors Heather and Eugene Caruso (who also happen to be married to each other), Leonard delivered his full spiel: "Improv is yoga for your social skills. Improvisation is loud group mindfulness. Improvisation is practice in abundant choices and agility and presence." He recalled:

> And when I finish, Heather says to me, "Kelly, we're behavioral scientists. We have decades and decades of research that shows us that people make bad choices for themselves. And what you're talking about is a pedagogy, an art form, a practice in allowing people to make better and different choices. Those two things have never been put together."

And now they have been put together, thanks to the Second Science Project. Here is one example of how we are marrying these two areas of expertise: the psychological theory of self-verification suggests that people feel reassured when their sense of self is supported by others. In our labs—our comedy classrooms—we are using this theory to create new improvisational exercises that let individuals see and hear the whole person across from them, not just the surface characteristics. Because being fully heard makes people feel valued. When they feel valued, they engage. And when they are engaged, they're at their best.

It seems that in a world where social disconnection has increasingly become the norm, all signs point to improvisation as being a remedy that reaches across human boundaries.

## The Second City's Next Act

"I remember when I first started at Second City in 1988, seeing all these matchbooks everywhere," said Kelly Leonard, "and on the inside, they said, 'The Second City: coming soon' to all these other cities. Almost all of them never happened." Despite the presumptive print, the essentially accurate truth is that The Second City has always succeeded by jumping into the unknown, embracing the crazy, and making it up as we go along. *Yes, and* there have been some misfires and (so far) one actual fire. But there's still so much ahead: new collaborations onstage and onscreen, a new home for The Second City Toronto, infinite discoveries in the ways that improv can improve lives, and the development of a new organization that will allow comedic artists take care of their own. The Second City is far from taking its final bow, and it will continue to make the world collectively laugh and think and illuminate (ideally, at the same time), just as it has for the last sixty wild, fiercely unpredictable years.

Inside The Second City Training Center space at North and Wells

# LASTWORD

After Harold Ramis passed away in 2014, President Barack Obama released this statement:

*Michelle and I were saddened to hear of the passing of Harold Ramis, one of America's greatest satirists, and like so many other comedic geniuses, a proud product of Chicago's Second City. When we watched his movies–from* Animal House *and* Caddyshack *to* Ghostbusters *and* Groundhog Day*–we didn't just laugh until it hurt. We questioned authority. We identified with the outsider. We rooted for the underdog. And through it all, we never lost our faith in happy endings. Our thoughts and prayers are with Harold's wife, Erica, his children and grandchildren, and all those who loved him, who quote his work with abandon, and who hope that he received total consciousness.*

The Second City has faith in happy endings, too, so it seemed fitting to close this book with Ramis's original "Lastword" from the 1999 edition.

FIRST SAW Second City in the summer of 1967. The actors were so accessible they were almost in your lap. I had this mixed feeling about the show: this is great, this is really funny. But I can do that. I've heard other people say that. In fact, when I was onstage, Betty Thomas was a waitress at Second City. I know she would look up onstage and say, "I can do that."

I enlisted in the workshop with Josephine Forsberg. An opening came up in the Touring Company, which Forsberg also directed. I honestly felt the place in the company should go to me. It wasn't just blind ambition. I thought I was doing good work. But she picked someone else. And I thought, "Well, I'm done." There was no angry blowup, no confrontation. Just me thinking "I'll go somewhere else." So I went around the corner to the Old Town Players Theater in St. Michael's Church. I started doing workshops there.

In the meantime, I started writing freelance features for the *Chicago Daily News*. I had approached Richard Christiansen, who edited the "Panorama" Sunday supplement, and I hounded him until he gave me some freelance work. After a while, he was publishing everything I wrote. In the summer of 1968, I sent some of my pieces to *Playboy*. They hired me to be the "Party Jokes" editor. That was their entry-level position.

One day, Richard Christiansen called me and said a friend of his, Michael Miller, was the new director at Second City, and he wanted me to meet him. I'd pretty much given up on Second City. I called Michael Miller, and he said, "All right, come down Saturday night for the second show. You'll go in the improv set." I hadn't been onstage in months. I figured this is it, either you do it or you don't. After the second show, we took suggestions. We went backstage. I volunteered for a number of pieces and went out and did them. Michael Miller was forming a new Touring Company, and, after seeing me improvise, he said, "All right, you're in." It was there I first met Brian Doyle-Murray and Joe Flaherty.

Bust of Harold Ramis
in 1959 Kitchen & Bar

This was in 1968, and Chicago was erupting. We had the race riots in the spring of 1968, the Democratic Convention in the summer, and then a year later the Chicago Seven trial. Abbie Hoffman used to come to The Second City then. He improvised with us as an alibi during the trial. When the Weathermen were in the streets, he was with us. He actually played Judge Hoffman onstage, which was cool.

In the Touring Company, we had started working up our anti-war material. Bernie Sahlins booked us into West Point. Our act was greeted with stony silence. Another time, Joyce Sloane booked us into a nightclub in Louisville, Kentucky. We had a lot of sacrilegious material and anti-war material in the show, and they hated us. Someone threw a glass at the stage, I remember. We rewrote the show. We basically took a lot of *Playboy* "Party Jokes" and acted them out onstage. It was the only safe thing we could think of. We also worked up a country western song called "If I'd a Known She Was Dead I'd Never Have Asked Her to Dance."

I worked at *Playboy* through 1968. Then Bernie Sahlins decided to move the current resident company to New York and moved us in as the new resident company. We worked up a show and called ourselves the "Next Generation." We looked like hippies, but we weren't really, and we weren't very good. We had a couple of good pieces. We improvised well. But our stuff was rough. I remember one of the columnists from the papers saw the show in previews and wrote, "If this is the 'next generation,' let's have the old generation back."

The first show wasn't very good. The second show we got a little better. After the third show, things started getting good. It was fun. I felt lucky to be at Second City during that time. It was the best job you could have in Chicago. What Second City taught me was how to play well with others. Those who get it, learn that.

Second City also makes it possible for performers to experience every actor's nightmare—to be in a play and not know what play you're in or what your dialogue is. We do that every night by choice at Second City. We go out there and put ourselves in the actor's nightmare. It inspires a general feeling of delightful hysteria.

HAROLD RAMIS
1999

# ACKNOWLEDGMENTS

**A** TREMENDOUS THANK-YOU to every single alum and staff member past or present who shared their memories and perspectives for this project, and especially to Catherine O'Hara; resident Second City historians and sounding boards Beth Kligerman, Kelly Leonard, Alison Riley, and Dionna Griffin-Irons; archival superhero Chris Pagnozzi; creative director of marketing and brand Bob Knuth; Lisa E. Reardon of Common Good Editorial; and Doug Seibold, Morgan Krehbiel, and Helena Hunt from Agate Publishing.

Thank you to all the fellow improvisers at the Chicago Fire Department, the City of Chicago, The Hartford, and everyone who opened their doors to us as comedy sanctuaries when Second City was smoked out, including A Red Orchid Theatre, Acting Studio Chicago, the Annoyance Theatre and Bar, Athenaeum Theatre, Bughouse Theater, Cards Against Humanity, Chemically Imbalanced Comedy, ComedySportz Theater, Corcoran's Grill and Pub, Gorilla Tango Theatre, Hotel Lincoln, Hot Tix, Hubbard Street Dance Chicago, iO, Jellyvision, Lifeline Theatre, Lincoln Park Zoo, the Old Town School of Folk Music, The Onion, pH Comedy Theater, The Public House Theatre, SPACE by Doejo, Stage 773, Steppenwolf Theatre, Theater Wit, Tribeca Flashpoint Media Arts Academy, Uptown Underground, Vagabond School of the Arts, and Zanies Standup Comedy Learning Center.

And finally, thank you to the millions of audience members who have allowed The Second City the privilege of making you laugh for sixty years (and counting).

Liz Kozak would also like to thank Andrew Alexander; Tyler Alexander; Joe, Posey, and Hazel Kozak; Noreen and Gerry Lekas; Joe Lekas; Jed Enlow; Ariel Christian; Billy Bungeroth; and Martin Short, for the pep talk after I didn't get into my high school's production of *Our Town* in 1993.

# THE ALUMNI

There is one fake name on this list of over 700.
Only four living people know which one it is.

**Playwrights Theatre Club and The Second City New York**

**1955–1959**

Alan Alda
Jane Alexander
Howard Alk
Alan Arkin
Larry Arrick
Rose Arrick
Ed Asner
Sandy Baron
Lloyd Battista
Walter Beakel
Shelley Berman
Haym Bernson
Roger Bowen
Hildy Brooks
R. Victor Brown
Jack Burns
Mona Burr
Loretta Chiljian
Del Close
Robert Coughlan
Barbara Dana
Severn Darden
Kornel Michael David
Bob Dishy
MacIntyre Dixon
Paul Dooley
Andrew Duncan
Tom Erhart
Theodore J. Flicker
Barbara "Bobbi" Gordon
Mark Gordon
Philip Baker Hall
Larry Hankin
Valerie Harper
Barbara Harris
Jo Henderson
Mo Hirsch
Kenna Hunt
Henry Jaglom
Linda Lavin
Martin Lavut

Sid Lazard
Mickey LeGlaire
Ron Leibman
Richard Libertini
Freya Manston
William Allaudin Mathieu
Elaine May
Paul Mazursky
Anne Meara
Lucy Minnerle
George Morrison
Mike Nichols
Tom O'Horgan
Robert Patton
Nancy Ponder
Diana Sands
Reni Santoni
Linda Segal
Omar Shapli
David Shepherd
Suzanne "Honey" Shepherd
George Sherman
Peg Shirley
Paul Sills
Viola Spolin
Leslie J. Stark
Jerry Stiller
Ron Weyand
Collin Wilcox
Mary Louise Wilson

**The Second City Chicago**

**1959**

Howard Alk
Roger Bowen
Severn Darden
Andrew Duncan
Barbara Harris
Mina Kolb
William Allaudin Mathieu
Sheldon Patinkin
Bernard Sahlins
Paul Sills
Eugene Troobnick

**1960**

Alan Arkin
Paul Sand
Joyce Sloane

**1961**

Bill Alton
John Brent
Hamilton Camp
Del Close
Melinda Dillon
Anthony Holland
Zohra Lampert
Alan Myerson
Irene Riordan
Joan Rivers
Avery Schreiber

**1962**

Mona Burr
Dennis Cunningham
Dick Schaal

**1963**

Jack Burns
MacIntyre Dixon
Ann Elder
Judy Harris
Melissa "Sally" Hart
Richard Libertini
Omar Shapli

**1964**

Ian Davidson
Eugene Kadish
Fred Kaz
Harv Robbin
David Steinberg

**1965**

Joan Bassie
Robert Benedetti
Alex Canaan
Sondra Caron
Josephine Forsberg
Judy Graubart
Robert Klein
David Paulsen
Fred Willard

**1966**

Bob Curry
Sid Grossfeld
Sandy Holt
Jon Shank
David Walsh
Penny White

**1967**

J. J. Barry
Peter Boyle
Martin Harvey Friedberg
Burt Heyman
Lynne Lipton
Ira Miller

**1968**

Murphy Dunne
Michael Miller
Carol Robinson

**1969**

David Blum
Martin de Maat
Brian Doyle-Murray
Jim Fisher
Joe Flaherty
Nate Herman
Pamela Hoffman
Roberta Maguire
Judy Morgan
Harold Ramis
Eric Ross
Cyril Simon
Paul Taylor

**1971**

John Belushi
Eugenie Ross-Leming
Dan Ziskie

**1972**

David Rasche
Ann Ryerson

**1973**

John Candy
Stephanie Cotsirilos
Tino Insana
Bill Murray

Jim Staahl
Betty Thomas

**1974**

Dan Aykroyd
Cassandra Danz
Don DePollo
Michael J. Gellman
Allan Guttman
Deborah Harmon
Richard Kurtzman
Eugene Levy
Raul Moncada
Rosemary Radcliffe
Gilda Radner
Mert Rich
Doug Steckler
Paul Zegler

**1975**

Bernadette Birkett
Miriam Flynn
George Wendt

**1976**

Will Aldis
Eric Boardman
Steven Kampmann
Shelley Long
Jim Sherman

**1977**

Cynthia Cavalenes
Larry Coven

**1978**

Jim Belushi
Tim Kazurinsky
Audrie Neenan
Lawrence J. Perkins
Maria Ricossa

**1979**

Danny Breen
Mary Gross
Bruce Jarchow
Nancy McCabe-Kelly

**1980**

Meagen Fay
Lance Kinsey
Rob Riley

**1981**
Susan Bugg
John Kapelos
Rick Thomas

**1982**
Nonie Newton-Breen
Cheryl Sloane
Craig Taylor

**1983**
Bekka Eaton
Ed Greenberg
Michael Hagerty
Isabella Hofmann
Richard Kind

**1985**
Andrew Alexander
Mindy Bell
Jim Fay
Mona Lyden
Len Stuart

**1986**
Dan Castellaneta
Rick Hall
Bonnie Hunt
Maureen Kelly
Harry Murphy

**1987**
Steve Assad
Kevin Crowley
Aaron Freeman
Ruby Streak
Barbara Wallace
Ron West

**1988**
Joe Liss
Mike Myers

**1989**
Chris Farley
Tim Meadows
Joel Murray
David Pasquesi
Judith Scott
Holly Wortell

**1990**
Tom Gianas
Bob Odenkirk
Tim O'Malley
Jill Talley

**1991**
Fran Adams
Cynthia Caponera
Steve Carell
Michael McCarthy
John Rubano

**1992**
Paul Dinello
Kelly Leonard
Ruth Rudnick
Amy Sedaris

**1993**
Stephen Colbert
David Razowsky

**1994**
Scott Adsit
Scott Allman
Jackie Hoffman

**1995**
Rachel Dratch
Jon Glaser
Jenna Jolovitz
Adam McKay

**1996**
Kevin Dorff
Tina Fey
Mick Napier
Lyn Pusztai

**1997**
Jim Zulevic

**1998**
Rachel Hamilton
TJ Jagodowski
Susan Messing
Jeff Richmond
Tami Sagher
Rich Talarico
Stephnie Weir

**1999**
Ed Furman
Beth Kligerman

**2000**
Craig Cackowski
Sue Gillan
Angela V. Shelton

**2001**
Debra Downing
Nyima Funk
Martin Garcia
Michael Kennard
David Pompeii

**2002**
Brian Boland
Joshua Funk
Al Samuels
Abby Sher

**2003**
Dan Bakkedahl
Lisa Brooke

Liz Cackowski
Antoine McKay
Jean Villepique

**2004**
Brian Gallivan
Robin Hammond
Maribeth Monroe
Alison Riley
Claudia Michelle
  Wallace

**2005**
Matt Craig
Molly Erdman

**2006**
Joe Canale
Ithamar Enriquez
Kirk Hanley
Marc Warzecha

**2007**
Matt Hovde
Brad Morris
Amber Ruffin

**2008**
Lauren Ash
Jimmy Carlson
Shelly Gossman
Anthony LeBlanc
Michael Patrick
  O'Brien
Emily Wilson

**2009**
Andy St. Clair
Monica Wilson

**2010**
Allison Bills
Timothy Edward Mason
Julie B. Nichols
Sam Richardson
Tim Robinson

**2011**
Edgar Blackmon
Billy Bungeroth
Holly Laurent
Katie Rich
Meghan Teal

**2012**
Tim Baltz
Jeremy Smith
Mary Sohn
Steve Waltien

**2013**
Ross Bryant
Bob Knuth
Tawny Newsome

**2014**
Ryan Bernier
Chelsea Devantez
John Hartman
Paul Jurewicz
Mike Kosinski
Jacob Shuda
Daniel Strauss
Christine Tawfik
Emily Walker

**2015**
Rashawn Nadine Scott
Sarah Shook
Jamison Webb

**2016**
Shantira Jackson
Kelsey Kinney
Martin Morrow
Vinnie Pillarella
Lesley Stone

**2017**
Ryan Asher
Tyler Davis
Jen Hoyt
Jeffrey Murdoch
Tien Tran
Nate Varrone

**2018**
Emma Pope
Kimberly Michelle
  Vaughn

**The Second City
Toronto**

**1973**
Andrew Alexander
Dan Aykroyd
Valri Bromfield
Brian Doyle-Murray
Jayne Eastwood
Gino Empry
Joe Flaherty
Fred Kaz
Gilda Radner
Bernard Sahlins
Gerry Salsberg
Sam Shopsowitz
Joyce Sloane

**1974**
John Candy
Todd Jeffrey Ellis
Piers Gilson
Allan Guttman
Eugene Levy
Catherine O'Hara
Sheldon Patinkin

Jim Patry
Rosemary Radcliffe

**1975**
Carol Cassis
Ben Gordon
Andrea Martin
John Monteith
Dave Thomas

**1976**
Peter Aykroyd
Brenda Donohue
Len Stuart

**1977**
Del Close
Robin Duke
Steven Kampmann
Robin McCulloch
Martin Short
Dave Thompson
Peter (PJ) Torokvei

**1978**
Scott Baker
Sally Cochrane
Cathy Gallant

**1979**
Maggie Butterfield
Don DePollo
Don Dickinson
Melissa Ellis
Derek McGrath
Tony Rosato
Kim Sisson
Mary Charlotte Wilcox

**1980**
Tom Baker
Gabe Cohen
Steve Ehrlick
John Hemphill
Kathleen Laskey
Denise Pidgeon
Wendy Slutsky

**1981**
Ken Innes
Jerrold Karch
Deborah Kimmett

**1982**
Michael J. Gellman
Don Lake

**1983**
Donald Adams
Bob Derkach
June Graham
Bruce Hunter
Ron James

Madelyn Keane
Debra McGrath
Lyn Okkerse
Peter Okkerse
Bruce Pirrie
Jane Schoettle
Blaine Selkirk
Adrian Truss

**1984**
Sandra Balcovske
Karen Poce

**1985**
Dana Andersen
Bob Bainborough
Kevin Frank
Linda Kash
Dorothy Tenute

**1986**
David Huband
Jeff Michalski
Mike Myers
Deborah Theaker
Mark Wilson

**1987**
Tamar Malic
Ryan Stiles
Audrey Webb

**1988**
Neil Crone
Wendy Hopkins
Lindsay Leese
Colin Mochrie
Alana Shields
Tim Sims

**1989**
Patrick McKenna

**1990**
Kathryn Greenwood
Karen Hines
Gary Pearson
Ed Sahely

**1991**
Christopher Earle
Nick Johne
Jenny Parsons
Judith Scott
Peter Sherk
Brian Smith

**1993**
Andrew Currie
Jackie Harris
Steve Morel
Paul O'Sullivan
Jonathan Wilson

**1994**
Lori Nasso
Janet Van De Graaff

**1995**
Tamara Bick
James Carroll
Kerry Garnier
Albert Howell
Nancy Marino
Teresa Pavlinek

**1996**
Jennifer Irwin
Mollie Jacques
Bob Martin
Jack Mosshammer

**1997**
Marc Hickox
Melody Johnson
Arnold Pinnock
Angela V. Shelton

**1998**
Gavin Crawford
Tracy Dawson
Andrew Dollar
Marypat Farrell
Jerry C. Minor
Doug Morency
Lee Smart
Gina Sorell
Jennifer Whalen

**1999**
Paul Bates
Lisa Brooke
Kevin Dorff
K. McPherson Jones

**2000**
Geri Hall
Sandy Jobin-Bevans
Carolyn Taylor

**2001**
Aurora Browne
Paul Constable
Jennifer Goodhue
Nathan David Shore

**2002**
Matt Baram
Pat Kelly

**2003**
Jamillah Ross
Naomi Snieckus

**2004**
Derek Flores
Rebecca Northan

**2005**
Lauren Ash
Steven Del Balso
Mick Napier
Anand Rajaram
Peter Schuller

**2006**
Jim Annan
Scott Montgomery
Matt Reid

**2007**
Marty Adams
Darryl Hinds
Karen Parker
Leslie Seiler

**2008**
Ashley Botting
Kerry Griffin
Reid Janisse

**2009**
Rob Baker
Dale Boyer
Adam Cawley
Caitlin Howden

**2010**
Inessa Frantowski
Kris Siddiqi

**2011**
Ashley Comeau
Jason DeRosse
Nigel Downer
Alastair Forbes
Carly Heffernan

**2012**
Craig Brown
Jan Caruana
Christina Cicko
Stacey McGunnigle
Allison Price

**2013**
Sophie Santerre
Connor Thompson
Kevin Vidal

**2014**
Sarah Hillier
Etan Muskat
Kevin Whalen

**2015**
Leigh Cameron
Kyle Dooley
Becky Johnson
Meaghan Maguire
Kirsten Rasmussen

**2016**
Roger Bainbridge
Lee Cohen
Brandon Hackett
Lindsay Mullan
Ann Pornel

**2017**
Nadine Djoury
Devon Hyland
Colin Munch
Paloma Nuñez
Georgia Priestley-
  Brown
Allana Reoch

**2018**
Jordan Armstrong
Jen Hoyt
Sharjil Rasool
Chris Wilson

**2019**
Christine Groom
Bob Knuth

## The Second City e.t.c.

**1983**
Bill Applebaum
Rob Bronstein
Don DePollo
Jim Fay
Susan Gauthier
Carey Goldenberg
Jeff Michalski
Jane Morris
Bernard Sahlins
Joyce Sloane
Ruby Streak

**1984**
Steve Assad
Dan Castellaneta
Isabella Hofmann
Maureen Kelly
Harry Murphy

**1985**
Andrew Alexander
Len Stuart

**1986**
Mark Belden
Mindy Bell
Kevin Crowley
Kevin Doyle
Joe Keefe
Barbara Wallace

**1987**
Chris Barnes
Madeleine Belden
Joe Liss

**1988**
Laura Hall
Judith Scott
Jill Talley
Holly Wortell

**1989**
Mark Beltzman
Dan Gillogly
Nate Herman
Michael McCarthy
Ruth Rudnick
Ron West

**1990**
Fran Adams
Steve Carell
Tom Gianas
John Rubano

**1991**
Rose Abdoo
Megan Moore Burns
Peter Burns
Ken Campbell
Jeff Garlin
Dave Razowsky

**1992**
Scott Allman
Stephen Colbert
Jimmy Doyle
Ian Gomez
Jackie Hoffman
Jenna Jolovitz
Kelly Leonard

**1993**
Scott Adsit
Michael Broh
Norm Holly
Nia Vardalos

**1994**
John Hildreth

**1995**
Adam McKay
Aaron Rhodes
Jeff Richmond
Dee Ryan
Brian Stack
Miriam Tolan
Jim Zulevic

**1996**
Neil Flynn
Laura Krafft

Jerry C. Minor
Horatio Sanz
Peter Zahradnick

**1997**
Aaron Carney
Matt Dwyer
Rachel Hamilton
Mick Napier
Rebecca Sohn
Rich Talarico

**1998**
Craig Cackowski
Kristin Ford
Noah Gregoropoulos
Tami Sagher

**1999**
Ali Farahnakian
Martin Garcia
Sue Gillan
Beth Kligerman
Jack McBrayer
David Pompeii
Lyn Pusztai
Klaus Peter Schuller
Angela V. Shelton
Trey Stone
Michael Thomas

**2000**
Andy Cobb
Debra Downing
Abby Sher

**2001**
Samantha Albert
Joshua Funk
TJ Jagodowski
Keegan-Michael Key

**2002**
Nyima Funk
Peter Grosz
Jean (Augustyn)
  Villepique

**2003**
Jeremy Wilcox

**2004**
Jen Bills
Lee Brackett
Frank Caeti
Matt Craig
Rebecca Drysdale
Ithamar Enriquez
Robin Hammond
Alison Riley

**2005**
Rebecca Sage Allen
Jimmy Carlson
Alex Fendrich
Robert Janas
Chad Krueger
Niki Lindgren
Nicky Margolis

**2006**
Amanda Blake Davis
Kirk Hanley
Andy St. Clair

**2007**
W. Shane Oman
Marc Warzecha

**2008**
Christina Anthony
Mike Descoteaux
Tom Flanigan
Megan Grano
Laura Grey
Matt Hovde
Timothy Edward Mason
Bruce Pirrie
Joseph Ruffner

**2009**
Beth Melewski

**2010**
Tim Baltz
Billy Bungeroth
Jesse Case
Brendan Jennings
Mary Sohn
Monica Wilson

**2011**
Kyle Anderson
Aidy Bryant
Jessica Joy
Michael Lehrer

**2012**
Ryan Bernier
Mike Kosinski
Tawny Newsome
Andel Sudik
Chris Witaske

**2013**
Carisa Barreca
Brooke Breit
Alex Kliner
Punam Patel

**2014**
Eddie Mujica
Asher Perlman
Tim Ryder

**2015**
Lisa Beasley
Bob Knuth
Anthony LeBlanc
Scott Morehead
Rashawn Nadine Scott

**2016**
Aasia LaShay Bullock
Laura Hum
Peter Kim
Katie Klein
Julie Marchiano
Lesley Stone

**2017**
Sayjal Joshi
Andrew Knox
Alan Linic
Jacob Shuda
Jasbir Singh Vazquez
Tien Tran

**2018**
Emily Fightmaster
Jen Hoyt
Katie Kershaw
Anneliese Toft

**2019**
Atra Asdou
E.J. Cameron
Mark Campbell
Laurel Krabacher
Chuck Norment

## The Second City Northwest (Rolling Meadows, Illinois)

**1988**
Fran Adams
Andrew Alexander
Jon Anderson
Mark Beltzman
Bill Cusack
Fred Kaz
Tim O'Malley
David Pasquesi
Ruth Rudnick
Cheryl Sloane
Joyce Sloane
Len Stuart

**1989**
Steve Carell
Christina Dunne
Jim Jatho
Sean Masterson

John Michalski
David Razowsky
John Rubano
Claudia Smith
Faith Soloway

**1990**
Ken Campbell
Kevin Crowley
Amy Sedaris

**1991**
Scott Allman
Megan Moore Burns
Stephen Colbert
Paul Dinello
Ian Gomez
Jackie Hoffman
John Holtson
Mick Napier
Charlie Silliman
Nia Vardalos

**1992**
Scott Adsit
Tom Gianas
John Hildreth
Norm Holly
Mark Levenson
Aliza Murrieta
Aaron Rhodes
Mitch Rouse
Jim Zulevic

**1993**
Peter Burns
Deborah Goldberg
Karol Kent
Kelly Leonard
John Thies
Tracy Thorpe

**1994**
Renee Albert
Pat Andrews
Bernadette Birkett
Martin Brady
Matt Dwyer
Jennifer Estlin
Pat Finn
Michael J. Gellman
David Koechner
Ron West

**1995**
Michael Bloom
Anne Libera
Theresa Mulligan
Todd Stashwick
Nancy Walls

## The Second City Edmonton

**1979-1982**
Andrew Alexander
Bob Bainborough
Sandra Balcovske
Lorraine Behnan
Gabe Cohen
Bob Derkach
Don Dickinson
Robin Duke
Michael J. Gellman
Christine Henderson
Sparky Johnston
Jerrold Karch
Gail Kerbel
Keith Knight
Don Lamont
David Mann
Kat Mullaly
Jeanette Nelson
Jan Randall
Mert Rich
Carol Sinclair
Kevin Smith
Veena Sood
Doug Stratton
Len Stuart
Adrian Truss

## The Second City London, Ontario

**1983-1992**
Donald Adams
Andrew Alexander
Dana Andersen
Elizabeth Baird
Sandra Balcovske
Jack Banks
John Bynum
Luc Casimiri
Alan Catlin
John Costello
Catherine Creary
Martin de Maat
Patrick Dubois
Todd Jeffrey Ellis
Kevin Frank
Michael J. Gellman
Mike Goran
Kathryn Greenwood
Allan Guttman
David Healey
Karen Hines
Shari Hollett
Wendy Hopkins
Bruce Hunter
Linda Kash

Madelyn Keane
Joe Keefe
Peter Keleghan
Deborah Kimmett
Elvira Kurt
Lindsay Leese
Frank McAnulty
Patrick McKenna
Steve Morel
Sue Morrison
Barbara Muller
Lori Nasso
Lyn Okkerse
Jenny Parsons
Bruce Pirrie
Karen Poce
Ed Sahely
Jerry Schaefer
Jane Schoettle
Devin Scott
Paul Scott
Blaine Selkirk
Tim Sims
Brian Smith
Mairlyn Smith
Rob Smith
Len Stuart
David Talbot
Deborah Theaker
Adrian Truss
Nia Vardalos
Audrey Webb
Jonathan Wilson
Mark Wilson

## The Second City Detroit

**1993**
Andrew Alexander
Robin Bucci
Colin Ferguson
John Holtson
Mark Levenson
Jerry C. Minor
Suzy Nakamura
Andrew Newberg
Lyn Okkerse
Tim Pryor
Jackie Purtan
Angela V. Shelton
Len Stuart

**1994**
Tom Gianas
Nancy Hayden
Chris Smith
Todd Stashwick

**1995**
Peter Burns
John Farley
Joshua Funk
Dionna Griffin
Grant Krause
Emily Rose Merrell
Ed Smaron
Rico Bruce Wade

**1996**
Larry Joe Campbell
Kim Greene
John Hildreth
Chad Krueger
Anne Libera
Trey Stone

**1997**
Eric Black
Margaret Exner
Andrew Graham
Brandon Johnson
Keegan-Michael Key
Joe Latessa
Catherine Worth

**1998**
Michael J. Gellman
Elaine Hendriks
Marc Evan Jackson
Mary Jane Pories
Ron West
Nyima (Woods) Funk

**1999**
John Edwartowski
Shatha Faraj
Joe Janes
Antoine McKay
Maribeth Monroe
Mary Vinette
Marc Warzecha

**2000**
Dexter Bullard
Jeff Fritz
Kirk Hanley

Cheri Lynne Johnson
David Razowsky

**2001**
Rob Chambers
Kiff VandenHeuvel

**2002**
Scott Allman
Suzan Gouine
Lisa Maxine Melinn
Topher Owen

**2003**
Jelly
Pj Jacokes
Shawn Handlon

**2005**
Ken Faulk
Jenny Hagel
Quintin Hicks
Matt Hovde
Tiffany Jones
Caroline Syran Rauch

**2006**
Jimmy Carlson
Amy Duffy
Nate DuFort
Brett Guennel
Shari Hollett
Tara Nida
Tim Robinson
Megan Wilkins

**2007**
Jaime Moyer

## The Second City Las Vegas

**2001**
Jean Augustyn
Dan Bakkedahl
Frank Caeti
Kay Cannon
Joshua Diamond
Matt Dwyer
Jennifer Estlin
Marypat Farrell
Sarah Gee
Karen Graci
Kelly Haran
Fred Hemminger

Joe Janes
Robin Johnson
Mike Lukas
Seamus McCarthy
Mick Napier
Phil Randall
Jason Sudeikis
Marc Warzecha
Mike Watkins

**2002**
Scott Allman
Ed Goodman
Brooke Schoening
Holly Walker

**2003**
Joe Kelly
Amy Rowell
Brian Shortall

**2004**
Lauren Dowden
Ithamar Enriquez
Martin Garcia
Shatha Hicks
Bridget Kloss

**2005**
Amanda Blake Davis
Paul Mattingly
David Novich
Craig Uhlir

**2006**
Ryan Archibald
Jimmy Carlson
Shelly Gossman
Katie Neff
Andy St. Clair

**2008**
Rob Belushi
Michael Lehrer
Robyn Lynne Norris
Bruce Pirrie

## The Second City Denver

**2006**
Dave Colan
Brendan Dowling
Jenny Hagel
Matt Hovde

Timothy Edward Mason
Beth Melewski
Amber Ruffin

## The Second City Cleveland

**2002**
Andrew Alexander
George Pete Caleodis
Maria Corell
Cody Dove
Colleen Doyle
Joshua Funk
Jack Hourigan
Kelly Leonard
Tommy LeRoy
Quinn Patterson
Dana Quercioli
David Schmoll
Ron West

**2003**
Dave Buckman
Katie Caussin
Nate Cockerill
Lauren Dowden
Randall Harr
Chad Krueger
Kiff VandenHeuvel
Joseph Ruffner

## The Second City Santa Monica

**1989**
Dana Andersen
Christopher Best
Mark DeCarlo
Andy Dick
Robin Duke
Teresa Ganzel
Michael Hagerty
John Hemphill
Bonnie Hunt
Richard Kind
Don Lake
Andrea Martin
Joseph Plewa
Ryan Stiles
Linda White

**NBC**     National Broadcasting Company, Inc.          Thirty Rockefeller Plaza
                                                          New York, N.Y. 10020   212-247-8300

March 7th

Dear Joyce and Jane and Bernie and the Entire Cast of Second
       City and the whole audience and Everyone Involved from
       the Ticket Taker to whoever sweeps up at night,

I had the best time being with you in Chicago. It was like
coming home and having ice cream and cookies in the kitchen
and laughing about stuff that happened in school that day.
So, this is a letter to say thank-you and a warning that I'll
be back to eat all your food and laugh at all your jokes.

I love you,

Gilda

Letter from Gilda Radner

# SELECTED BIBLIOGRAPHY

## BOOKS

Fey, Tina. *Bossypants*. New York: Reagan Arthur Books / Little, Brown and Company, 2011.

Leonard, Kelly, and Tom Yorton. *Yes, And: How Improvisation Reverses "No, But" Thinking and Improves Creativity and Collaboration—Lessons from The Second City*. New York: Harper Business, 2015.

Libera, Anne. *The Second City Almanac of Improvisation*. Evanston, IL: Northwestern University Press, 2004.

Napier, Mick. *Improvise: Scene from the Inside Out*. 2nd ed. Denver, CO: Meriwether Publishing, 2004.

Patinkin, Sheldon. *The Second City: Backstage at the World's Greatest Comedy Theater*. Naperville, IL: Sourcebooks, 2000.

Poehler, Amy. *Yes Please*. New York: Dey Street Books, 2014.

Rivers, Joan, and Richard Meryman. *Enter Talking*. New York: Delacorte Press, 1986.

Sahlins, Bernie. *Days and Nights at The Second City*. Chicago: Ivan R. Dee, 2001.

Spolin, Viola. *Improvisation for the Theater: A Handbook of Teaching and Directing Techniques*. 3rd ed. Evanston, IL: Northwestern University Press, 1972.

Sweet, Jeffrey. *Something Wonderful Right Away*. 3rd Limelight ed. New York: Proscenium Publishers Inc., 1996.

Thomas, Dave. *SCTV: Behind the Scenes*. Toronto, ON: McClelland & Stewart, 1996.

Thomas, Mike. *The Second City Unscripted: Revolution and Revelation at the World-Famous Comedy Theater*. Evanston, IL: Northwestern University Press, 2012.

Wasson, Sam. *Improv Nation: How We Made a Great American Art*. New York: Houghton Mifflin Harcourt, 2017.

Woodward, Bob. *Wired: The Short Life and Fast Times of John Belushi*. New York: Simon & Schuster, 1985.

## MAGAZINE ARTICLES

Dratch, Rachel. "Amy Poehler on Babies, Boys & Tarantulas." *BUST*, December/January 2010.

English, T. J. "Bill Murray: The King of Comedy." *Irish America*, November 1988.

Galloway, Stephen. "Jordan Peele Reveals Plans to Shoot Next Movie Later This Year." *Hollywood Reporter*, January 19, 2018.

Heilpern, John. "Cecily Strong Shares the Secret to Her *Saturday Night Live* Success." *Vanity Fair*, February 2016.

Lahr, John. "Fortress Mamet." *New Yorker*, July 28, 2014.

Rader, Dotson. "Life Is Easier If You Can Share the Burdens." *Parade*, February 21, 1999.

Rooney, David. "'The Waverly Gallery': Theater Review." *Hollywood Reporter*, October 25, 2018.

Spitznagel, Eric. "An Interview with Tina Fey." *Believer*, November 1, 2003.

Syme, Rachel. "When in Doubt, Play Insane: An Interview with Catherine O'Hara." *New Yorker*, January 23, 2019.

Semley, John. "Hall Pass." *NOW Toronto*, December 5, 2013.

Tucker, Ken. "The Ben Stiller Show." *Entertainment Weekly*, October 16, 1992.

## NEWSPAPER ARTICLES

Ali, Lorraine. "'Veep' Breakout Sam Richardson Takes His Sweetly Off-Kilter Comedy to 'Detroiters.'" *Los Angeles Times*, February 7, 2017.

Bommer, Lawrence. "It Was Thirty Years Ago Today." *Chicago Reader*, October 19, 1989.

Burrill, William. "Second City Begins a New Life." *Toronto Star*, October 13, 2005.

Caro, Mark. "Chicago's Mick Napier: Master of Annoyance." *Chicago Tribune*, May 16, 2014.

Caro, Mark. "The Incredible Steve Carell." *Chicago Tribune*, March 11, 2013.

Chapman, John. "Chicago Revue Semi-Pro." *Chicago Tribune*, September 27, 1961.

*Chicago Tribune*. "Improv Pioneer Josephine Forsberg Dies." October 3, 2011.

Columbia *Chronicle*. "Beloved Professor Sheldon Patinkin Dies at 79." September 29, 2014.

Iglarsh, Hugh. "An Invitation to Drama and Drinks: Sixty Years Ago, Chicago's Compass Reinvented Comedy." *Newcity*, March 5, 2015.

Jergensen, John. "The New Face of Second City." *Wall Street Journal*, July 7, 2016.

Jones, Chris. "'The Art of Falling' Positively Dances with Life-Affirming Fun." *Chicago Tribune*, June 10, 2016.

Jones, Chris. "'Bernie' Sahlins, Co-founder of Second City, Dies at 90." *Chicago Tribune*, June 17, 2013.

Jones, Chris. "Fred Kaz, Music Director at Second City, Dies at 80." *Chicago Tribune*, March 12, 2014.

Jones, Chris. "'Hilarious,' 'Lovable' Second City Alumnus Jim Zulevic." *Chicago Tribune*, January 7, 2016.

Jones, Chris. "Joyce Sloane Dies at 80; Beloved Powerhouse of Second City Improvisational Theater in Chicago." *Chicago Tribune*, February 5, 2011.

Jones, Chris. "Laughs Come Thick and Fast in Shakespeare Parody." *Chicago Tribune*, May 21, 2004.

Jones, Chris. "Next Stop, Japan . . . Second City Extends Its Reach to Second Continent." *Chicago Tribune*, February 15, 2012.

Jones, Chris. "Paul Sills: 1927–2008." *Chicago Tribune*, June 3, 2008.

Jones, Chris. "Second City and the Democratic Convention: When Abbie Hoffman Improvised about Himself." *Chicago Tribune*, August 31, 2018.

Jones, Chris. "'South Side' Sidesplitting as It Plumbs Chicago's Depths." *Chicago Tribune*, April 11, 2011.

Kaufman, Joanne. "Fifty Years of Second City." *Wall Street Journal*, December 9, 2009.

Kogan, Rick. "Comedy Rules at Second City's Northwest Club." *Chicago Tribune*, November 14, 1990.

*Las Vegas Sun*. "Second to None: 'The Second City' Chugs Along at Flamingo Las Vegas." August 29, 2002.

Mahlman, Howell J., Jr., "Second City Notches the Belt with 'Paradigm Lost.'" *Chicago Tribune*, February 17, 1997.

Metz, Nina. "Embryos on Ice! Or Fetus, Don't Fail Me Now." *Newcity*, September 27, 2001.

Metz, Nina. "'Tasty Radio' Extends Mike O'Brien's Sketch Comedy beyond 'SNL.'" *Chicago Tribune*, October 28, 2015.

O'Donnell, Maureen. "Actress Barbara Harris Dies; Second City Alum Became Toast of Broadway, Movies." *Chicago Sun-Times*, August 21, 2018.

Pela, Robrt L. "Barbara Harris Knew Bill Clinton Was White Trash." *Phoenix New Times*, October 24, 2002.

Shales, Tom. "'SCTV' Goes Cable." *Washington Post*, May 18, 1983.

Smith, Sid. "2nd to None." *Chicago Tribune*, May 20, 2007.

Smith, Sid. "In 'Pinata,' Troupe Takes Daring Step, Breaks Out of Second City Mold." *Chicago Tribune*, June 23, 1995.

Whipp, Glenn. "Director Adam McKay and Steve Carell Cash In on 25 Years of Funny Friendship in 'The Big Short.'" *Los Angeles Times*, December 29, 2015.

Williams, Albert. "Holy War Batman! Or the Yellow Cab of Courage." *Chicago Reader*, November 15, 2001.

Williams, Albert. "Second City's 50th Anniversary Celebration." *Chicago Reader*, December 17, 2009.

Williams, Kevin M. "'Words' Uniquely Celebrates Diversity." *Chicago Tribune*, February 22, 2002.

## WEBSITES

Albini, Steve. "Why I Haven't Had a Conventional Christmas in 20 Years." *Huffington Post*. November 23, 2015. https://www.huffpost.com/entry/why-i-havent-had-a-conventional-christmas-in-20-years_b_8614568.

Bergren, Joseph. "'Wayne's World' 25 Years Later: How Mike Myers and Dana Carvey Found Their Inner Rock Stars." *Entertainment Tonight*. February 14, 2017. https://www.etonline.com/features/210430_wayne_world_turns_25_looking_back_with_mike_myers.

Carra, Mallory. "'At Home With Amy Sedaris' Star Amy Sedaris' Best & Most Complex Character Is Herself." *Bustle*. Retrieved February 26, 2019. https://www.bustle.com/p/at-home-with-amy-sedaris-star-amy-sedaris-best-most-complex-character-is-herself-15959568.

Carter, Adam. "Star-Studded SCTV Reunion Raises Funds for Ian Thomas's Son." CBC. June 4, 2017. https://www.cbc.ca/news/canada/hamilton/sctv-1.4145545.

Harris, Will. "Joel Murray on Vampires, One Crazy Summer, and Freddy Rumsen's Zipper." *A.V. Club*. September 5, 2015. https://film.avclub.com/joel-murray-on-vampires-one-crazy-summer-and-freddy-r-1798285340.

Harris, Will. "Richard Kind on Red Oaks, Spin City, Larry David, and Being Bing Bong." *A.V. Club*. October 9, 2015. https://tv.avclub.com/richard-kind-on-red-oaks-spin-city-larry-david-and-b-1798285671.

Jung, E. Alex. "In Conversation: Catherine O'Hara." *Vulture*. March 20, 2019. https://www.vulture.com/2019/03/catherine-ohara-on-schitts-creek-and-sexism-in-comedy.html.

Murray Bros. "Caddyshack Charity Golf Tournament." Retrieved April 4, 2019. https://murraybrosgolf.com.

Nero, Dom. "You Probably Didn't Watch *SCTV*, But It Shaped the Comedy You Love Today." *Esquire*. April 12, 2018.

Newman, Jason. "Flashback: Martin Short, John Candy Go Punk as 'The Queenhaters' on 'SCTV.'" *Rolling Stone*. May 22, 2019.

Rabin, Nathan. "Stephen Colbert." *A.V. Club*. January 25, 2006. https://tv.avclub.com/stephen-colbert-1798208958.

Sepinwall, Alan. "'Detroiters' Stars Sam Richardson and Tim Robinson Are Best Friends in Real Life, and on TV." *Uproxx*. February 6, 2017. https://uproxx.com/sepinwall/detroiters-comedy-central-sam-richardson-tim-robinson.

Shanoff, T. J. "Rod Blagojevich Superstar." *Oy!Chicago*. June 15, 2009. http://oychicago.com/article.aspx?id=3264&blogid=132.

Shivji, Salimah. "'How's It Going, Eh?' Bob and Doug McKenzie Help Raise $325K in Special Show." CBC. July 17, 2017. https://www.cbc.ca/news/entertainment/how-s-it-going-eh-bob-and-doug-mckenzie-help-raise-325k-in-special-fundraiser-1.4210544.

Winchell, Stephen. "Inside the Second City's Comedy Studies Program." *Vulture*. August 30, 2012. https://www.vulture.com/2012/08/inside-the-second-citys-comedy-studies-program.html.

Wright, Megh. "This 20-Year-Old Amy Poehler Pilot Is the Stuff of Comedy Nerd Dreams." *Vulture*. February 25, 2015. https://www.vulture.com/2015/02/this-20-year-old-amy-poehler-pilot-is-the-stuff-of-comedy-nerd-dreams.html.

## PODCASTS

Libera, Anne, and Kelly Leonard. "An Education in Comedy." *Getting to Yes, And*. Podcast audio. February 23, 2018. https://www.secondcityworks.com/podcast-posts/guest-anne -libera-and-kelly-leonard.

McKay, Adam. Interview by Jimmy Carrane. *Improv Nerd*. Podcast audio. December 21, 2015. http://jimmycarrane.com /168-adam-mckay.

## RADIO INTERVIEWS

Key, Keegan-Michael. Interview by Cynthia Canty. *Stateside*. Michigan Radio, December 19, 2016.

Mochrie, Colin. Interview by Jason Fraley. WTOP, September 14, 2016.

Napier, Mick. Interview by Justin Kaufmann. *The Download*. WGN Radio, December 8, 2015.

Warzecha, Marc. Interview by Elizabeth Blair. *All Things Considered*. NPR, July 22, 2009.

Willard, Fred. Interview by Justin Kaufmann. *The Download*. WGN Radio, September 14, 2016.

## TELEVISION INTERVIEWS

Carell, Steve. Interview by Conan O'Brien. *Conan*. Season 6, episode 26, "Steve Carell/Mike Schultz." Aired January 12, 2016, on TBS.

Carell, Steve. Interview by Steve Kroft. *60 Minutes*. Season 47, episode 8, "The Ebola Hot Zone/Cleaning Up the VA/Steve Carell." Aired November 9, 2014, on CBS.

Fey, Tina. Interview by Brian Williams. *Rock Center with Brian Williams*. Season 1, episode 2, "Greek to Me/State of Shame/ Tina Fey." Aired November 7, 2011, on NBC.

Louis-Dreyfus, Julia. Interview by Stephen Colbert. *Late Night with Stephen Colbert*. Season 1, episode 127, "Julia Louis-Dreyfus/Nikolaj Coster-Waldau/Sam Morril." Aired April 22, 2016, on CBS.

Rivers, Joan. *Make 'Em Laugh: The Funny Business of America*. Aired January 28, 2009, on PBS.

Sedaris, Amy. Interview by Stephen Colbert. *Late Night with Stephen Colbert*. Season 4, episode 102, "Jake Tapper/Amy Sedaris/The Claypool Lennon Delirium." Aired February 18, 2019, on CBS.

## FILMS

Hoffman, Matt, dir. *Second to None*. Des Plaines, IL: HMS Media, 1999.

*Howard Alk: A Life on the Edge*. Film retrospective. Chicago: Chicago Film Archives, 2009.

Levy, Eugene, dir. *The Second City Toronto 15th Anniversary*. Showtime, 1988.

Siska, Mark, dir. *Compass Cabaret 55*. Siska Films, 2014.

# PHOTO CREDITS

All photos and artwork are from The Second City's archives, except those listed below:

# INDEX

*Italicized* page numbers indicate illustrations and photographs.